Practical Magic for Crafting Powerful Work Relationships

Bc
BUSINESS
CHEMISTRY®

Kim Christfort
Suzanne Vickberg

Page Layout Designers: Patricia Mozetic and Randy Okamura

Library of Congress Cataloging-in-Publication Data

Names: Christfort, Kim, 1974- author. | Vickberg, Suzanne, 1971- author.
Title: Business chemistry : practical magic for crafting powerful work relationships / Kim Christfort, Suzanne Vickberg.
Description: Hoboken : Wiley, 2018. |
Identifiers: LCCN 2018007684 (print) | LCCN 2018010237 (ebook) | ISBN 9781119501640 (epub) | ISBN 9781119501626 (pdf) | ISBN 9781119501565 (hardback)
Subjects: LCSH: Leadership. | Employee motivation. | Career development. | BISAC: BUSINESS & ECONOMICS / Management. | BUSINESS & ECONOMICS / Leadership. | BUSINESS & ECONOMICS / Accounting / General.
Classification: LCC HD57.7 (ebook) | LCC HD57.7 .C523 2018 (print) | DDC 658.3/14–dc23
LC record available at https://lccn.loc.gov/2018007684

Printed in the United States of America.
V10002353_071218

SUZANNE

To my mom and dad, who have shown me I can go anywhere, do anything, and be anyone I want.

KIM

To my family, for their unwavering love and support.

Contents

BUSINESS CHEMISTRY APPLICATIONS

ADDITIONAL CONTENT

Foreword

BY PUNIT RENJEN

I spend much of my time on the road, meeting and working with business leaders from around the world. The insights I gain—about the world, about people, even about myself— are a constant source of learning and inspiration.

Probably the most valuable insight for me thus far concerns what it takes to *effectively* connect with other people. And it is not what you might think.

While my experience has shown me that, as human beings, we are more alike than we are different, it has also helped me to see that similarities are not the only basis for connection. It is when we understand and effectively navigate our differences that some of the most meaningful connections are made. That is what makes Business Chemistry such an effective tool.

Consider all of the different types of people you encounter in the course of your day-to-day interactions. People who prioritize diplomacy, and others who prefer candor; people who focus on the big picture, and others who live in the details; people who like the slow play, and others who want to cut to the chase. Business Chemistry provides a framework for identifying these different types of people so that you know quickly what approach to take and when. Have you ever tried to walk through a detailed slide deck with a big-ideas person? Not fun. And more importantly, not effective.

By helping to identify people's working styles, Business Chemistry produces the kind of seamless collaboration that normally takes years of working together to develop. And it does so not by forcing us to find common ground, but by drawing on the strength of our diversity as a global business community. Proof positive that people can think differently and still come together.

I know what Business Chemistry has done for my team, a robust mix of all four identified types: Pioneers, Integrators, Guardians, and Drivers (my category, which is probably not a surprise to those who know me). I would encourage everyone to add it to their bag of tricks for building highly effective relationships—both within and outside of their organizations.

It has been said that it takes all types to make the world go round. I believe that to be true, particularly when it comes to business. We need the doers and the dreamers, the hard drivers and the relationship builders, the extroverts and the introverts. Each has a role to play, but it's not enough for them to have a seat at the table. It's their ability to work together that completes the picture.

Punit Renjen is the chief executive officer of Deloitte Global.

The Power of Chemistry

"It's just like dating!" my colleague exclaimed as he rushed into the room. A recent divorcé, Brian had just discovered online matchmaking websites, so it was with some trepidation that I asked him, "What's just like dating?"

"Business relationships," he replied.

At that point I was dubious about where the conversation was heading, but then he continued, saying, "It's all about the chemistry."

Chemistry. A powerful word used to represent that magical *something* that can exist between people—and not just the romantically inclined. The term is applied broadly, from successful sports teams to highly rated news anchors to popular political leaders. In most cases its presence is obvious, but mysterious. It is hard to know exactly what's behind it. It's just there.

Of course, chemistry is also a branch of science that explores what matter is made of and how those ingredients interact, combine, and change. As a former pre-med student, I vividly recall my afternoons in the organic chemistry lab, carefully titrating *this* and heating *that* to create the perfect cocktail that would bring about the particular transformation I was hoping for (rather than an explosion). This other definition of chemistry pertains to the precise, analytical, and measured (literally). And yet the result still somehow feels magical.

Brian's words about business relationships made something click for me. He was right; chemistry is a huge factor in business. And not just in established working relationships, but in any interaction between people, whether they know each other well or not. Once you start looking, its presence or absence is noticeable everywhere. With that colleague you seek out when you want to riff on a new idea versus the one you avoid because he's *so* difficult to work with. With the client who will work with no one but you, versus the one you can't seem to click with. With the teams that achieve outsized success, versus those that churn and churn and never make progress. Time and again we've seen how chemistry can be the invisible force tilting the outcome in one direction or the other.

We often consider the great chemistry in these situations to be something we either have or don't. We think of it like luck, an abstract boon to wish for but not something to expect. However we rarely question whether there's a way we could concoct it ourselves. What if instead we viewed it as a discipline, one that explores the elements behind human interactions and how they might be brought together to minimize explosions and maximize positive outcomes? What if we took a scientific view on the art of business relationships?

That question kicked off the development of the Business Chemistry Project at Deloitte, which has become a seven-year exploration into *what* makes people click or clash, *why* some groups excel and others fumble, and *how* leaders can make or break team potential. What is Business Chemistry?

*
- **WHAT MAKES PEOPLE CLICK OR CLASH**
- **WHY SOME GROUPS EXCEL AND OTHERS FUMBLE**
- **HOW LEADERS CAN MAKE OR BREAK TEAM POTENTIAL**

In short, it is an analytics-driven tool for understanding and leveraging differences between people. It has been used by hundreds of thousands of professionals around the world to build healthier teams, enhance customer engagement, and become more effective leaders.

*
- **BUILD HEALTHIER TEAMS**
- **ENHANCE CUSTOMER ENGAGEMENT**
- **BECOME MORE EFFECTIVE LEADERS**

This book is dedicated to helping you use the principles of Business Chemistry to build your own powerful relationships, high-performing teams, and exceptional organizations.

As one of the original architects of the system, I'm writing this first chapter to lay some groundwork for why we developed this tool in this first place. In the rest of the book my co-author, Suzanne, will join me in sharing some of the most important ways in which people differ, and how those differences can cause conflicts between individuals and inconsistent performance on teams. Think your colleague doesn't *get it*? Their working style may simply be the opposite of yours. Think some of your team members lack commitment? Your team norms might be draining their energy and sapping their potential. Throughout this book we'll provide you with practical strategies for creating better business chemistry with those you work with, improving the performance of everyone involved. We'll share ideas for how to manage, motivate, and influence different types of people. We'll offer strategies for earning their trust and respect. And we'll explore how to lead your teams so that everyone can excel and deliver their best performance. But in order to get there, it helps to understand first things first.

Origins

The truth is, that early conversation I had with Brian catalyzed a mass of existing interest around this topic within our team. We had noticed that certain people in our organization were consistently outperforming the average, a trend that stayed true even when they switched from one client to another. So we embarked on an effort to better understand what made these individuals special and whether we could help others to perform like them. Our corporate sleuthing revealed that, for the most part, what these outliers were doing was similar to everyone else. They performed the same types of work, on the same size projects, with the same level of expertise. What *wasn't* the same was their approach to working with others. These star performers weren't just delivering services, they were building relationships—with clients, with their teams, and with one another. Not only that, but it seemed they were what you might call *relationship naturals*. They didn't appear to consciously think about *why* they should build relationships or *how* to build them, they just did it and did it well. They each seemed to be highly attuned to their clients' individual needs, and would frequently talk about "walking in their clients' shoes." When we spoke with their clients, they couldn't really identify why the relationships were so strong. They would say things like, "He just gets me" or "We complement one another."

We suspected that the secret sauce for each of these individuals was *empathy*. Decades of studies have shown that empathy is integral to effective human connection[1], and recent research further demonstrates links between empathy and leadership performance[2] [3], as well as commercial success at the organizational level.[4] Our high-performing people seemed to have an extra dose of this important quality, which translated into great chemistry with their clients, colleagues, and teams.

So our hypothesis about empathy was all fine and good, but now we were up against a daunting challenge. We were an organization of well over a hundred thousand people, and growing. If we wanted to scale the success of our high-empathy stars, we'd need to rely on something more than just natural empathic ability. But it wasn't immediately clear what we should do next. After all our digging, we wondered if our investigation had reached a dead end. But it turns out the answer, dear readers, was elementary.

Diamonds are a firm's best friend

Sadly I've forgotten much of what I learned in my college science courses, but my conversation with Brian about parallels between business and dating did unearth one relevant gem of knowledge from the depths of my brain, specifically, a fact about diamonds. See, organic chemistry hinges around the core element carbon. And in its pure state, carbon has two well-known forms, coal and diamonds. (Let's hope Santa doesn't confuse the two when he visits my house this year.)

Naturally occurring, the diamond form of carbon has always been highly valued due to its rarity. As a result, people have long been experimenting with how to transform lesser forms of carbon into high-worth diamonds. The earliest recorded attempts to do so date back to 1797.[5] Then finally, in 1954, GE created the first commercially successful synthesized diamond.[6] The interesting thing about these cultivated diamonds was that they weren't imitations; they were the real deal, pure carbon crystallized in isotropic 3D forms. In fact, these synthetic diamonds actually possessed some properties that made them superior to naturally formed diamonds, particularly for industrial applications, which require hardness, thermal conductivity, and electron ability.

Thinking about these various forms of carbon, I realized that our outlier performers were "diamonds in our midst." They possessed something highly valuable and naturally occurring: gem-grade empathy. But if we wanted to raise the performance of all our people to their level, we couldn't rely on nature; we needed to follow the example of the synthetic diamond innovators and figure out a way to cultivate it. And like lab-created diamonds, our cultivated empathy would not only be authentic, we hoped, but superior to organic empathy for business applications. With that clarity, we set off on a journey to figure out how we might help our people become more empathic.

A matter of style

If you're going to try to cultivate empathy, it helps to first be clear about what you mean by it. We define empathy as *understanding and identifying with another person's perspective*. It was this ability we wanted to nurture in our leaders and professionals across the organization. But like bumper sticker advice, this seemed easier said than done. Unless you know someone really well (which often isn't the case in a business environment), you may not even be aware of what their perspective is, let alone really understand or identify with it. And as for coming straight out and asking someone to tell you all about how they see and experience the world? Awkward.

What we needed was a simple way to help people develop empathy—some clue they could detect in a business environment without asking a lot of questions. Something they could directly observe that would correlate strongly with an individual's distinct perspective. That clue turned out to be *working style*.

 WORKING STYLE IS ESSENTIALLY YOUR PERSONALITY MANIFEST IN A BUSINESS SETTING.

Working style is essentially your personality manifest in a business setting. It's a composite of how you process information, make decisions, connect with people, and a multitude of other facets that reflect your unique perspective. By observing whether someone's working style is more spontaneous or structured, more diplomatic or direct, more conceptual or concrete, you can start to get a pretty clear picture of their perspective on things. And while it seems obvious that individuals' working styles differ in significant ways, people often overlook these differences, or see them as nuisances to be tolerated rather than clues to be understood, appreciated, and leveraged. To cultivate empathy, you need to recognize these differences for what they are—useful signals about an individual's perspective, and the building blocks of powerful working relationships.

But in order to fuel that magical chemistry of great business relationships, you need gem-grade empathy. That requires going beyond simply acknowledging differences and building understanding, to acting on that knowledge. As it turns out, those kindergarten lessons to *treat others the way you want to be treated* only go so far in an environment where the way you like to think, behave, and work is different from what I like. With the kindergarten's Golden Rule in mind, we often default to our own personal working styles and assume others process information, make decisions, and connect with people the same way we do. Then we wonder why that yields mostly frustration, misunderstanding, and wasted potential.

*

GEM-GRADE EMPATHY

We developed Business Chemistry to highlight some of these important differences in the name of empathy-building. Our goal was to help our people quickly identify someone's working style, understand how it's different from or similar to their own, and then to act on that knowledge by flexing their own style relative to the other person. In other words, treat others as *they* want to be treated. *That's* gem-grade empathy. Ultimately, with Business Chemistry we created a working style assessment and framework that makes practical the seemingly magical practice of crafting powerful work relationships.

Building a better mouse trap

Ok, we get it—the idea that people have different personalities, working styles, and ways of being is not exactly new. Since the ancient Greeks, at least, humans have tried to categorize and catalog thoughts and behaviors, feelings and preferences. And we realize that in today's modern times there is no shortage of systems, assessments, and tools available for classifying people's styles, whether in the workplace or in more personal realms, and whether serious and practical or fun and frivolous. (How many online quizzes did you take last month?) We're very aware of the ubiquity of these sorts of surveys and we often start with the following request when introducing Business Chemistry to a group: "Raise your hand if you've taken a personality or working style assessment before." Rarely does a hand fail to rise.

But then we ask a question: "How many of you, regardless of the assessment you took, can remember what type you are and what that means?" About half the hands go down and the previously self-satisfied expressions turn a bit sheepish. And then we throw out one more question: "How many of you could guess the type of the person next to you, based on a few key observations, and would know how to tailor your interactions accordingly?" At this point eyes look down, heads begin to shake, and perhaps just one or two hesitant hands remain raised at half-mast.

Right. So the concept isn't new, and most everyone has been exposed to these kinds of tools before. However, we've found that: 1) many people don't remember what they learned about themselves much less what they learned about others, and 2) most people don't know or can't remember how to apply that information to create chemistry in their own work relationships.

This is why we set out to develop a new system—one that would be both memorable and actionable. What you'll find is that Business Chemistry is powerful not because it invalidates existing theories or reveals some groundbreaking new discovery about human nature. Quite the opposite, in fact. This system is powerful because it takes a fresh approach to an age-old topic. Built for business, it's purposely designed to be practical and sticky, distilling an often murky subject down to the essence of what really matters for people in a work environment.

The basics of Business Chemistry

The Business Chemistry types are the focus of the rest of this book, so you're about to learn all about them. For now, though, I'll tide you over with a quick summary. Do you recognize yourself or your colleagues in any of these descriptions?

Pioneers value possibilities and they spark energy and imagination. They're outgoing, spontaneous, and adaptable. They're creative thinkers who believe big risks can bring great things.

Guardians value stability and they bring order and rigor. They're practical, detail-oriented, and reserved. They're deliberate decision-makers apt to stick with the status quo.

Drivers value challenge and they generate momentum. They're technical, quantitative, and logical. They're direct in their approach to people and problems.

Integrators value connection and they draw teams together. They're empathic, diplomatic, and relationship oriented. They're attuned to nuance, seeing shades of grey rather than black and white.

Of course, we don't all fit neatly into one of these categories. In fact, we are each a unique combination of all four, and depending on the context or situation in which we find ourselves, we may demonstrate behaviors associated with any of the types. Yet most of us find that in general we strongly associate with one or two of the types and that our behavior will be relatively consistent across various situations. For ease of use in this book we'll refer to these four types, and to people resembling them, by using the simple labels of Driver, Integrator, Guardian, and Pioneer. We trust that you, as our readers, will understand that we're using a shortcut. When we refer to someone as a Driver, what we really mean is a person with lots of characteristics closely associated with the Driver type, who thinks and behaves like a Driver much of the time. While the former isn't perfectly accurate, the latter is prohibitively awkward. We thank you in advance for remembering that we're simplifying. (And speaking of simplifying, I know that some of you are really interested in the details about how the system was created and the specifics behind its application. You can find all of that in the appendix.)

Activating the power of diversity

Ultimately, the magic of Business Chemistry is not in the types individually, but in their combinations collectively. As you may have already discerned, Guardians and Pioneers have opposite working styles, as do Drivers and Integrators. Business Chemistry can be particularly valuable with diversity like this, helping people work across these kinds of stark differences. But even when differences are more subtle, understanding how to reconcile them and use them to your advantage is crucial for creating great chemistry.

Diversity in the broadest sense—of thought, background, or experience—is often lauded as a driver of performance.[7] And most teams and organizations have some level of diversity to draw upon. But even when many different perspectives are represented, leaders often treat people as if they're all the same (that good old kindergarten lesson we mentioned earlier). As a result, they fail to tap into diversity's powerful potential. Furthermore, they inadvertently foster environments that marginalize or neglect to nurture those who are different. And we find they often don't realize they're doing this and don't recognize the negative impact it's having.

In our work with thousands of executives and professionals, we've seen this challenge over and over again: A CEO beats her head against the wall because her team keeps derailing and can't deliver on the strategy. A VP doesn't understand why her team members constantly undercut one another's efforts. A CFO feels his own contributions aren't being valued. These situations could be attributed to sub par talent, incompetent leadership, or poor organizational models, but they could also be caused by unrecognized and underleveraged differences between working styles.

Contrast those scenarios with leaders and teams that actively manage diversity: An executive team dramatically increases effectiveness by tapping into complementary strengths. A CHRO improves performance by letting individuals tailor their work environments to their needs. A director becomes a key contributor to the leadership team by shaping his interactions with others according to their individual styles. In these stories of success, people appreciate diversity, and adapt to make the most of it.

The most successful leaders and teams we've worked with take it one step further. They don't just respond to the working style differences around them, but they actively cultivate diversity—in leadership pairings, within teams, and across organizations—bringing together complementary strengths through thoughtful management. They go beyond flexing on a one-on-one basis to actively appreciating and leveraging the multi-dimensionality of their teams. They create environments that both empower and compel people to make their very best contributions.

 WHILE THE BENEFITS OF DIVERSITY ARE REAL, THEY'RE FAR FROM AUTOMATIC; THEY MUST BE ACTIVATED.

This is the true mission of Business Chemistry. To provide a simple, practical way to identify meaningful differences between people's working styles. To grasp where others are coming from, appreciate the value they bring, and determine what they need in order to excel. And finally, to offer ways to act upon that information in order to be more effective as individuals and as leaders. Because while the benefits of diversity are real, they're far from automatic; they must be activated. Each style must be recognized, valued, nurtured, and integrated to create an overall environment where all can thrive.

REFERENCES

1. Harvard Business Review. *Empathy*. Brighton, MA: Harvard Business Review Press, 2017.

2. Sinar, Evan, Rich Wellins, Matthew Paese, Audrey Smith, and Bruce Watt, "High-Resolution Leadership: A Synthesis of 15,000 Assessments into How Leaders Shape the Business Landscape." Development Dimensions International, Inc, 2016.

3. Ovans, Andrea. "How Emotional Intelligence Became a Key Leadership Skill." *Harvard Business Review*. May 05, 2015. https://hbr.org/2015/04/how-emotional-intelligence-became -a-key-leadership-skill.

4. Parmar, Belinda. "The Most Empathetic Companies, 2016." *Harvard Business Review*. December 20, 2016. https://hbr.org/2016/12/the-most-and-least-empathetic -companies-2016.

5. Boser, Ulrich. "Diamonds on Demand." Smithsonian .com. June 1, 2008. https://www.smithsonianmag.com/ science-nature/diamonds-on-demand-48545144/.

6. Kellner, Tomas. "Diamonds Weren't Forever in the GE Store, but Carbon Will Be." *GE Reports*. May 21, 2015. https://www.ge.com/reports/post/119548896365/ diamonds-werent-forever-in-the-ge-store-but/.

7. Page, Scott E. *The Difference: How the Power of Diversity Creates Better Groups, Firms, Schools, and Societies*. Princeton, NJ: Princeton University Press, 2007.

The Lay of the Land

Before we jump into the rest of the book, we thought it might help to provide a brief lay of the land—particularly for those of you who like context or are impatient to know what's ahead (we bet we know who you are). Broadly speaking, we've organized the chapters into three sections: Business Chemistry Core, Business Chemistry Electives, and Business Chemistry Applications. Consider the order in which we present the chapters to be a suggestion. You might prefer to read them in a different order, or (gasp) you might even skip a chapter or two. That's perfectly fine. Not everyone is interested in the same things!

Business Chemistry Core

This first section of the book is dedicated to helping you build a solid understanding of Business Chemistry.

Chapters 3 through 6 each feature one of the Business Chemistry types and should provide you with enough information to identify your own type with confidence. We'll tell you about the key traits and characteristics of the type and outline people's complaints about them. Think no one could possibly criticize your type? Think again! Each of these chapters ends with the good stuff: describing the particular value that type brings to a team. This is one reason you should read all of these chapters, even if you start with the one that sounds most like you.

In Chapter 7 we'll teach you how to make an educated guess about someone's Business Chemistry type, even with limited information. You can use these techniques to hypothesize about your colleagues', customers' or even your own type. You'll learn about some of the traits shared between types and why it's so important to consider context when attempting to intuit someone's type.

Chapter 8 offers some guidelines for using Business Chemistry responsibly. We'll address the issue of stereotyping and discuss the difference between unconscious bias and conscious categorization. Then we'll caution you about some possible pitfalls of using Business Chemistry carelessly, and suggest strategies for avoiding them.

Business Chemistry Electives

The second section of the book offers a richer view of the types. It explores many of the questions people routinely ask about how the types differ and how they relate to various other key topics. While this information will enrich your understanding of the third part, "Business Chemistry Applications," you could go on to apply the principles without reading this section. For that reason we frame these chapters as electives. For those of you who crave numbers and graphs, there is a lot of data in this section to quench that thirst.

Chapter 9 addresses the popular topics of introversion and extroversion. We'll share how this particular lens relates to Business Chemistry and adds a level of nuance to how we see the types. We'll also illustrate some ways in which an Introvert is not just an Introvert—there are differences between our introverted types—nor is an Extrovert just an Extrovert—we see differences between those types as well.

Chapter 10 will help you develop an even deeper understanding of the types and the many ways in which they differ from one another. We'll share findings from our large-scale research studies and highlight how Business Chemistry relates to responses to stress, psychological safety, locus of control, career aspirations and priorities, and the conditions under which the types thrive. We'll also discuss when and how the distinction between Introverts and Extroverts adds an important perspective on our findings.

This section ends with Chapter 11, which addresses the age-old question of where our differences come from. Are we born with a preference for spreadsheets or whiteboards? Do we learn directness or diplomacy in childhood? Is our comfort level with ambiguity a reflection of our role at work? We'll explore these questions by viewing our Business Chemistry data through the lenses of gender, generation, organizational level, and leadership.

Business Chemistry Applications

The final part of this book will serve as your guide for applying all the understanding you gained in the first two parts. As Ralph Waldo Emerson said, "An ounce of action is worth a ton of theory."

Chapters 12 through 15 take you through key things *not* to do with each of the types, by sharing stories of "workplace hell" from each type's perspective. These examples bring to life common scenarios that sap the energy and potential of the different types in ways that can lead to lower levels of engagement, commitment, and performance. Then you'll get an insider's view into our own thoughts and perspectives about each story—what went wrong and what could work better—presented through a pen-pal–style conversation between us. Through these discussions we'll offer lots of advice for how to make your team and workplace more palatable for each type so they can perform at their best. And you'll get a good sense of how Suzanne's view of things as a Guardian-Integrator differs from Kim's as a Pioneer-Driver. We end each of these chapters with strategies that can be employed by the featured type to improve their own situation because, while it would be great if everyone's manager were a Business Chemistry expert, sometimes you have to take care of things yourself.

Chapter 16 is focused on what you can do to flex your style in order to create powerful working relationships with others. We start with suggestions for interacting with your opposite type, which is often the most challenging. We also provide tips for how to be more effective with those who are the same type as you, and those who are a different type but share key traits with you.

Chapter 17 addresses questions about the best team composition and the greatest of all Business Chemistry challenges—creating an environment where all types can thrive at the same time. Because while you're focused on meeting the needs of one type, you're often in danger of turning off another, and getting consistently high performance from a team requires balancing the needs and preferences of all types.

After some concluding thoughts in Chapter 18, we'll share a bit about ourselves and what it's like working together across our own Business Chemistry differences. Then, for you detail die-hards, we've got a data-rich appendix that outlines the specifics of the Business Chemistry system. It includes information about our process for developing the system and scoring the assessment, our research samples and methodologies, and the properties of Business Chemistry.

———

Personal business

One last point before we dive in: For us, writing this book was not a purely academic exercise. It was an acknowledgment of the power of Business Chemistry that we've experienced in our own day-to-day lives. As you will learn, we're opposites. Kim is a Pioneer and a secondary Driver, while Suzanne is a Guardian and a secondary Integrator. And although we work together on the same team within Deloitte, we go about delivering on our mission in quite different ways.

As the National Managing Director of Deloitte Greenhouse Experiences, Kim's role is diverse and ever changing. Whether she's designing immersive sessions to help executives get to breakthrough, or negotiating sometimes rocky political terrain, or envisioning the *next big thing* for client experiences, she thrives on the pace and variety of her job. And if someone proposes karaoke at the end of the day, far be it for her to say no. These kinds of things suit her Pioneer tendencies.

Suzanne leads Deloitte's Business Chemistry research and thought-leadership efforts. She appreciates being able to concentrate deeply on one thing and to dedicate all her resources to doing it well—without disruption or distraction. From analyzing data sets to engineering survey questions to writing blogs, she thrives on the clarity and focus of her job. And the large, loud team events are not for her—especially not karaoke! She'd much prefer to grab a cup of coffee or a glass of wine with a teammate or two. These kinds of things suit her Guardian tendencies.

So we're not just authors, we're believers too. As opposites, we don't always agree. And yet we know our different perspectives make our joint work richer. To that end, we haven't tried to mask our individual styles in writing this book by blending them into a neutral composite. Rather, we're offering you readers an inside view of our thought processes, our conversations, and our perspectives. We're hopeful that these different lenses—combined with data-driven context and practical advice—will make it easy to put diversity to work for you. As we like to say, it's not rocket science, but it is Business Chemistry.

Ready to get started?

Business Chemistry Core

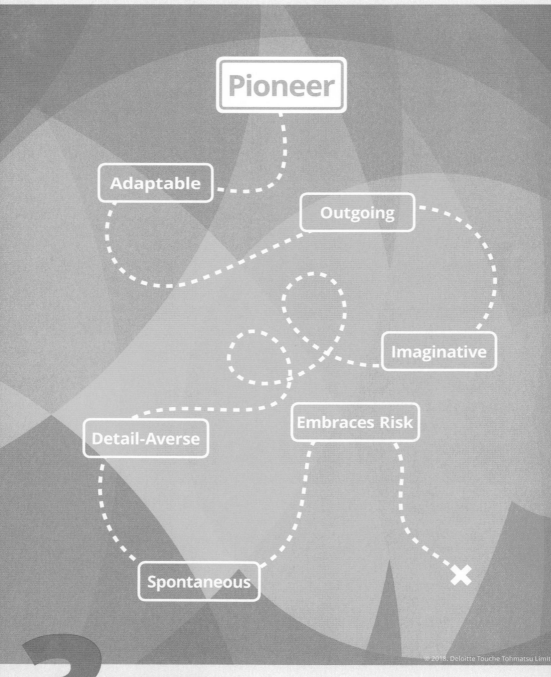

3 PIONEERS
Value Possibilities and Spark Energy and Imagination

If we could capture the essence of the Pioneer in one word, it would be **POSSIBILITIES**. Pioneers love imagining what could be and don't hesitate to reach beyond the status quo. Expressions like "What if...?", "Picture this...", "Yes, and...", and "Why not?" are music to a Pioneer's ears, and often are lead-ins to lively brainstorms. Pioneers are big fans of collaborative idea generation. They're very comfortable with ambiguity, and highly adaptable to change—whether they're the ones initiating it, as is often the case, or not.

Strong Pioneers tend to be easy to spot because they're typically high energy and outgoing. They're the ones you can hear all the way down the hallway before you even get to the conference room. Or more likely, you'll hear them coming down the hallway as you wait in the conference room, because they'll be running late. They have little regard for rigid structure, and an almost allergic aversion to details. That agenda the team put together so painstakingly? Don't expect the Pioneers to follow it. Their thinking can be non-linear and resists constraint. That detailed review of the pivot table analysis you had planned? Their eyes will blur and their minds will wander as you strain what paltry patience they possess. But give them a juicy, open-ended challenge and a whiteboard, and they'll be formidable idea generators.

Pioneers often think while speaking, formulating their opinions as they talk. It's one reason they like working in teams (after all, a Pioneer in a fishbowl office talking to him or herself can look a little strange). Those able to follow a Pioneer's vocal stream of consciousness will note the non-linear way they tend to jump from one thought to the next. And don't expect any long, awkward pauses in conversation—a Pioneer will be only too happy to fill them.

Don't expect Pioneers to stick to any one task or activity for long. They tune out and are easily distracted. In their eagerness to move onto the next thing (same old same old is sooooo boring), Pioneers usually make decisions quickly and spontaneously, based on gut feel versus any careful consideration of the data. Pioneers are very comfortable with risk, and are likely confident that their inherent adaptability will carry them through, regardless of where they land.

Overall the Pioneer working style is fast, fun, and free of inconvenient facts that might inhibit possibilities. Indeed, there are few things that Pioneers dislike more than someone raining on their parade. For a Pioneer, it's more important to expand upon what *could be* than to analyze why it can't be, because for Pioneers, there is rarely such a thing as a dead end. Isn't there always another option, another path that hasn't been considered? That's how Pioneers see it. They generally believe that where there's a will—and a great idea—there's a way. The problem is, finding the way usually entails a devil of details that the Pioneer has little tolerance for, and thus leaves (dumps) in the hands of others.

Pioneers have more fun. No really, it's true, and fun is a word they use frequently as if to reinforce the point. These free-wheeling, idea-sparking, optimistic individuals bring positive energy to everything they do, and because they value diverse opinions and love to collaborate, they happily bring others along on their wild ride. Better still, since they mostly hang out in the rarified air of lofty ideas and big-picture thinking, they don't tend to stress about the pesky details or complex processes lurking underneath. Indeed, Pioneers are the least stressed of all types. So is it any great surprise that our research shows that, given a choice, more people would wish to be a Pioneer than any other type? (And that includes those who actually *are* Pioneers.) But they're also the type others find most challenging to work with.

Which brings us to...

The problems with Pioneers

TOO MUCH OF A GOOD THING

Yes, all that energy and passion can be great, but it can come across as frenetic chaos. A Pioneer jumping from topic to topic, often without warning ("Ooh look, a squirrel!"), can be perceived as scattered, erratic, and unfocused. Their tendency to think as they talk instead of beforehand can be irritating for those who like to process silently to ensure they have something valuable to say before they speak. Idle Pioneer chatter doesn't leave much room for others to get a word in edgewise. And for someone looking for clear direction, a Pioneer's 30,000-foot vision filled with limitless options can be hard to translate into actual tasks and tangible outcomes on the ground.

IT'S ALL FUN AND GAMES UNTIL…

Pioneers tend to be really comfortable taking risks—*not* because they've calculated probable outcomes and impacts and are consciously accepting those as costs of action, but simply because *it feels like a good idea*. This confidence in their own intuition as the basis for risk-taking can make Pioneers appear reckless. Frequently they're faulted for being opportunistic, and for not considering the full impact on others in their quest for the next new thrill. And typically they don't have much empathy for those who are reluctant to embrace change.

YOU'LL TAKE CARE OF THAT, RIGHT?

Ultimately, even the best idea is only as good as its execution, and here's where Pioneers get the most criticism. Their strong dislike of rules, process, and pragmatic realities sometimes makes them come across as impractical and unable to get things done. Worse, they often expect others to carry out their unrealistic visions, putting the burden of implementation on them without worrying about whether what they're asking for is really possible. And since they don't tend to personally value meticulous planning and structured execution, the people doing that work are often underappreciated and under-celebrated.

But before you write them off as frivolous or clueless, consider...

The promise of Pioneers

In spite of the fact that people report Pioneers are the most challenging type to work with, there is an almost universal appreciation for their value on a team.

LIGHT MY FIRE

Pioneers often provide the spark that ignites others' creativity. Their out-of-the-box thinking and "insanely creative ideas," as one executive aptly described it, catalyze innovation for teams and organizations. Have a great idea yourself? Pioneers will rarely be the naysayers, so they're great to have on your side if you're looking to garner enthusiasm about something. And of course they'll add in their own slew of suggestions to build on those ideas along the way.

WE'VE GOT THIS

Pioneers' idea generation is not only helpful for fueling an organization's aspirations, but it also bolsters them in times of challenge. When a team is backed against a wall, Pioneers are the ones who see a window, or suggest a ladder. Their peers recognize the importance of this can-do spirit and positivity, which inspires teams in times of opportunity and buoys them in times of trouble.

The Pioneer's tendency to leave the details to others isn't always a bad thing. Some of the other types love the problem solving needed to bring a fantastic idea to life. A Pioneer paired with such a teammate is the perfect yin yang of vision and implementation.

TURN ON A DIME

Pioneers' adaptability and flexibility is seen as a real asset in times of rapid change. Their boldness and ability to pivot makes them effective on the front lines of disruption, rapidly formulating response options while the organization catches up in the trenches.

LEADER OF THE PACK

Not only willing, but eager to step up into leadership roles, Pioneers are more common in the C-suite than any other type. They are often captivating individuals, social and networked. When you think of a natural leader, do you think of charisma, confidence, decisiveness, and outgoing engagement? If so, you are thinking not only of the common stereotype that exists in many business cultures, but also of many traits that characterize the Pioneer style.

PIONEERS ARE...

- Outgoing, spontaneous, and adaptable
- Imaginative thinkers who believe big risks can bring great things
- Intuitive decision makers, open to new ideas but prone to changing their minds

PIONEER MOTTO | YOLO (You only live once.)

"It is in our nature to explore, to reach out into the unknown. The only true failure would be not to explore at all."

ERNEST SHACKLETON

Explorer

In 1914, Ernest Shackleton was soliciting funds and crewmates for a daring polar expedition—to sail a thousand miles through the Antarctic unknown. Promises of meager wages, months of bitter cold in dangerous conditions, and no guarantee of safe return, wouldn't make you think men would be lining up to jump aboard. And yet, more than 5,000 applications poured in for spots on the expedition, and so did today's equivalent of millions of dollars in funding.

Why? In large part because Ernest Shackleton was a courageous leader with a magnetic way about him. He inspired confidence, stirred a sense of adventure, and captivated people's imaginations with his big ideas and daring quests.

These traits are characteristic of the **PIONEER.**

Shackleton itched for discovery. He chased new ideas, tough challenges, and risky business opportunities that other investors balked at—the tobacco company, the troop transport company, the Hungarian mining concession.

He often made decisions spontaneously, relying on gut feel over logic. While interviewing applicants for his Antarctic journey, he was known for asking eccentric questions, believing a man's character to be just as important as his technical ability. For instance, physicist Reginald James was asked if he could sing. Other applicants were accepted after extremely brief interrogations or on sight—simply because Shackleton liked the look of them.

Shackleton believed in the power of entertainment, of fun. He was referred to as the "life and the soul" of the ships he sailed on, lifting the spirits of the crew through his antics and his spontaneous, optimistic, and unflagging spirit. His crew became trapped at sea with their vessel, *The Endurance*, wedged tightly between miles of solid ice in the dead of winter. While they lived on the polar ice pack for months and months Shackleton devised elaborate diversions to maintain morale. He organized activities like dog races, talent shows, and nightly sing-alongs.

When *The Endurance* was eventually crushed by the ice and sank—taking Shackleton's plans down with it—he pivoted, brainstormed, and pursued new tactics. For the next five months, his men rode ice floes northward until they found a desolate frozen island.

Shackleton had seemingly unsinkable energy. Leaving his exhausted crew to rest on the island, he completed one of history's most incredible journeys, sailing in an exposed dinghy an additional 800 miles across open ocean, enduring a hurricane and scaling miles of frozen mountains to find help.

He eventually found help at a whaling station on South Georgia Island, a British territory just beyond the Antarctic. But he was back on the water within three days, in a borrowed ship, starting what became a three-month mission to rescue his stranded companions.

Although many of Shackleton's endeavors were not successful (OK, in this case, spectacularly unsuccessful), his boundless energy and pioneering spirit always drove him on to the next adventure.

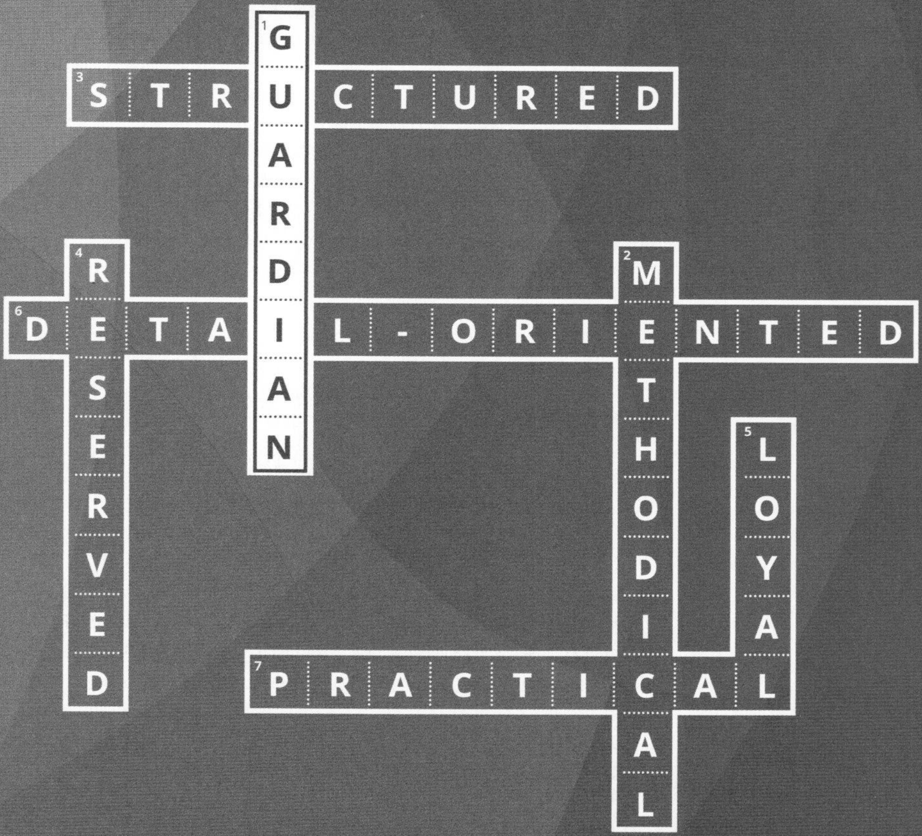
1 GUARDIAN
2 METHODICAL
3 STRUCTURED
4 RESERVED
5 LOYAL
6 DETAIL-ORIENTED
7 PRACTICAL

4 GUARDIANS Value Stability and Bring Order and Rigor

If we had to pick one word to represent what the Guardian values, it would be **STABILITY**. A Guardian knows it's essential to forge a solid foundation before building anything skyward. And when it comes to how the Guardian does things, many aspects of their working style serve to establish and maintain such stability. They're methodical, careful, disciplined, meticulous, and exacting. (How else to ensure a foundation is sound?) Guardians believe it's important to follow a structured process when completing a task, and they like a bit of structure in their work environments and meetings too.

Spontaneity? New environments? Ambiguity? A Guardian will likely say *no thanks*, because spontaneity, newness, and ambiguity all threaten stability.

When they simply *must* embark on something new, Guardians seek to first understand as much as possible. They don't jump in feet first, but conduct their due diligence and hatch a plan for moving forward. In fact, they say they actually *enjoy* planning. Guardians like to get cozy with the details, digging in to see what's what. And they're not going to trust anyone else to worry about those details for them— they'll do the worrying themselves, thank you very much.

Planning a big brainstorming session? That's not really the Guardian's thing. In their opinion, learning from past approaches is better than trying something new. Why not take advantage of all that we already know and use tactics that have worked in the past? And don't expect a Guardian to give you points for being original or imaginative while you brainstorm. They're an unapologetically practical type. If it ain't broke, why brainstorm creative ways to fix it? Guardians also tend to see things as absolutes—more black and white than gray. Sometimes that black and white approach means they get frustrated when others don't do things the right way. And to a Guardian, *right* is synonymous with the way things have always been done.

Guardians are most comfortable when the waters are calm and no big waves are rocking their boat. And they themselves often serve as anchors. Depending on who you ask, they're anchors that thwart progress, or anchors that prevent aimless drifting or even being lost at sea. Guardians don't always see a big risk as the path to great things, but they also don't reject risk entirely. They only want to thoroughly consider the possible implications before taking a risk. Likewise, they take their time when making decisions and they're not sorry about it. To a Guardian, their decision-making pace is just right to ensure that they come to the correct decision. On occasions when they take a risk that doesn't pay off or make a decision that backfires, they tend to beat themselves up about it. A Guardian will turn a mistake over and over in their mind to try and figure out what they missed or should have done differently; all the better to avoid making a similar mistake next time.

Guardians tend to be introverted and reserved, both socially and emotionally. You won't usually find a Guardian at the center of a large group of colleagues and they don't need to be in charge. Instead, they often contribute in other, less out-front and obvious ways. Of course they work on teams— who doesn't these days?—but they're also quite comfortable working alone. And Guardians tend to be particularly quiet around new people. (Who *are* those strangers?) In groups they may be uncomfortable expressing their emotions, or sometimes even their opinions. They're unlikely to fight for the floor and they generally prefer to avoid any kind of confrontation. If you want to know what a Guardian thinks, you'll often have to inquire.

When asked which type they'd least want to be, people tend to say Guardian. While this doesn't seem like a great compliment, the same people characterize Guardians as the most underappreciated type. And they further suggest that this lack of appreciation is because the Guardian's work, while critical, is often conducted behind the scenes. So it makes a lot of sense that people might not wish to be Guardians—who wants to be underappreciated? But people also grumble about some specific characteristics of their Guardian colleagues.

Which brings us to...

The gripes about Guardians

CAN'T WE BE FRIENDS?

Because of their reserved nature, others sometimes complain that Guardians are tough to get to know. They're seen as holding things too close, withholding personal details, and even being uninterested in getting to know others. It's a bit like trying to get friendly with an armadillo. And this isn't the only complaint we hear about Guardians.

PICKY, PICKY, PICKY

Guardians are also viewed as sticklers for the rules. They tend to think rules are there for a reason and it's certainly not to break them. Further, it's important to a Guardian to follow the letter of the law, not just the spirit. For these reasons Guardians are sometimes considered rigid, inflexible, and closed minded. If there's a process in place, then *all* the steps of the process should be followed, and *in order*. The Guardian does things this way and thinks everyone else should too. Guardians are sometimes seen as too perfectionist or are accused of micromanaging others because they're hung up on "unnecessary details" and their own overwhelming need for structure and stability.

STUCK IN A RUT

People also complain that Guardians are stuck in the status quo like tractors in a field of mud. As the pace of change quickens everywhere some see Guardians as unable to free themselves and adapt, and wonder if they, perhaps, like being stuck in the mud. They're considered too careful and too conservative, resistant to progress, and unwilling to accept any exposure to risk—a roadblock covered in caution signs. Together, these complaints culminate in the claim that Guardians move at a glacial pace, slowing everyone and everything around them.

But before you decide to vote all those boring Guardians off the island, consider...

The gifts of Guardians

Given all those complaints, why on earth would anyone want to work with a Guardian? Because, of course, Guardians have a lot of value to offer, even if it's not always appreciated in the moment. In fact, they're indispensable.

WALK THE TALK

When people *do* express their appreciation, they report that they value the Guardian's commitment to follow-through. They know they can count on a Guardian to do what they say they're going to do and to be accountable. People describe Guardians as dependable, responsible, persistent, and loyal. Guardians value loyalty because knowing who they can trust provides the predictability they crave. And they pay back loyalty by being loyal in return, so you know you can count on a Guardian (as long as they know they can count on you).

BETTER SAFE THAN SORRY

People also appreciate Guardians for keeping them out of trouble. Because they're less likely to embrace risk, Guardians will often insist that proper due diligence be conducted when other types might skip it. Likewise, Guardians make decisions deliberately, considering various options, thinking through details, and identifying potential consequences. It's as if Guardians spend more time than others engaging in System 2 thinking—the deliberate kind of conscious thinking we use when we analyze something.[1] Since many errors are due to snap judgments we make when using System 1, or more automatic thinking, it can be helpful to have someone around who spends a bit more time in System 2.

EAGLE EYES

There's also something to be said for the Guardian's organizational skills and their attention to detail. And seriously, someone has to be paying attention to these things! Guardians have a way of spotting subtle inconsistencies, imagining potential implications, conceptualizing how a process could unfold, and understanding how and why little things matter. Sometimes people say they're thankful for these strengths because Guardians do the work that others can't or don't want to do. If you're not a methodical person but you need quality control, where will you look for help? Probably to a Guardian. If you have little patience for thinking through the details and possible implications of a plan, where would you go? Again, to a Guardian.

A DOSE OF REALITY

Let's say you're really good at coming up with outlandish ideas—no one is more creative than you! But if your success depends on making those ideas a reality, a Guardian can help. Guardians are known for their realism and practicality, which can be a great balance for creativity. They're terrific at envisioning just what it would take to implement an idea, and then putting in place the structure and plan to make it happen. To harness the power of this Guardian strength, ask, "How can we make this happen?" instead of framing your question around whether an idea is good or realistic. (Chances are, a Guardian will point to a few reasons why it's not.)

GUARDIANS ARE...

- Practical, reserved, and loyal
- Detail - and process-oriented thinkers who focus on the how
- Deliberate decision-makers apt to stick with the status quo

GUARDIAN MOTTO | It's all in the details.

© 2018. Deloitte Touche Tohmatsu Limited

REFERENCES

1. Kahneman, Daniel. *Thinking, Fast and Slow*. New York: Farrar, Straus and Giroux, 2015.

"Great events make me quiet and calm; it is only trifles that irritate my nerves."

QUEEN VICTORIA

British Monarch

In 1851, Queen Victoria's foreign secretary, Lord Palmerston, sent a telegram to Napoleon III. Lord Palmerston had the approval of England's prime minister, so he saw no reason to clear the telegram with the Queen before sending it. She signed the thousands of dispatches that went out in her name every year, but he couldn't imagine she read all of them. But that is exactly what she did. Queen Victoria read everything. And she didn't appreciate someone skirting her authority. Soon enough, Lord Palmerston was sacked.

Having taken the throne at only 18 years of age, this young queen set out to do her job right, to understand her obligations, and to fulfill every detail of them meticulously and dutifully, to a T.

This approach is characteristic of the **GUARDIAN**.

It was important to Queen Victoria that she know every detail of what was going on in her empire. She cared about order, tradition, and getting each particular just right. She also had the patience and fortitude to make that happen. She paid close attention, deliberately assessing each issue and weighing in when she deemed her royal opinion to be warranted. The issue might be big or small—whether to send forces into war, or whether sailors should be permitted to grow beards—but she kept a pulse on everything, and often expressed a strong and well-reasoned opinion.

Queen Victoria's remarkable diligence could be seen across all aspects of her life. When she was 13, her mother gave her a journal, and from that day on, she wrote a diary entry almost every day until a week before her death at age 81. As a meticulous planner, she left no detail up to chance, even when it came to her death. In her will, she outlined every aspect of her funeral, from the steps in the procession to the color of the casket.

She was calm, controlled, and dignified; she didn't need to be flamboyant or charismatic to demand complete respect from those around her. And as it turned out, Queen Victoria was no firebrand. She would never be the one to launch the ship of state on a reckless adventure. But, despite her calm demeanor, anyone who expected her to be a wallflower was in for a surprise.

She was the most powerful person in any room she walked into. At a time when women the world over could not vote, Queen Victoria was the ruler of the world's greatest empire. And for six decades she maintained firm and principled oversight, successfully shepherding her nation through a time of previously unparalled social and technological change, as well as global and economic expansion.

Queen Victoria was one of the longest-reigning British monarchs in history, and the second longest-reigning female monarch anywhere. Talk about tried and true–there was an entire era named after her! With her steady, disciplined, and meticulous style, the *Grandmother of Europe* is a great example of a Guardian.

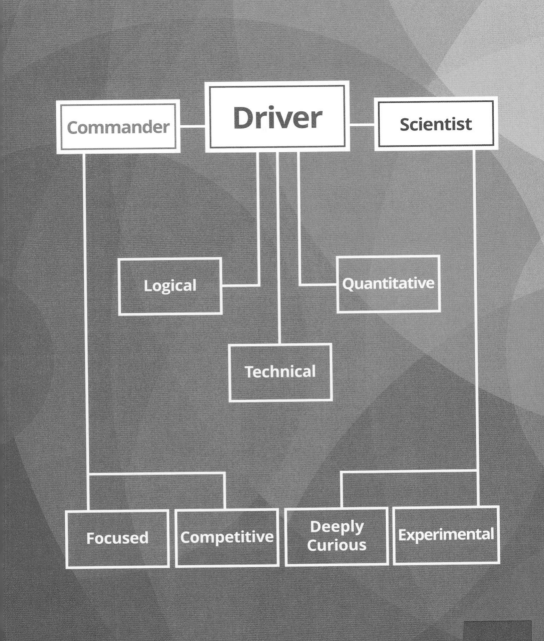

Commander — **Driver** — Scientist

Logical

Quantitative

Technical

Focused — Competitive — Deeply Curious — Experimental

DRIVERS
Value Challenge and
Generate Momentum

Ask people the best thing about Drivers, and a clear theme emerges: They get sh*t done. Even when it's difficult. Especially when it's difficult. Because if you had to capture the spirit of Drivers in a word, it would be **CHALLENGE**. Drivers love a challenge, and they love *to* challenge. They are focused and competitive. To get the results they want, Drivers will calculate the shortest possible path and stay on course despite whatever, or whoever, gets in their way. This directness infuses everything they do, from the way they make decisions to the way they interact with others. They like to get to the point.

Drivers are not the warmest and fuzziest of the types. They don't mince words and they don't sugarcoat. Expecting small talk? Drivers see it as a waste of time. No clear agenda? Come back when you have one. Vague ambitions? Intuitive conclusions? Emotional interpretations? Good luck with that. Drivers are logical, technical, and quantitative. They want data and structure. Try to engage them without these things, and they have no qualms voicing their displeasure. Even if you do arrive armed with facts, don't expect Drivers to accept them at face value. They will likely question your data, dispute your premise, and argue with your conclusion. But often that's not a bad sign. Drivers are competitive and love to debate. They respect someone that can go toe to toe with them—and they don't give out points to people who are self-effacing. Tell a Driver you're not that good at something and, chances are, they will believe you.

Drivers won't waste a lot of time digging into your motives, or questioning their own. It's not that they lack curiosity—in fact quite the opposite. But their interests are more pragmatic than philosophical; more "How does this clock work?" than "What is the meaning of time?" Drivers are deeply inquisitive and experimental. They will often ask "Why?" and then determine a way to find out.

Drivers dislike ambiguity, so they quickly look for patterns and move forward with solutions. They want to figure out the reason for everything, and if they can't find one, they assume it must not be important. They make decisions swiftly, discarding what they consider extraneous to zero in on an answer, even if it's unpopular. For Drivers, if the facts suggest a particular choice then any feelings about it are irrelevant. They're also comfortable with risk, as long as it's calculated.

There are two sub types of Drivers: Commanders and Scientists. Commanders are the take-charge, more extroverted type. Scientists are the cerebral, more introverted type.

Commanders

As the name suggests, Commanders are disciplined and tough minded, ready to lead the troops toward the goal. They like to be in charge, and even when they are not the official leader, their dominant presence is hard to miss. Commanders are not reserved; they tend to be energetic, quick speaking, and outgoing.

Compared to their Scientist counterparts, Commanders are more focused. Once they've got the scent of a goal in their nostrils, it's hard to distract them from their track. Their bias is for action versus deliberation. And while Drivers in general are competitive, Commanders take it to the extreme. Even if there's no explicit competition, Commanders will often create one. That could be as obvious as a "my [insert noun] can [insert verb] better / faster / cheaper than yours" kind of standoff, or it could be more subtle, like jockeying for status, titles, compensation, and resources.

Scientists

Scientists have a more inward orientation than Commanders. They aren't hierarchical and don't put particular value on relationships or social networks. Rather, they're focused on ideas. They tend to be very intellectual.

Scientists are more curious than their Commander counterparts. They love to explore, to probe, to experiment. For them, the goal is as much about gaining understanding or solving a puzzle as it is about achieving a specific objective. They are highly visual, picturing problems in their mind in order to dissect them. Scientists also tend to be less traditional, willing to try new things in order to tease out hidden truths.

―――――

Overall, Drivers are direct, unapologetic, and compelled more by logic than emotion. They approach work much like an algorithm, analyzing options and outcomes unencumbered by second-guessing, fear of conflict, or worry about collateral damage. For a Driver, these costs are necessary to getting things done.

When Drivers see a mountain, they don't see an insurmountable obstacle. They see a challenge they can climb over, tunnel through, or move if needed—and then perhaps boast about. Drivers have a laser focus on achieving objectives, which makes them incredibly useful for a team. Indeed, of all the types, our research shows Drivers are the type that people say they most value. And yet, they are also considered the least enjoyable type to work with.

Which brings us to...

―――――

The difficulties with Drivers

――

WHAT A JERK

Drivers are impatient, and don't particularly value social niceties. Add to that their single-minded focus and direct speaking style, and it's not surprising that Drivers often come across as blunt and abrasive. Drivers also tend to either not notice or not care about how this behavior makes others feel. In Drivers' complex calculus, personal feelings and individual implications are given significantly less weight than other considerations. They are the least empathetic of the types.

THEIR WAY OR THE HIGHWAY

Drivers are quite focused, but this can look like "tunnel vision" to those who view the world from a broader vantage point. It can be difficult to shift Drivers' perspectives, particularly if they've already made up their minds. For Drivers, every decision they make is based on a logical analysis of facts. So unless the facts change, their logic is, from their standpoint, irrefutable. This makes Drivers seem very inflexible and unyielding.

Drivers also tend to roll their eyes at softer activities like building consensus, gaining buy-in, and practicing diplomacy. So while they're really great at driving the metaphorical bus, they're not so good at making sure anyone else is on it with them.

WINNING IS EVERYTHING

Drivers tend to want to be leaders, and strive for advancement and achievement. They think second place is for losers. Drivers like to know how they measure up, and how they can move on up. As a result, they're often accused of being self-interested and self-serving, maneuvering to be at the top of the heap whether organizationally (for the Commanders) or intellectually (for the Scientists).

Drivers can also be accused of having a bit of a killer instinct, due to their competitive streaks, passion for debate, and comfort with confrontation. They can sense weakness, and when they do, they don't pull their punches. But at least they'll punch you in the face, rather than below the belt. Drivers love to win, but they want to win fair and square.

But before you decide that Drivers are a little too rough around the edges, consider...

The deftness of Drivers

Yes, people say that Drivers are less enjoyable to work with. But remember they're also the type that people value most. Here's why.

MAKE IT REAL

Drivers possess a unique combination of originality and pragmatism, which helps them to translate vague visions into actionable strategies. They'll make sure discussions are grounded in facts, without getting bogged down in too many details. And while their straight-shooter style might occasionally offend, it also gets the truth out quickly. Sometimes you need someone who can call out the elephants in the room. —and volunteer to subdue them. They're also great at testing concepts early on to make sure they hold water, playing devil's advocate and challenging assumptions so that the ultimate outcome is viable.

TACKLE THE TOUGH CHOICES

Drivers are particularly good at making tough choices. They don't mind being unpopular in service of results. If you've been tiptoeing around an unpleasant decision, it's great to have a Driver who can boldly step up and deal with it. And Drivers don't do a lot of introspective second-guessing, so they're also great at making a decision and moving on rather than dwelling on the would haves, could haves, and should haves.

GET IT DONE

More than anything, Drivers are great at getting results. This is perhaps why they are the second most prevalent type in the C-suite (after Pioneers). As leaders they channel the energies of the rest of the team into productive progress toward goals. They keep everyone on task and don't waste time. In the face of daunting odds, their motivation fuels them. This is a type that doesn't take *no* for an answer.

DRIVERS ARE...

- Technical, quantitative, and logical; direct in their approach to people and problems

- Analytical thinkers who look for patterns in complex systems

- Quick to judge and then reluctant to revisit decisions

DRIVER MOTTO | It's not personal; it's just business.

"The boy who is going to make a great man must not make up his mind merely to overcome a thousand obstacles, but to win in spite of a thousand repulses and defeats."

THEODORE ROOSEVELT

26th President of the United States

In 1912, Theodore Roosevelt was on the campaign trail pursuing the presidential nomination. He was proposing a bold, progressive platform, and was determined to win in spite of his unpopularity with certain voters. This dislike turned nearly lethal though when he was shot at a campaign event. But what did Roosevelt do? Back off? Give up? Of course not. He went on to deliver a 90-minute speech anyway. After all, it was only *one* bullet.

Roosevelt was a resolute, take-charge, never-say-die leader. He was determined to pursue his goals regardless of the obstacles in his path, and he achieved great things as a result.

These traits are characteristic of the **DRIVER.**

Theodore Roosevelt was a sickly child, and he was home-schooled due to his constant illness. But, he never let his illness get in the way of doing what he wanted to do. Despite repeated bouts of asthma, he convinced his father it would be a good idea to develop a rigorous physical routine, so he began weightlifting and boxing to build his physical strength. He was focused, disciplined, and full of determination.

When his father died, Roosevelt channeled his grief into hard work, graduating *magna cum laude* from Harvard. Ambitious and goal oriented, he left law school early to join the New York State Assembly as a representative from New York City—becoming the youngest person to serve in that position. Almost 20 years later, when he was 42, he became the youngest president in U.S. history. And, eventually, he became the first American to win the Nobel Peace Prize.

Roosevelt's no-nonsense nature became a trademark of his presidency. Famously, he used the expression, "Speak softly and carry a big stick," to illustrate his approach to foreign policy. He wanted to show the world that he wasn't afraid to use his power, if tested.

He put his Driver spirit to use in 1904 when he decided to build the Panama Canal, despite previous failed attempts by the French. His opponents were merciless in their criticism of his approach, but he ignored their skepticism and did it his way.

He inspired thousands of Americans to come work on the canal with the words, "Make the dirt fly!", but still he faced an uphill battle. Yellow fever threatened the American workers. Not to let anything stand in the way of his plan, Roosevelt declared war on the mosquito that spread the disease—and won. He then took on the engineering challenges that had doomed the French, pursuing a radical new design that would lift ships above Panama's mountains through a complicated system of locks, rather than dredging a pathway at sea level.

Ten years later, Roosevelt's vision was realized. The Panama Canal was an engineering marvel. As a result of his steadfast will, ships trimmed almost 8,000 miles off of the journey from New York to San Francisco—with a route that was cheaper, faster, and safer.

Like Drivers before him and those who have followed, Roosevelt, pushed by his competitive nature, stopped at nothing to achieve his goals.

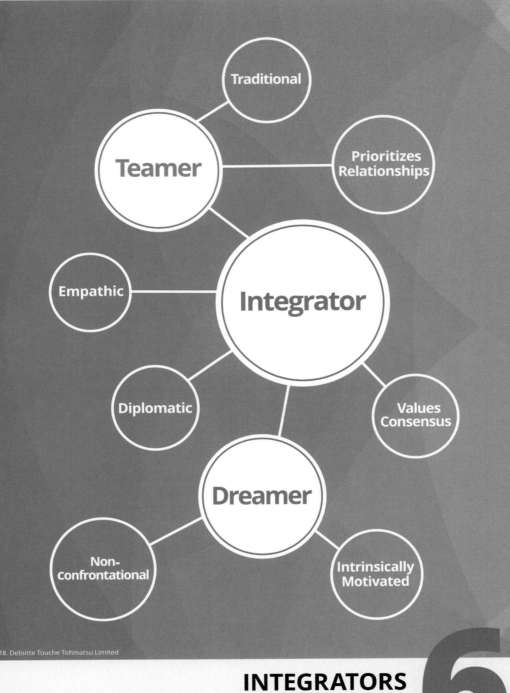

INTEGRATORS
Value Connection and
Draw Teams Together

6

CONNECTION—that's what it's all about for Integrators, and connector is the role they often play on a team. Sometimes an Integrator is focused on creating connections between people, and other times on connections between ideas. Either way, Integrators like working on teams more than toiling away in solitude. They're trusting and they forge deep relationships—beyond networking or teamwork—getting up close and personal to form real friendships with colleagues.

And there are lots of reasons you'd want to be friends with an Integrator. For one thing, they go out of their way to be helpful. You know that one colleague who's always happy to pitch in and does so with a smile? They're probably an Integrator.

Integrators are great listeners and observers too. They pay close attention to what's being said and can often sense even unspoken emotions and reactions. And then they take others' feelings into account. An Integrator knows that sticks and stones aren't the only things that can hurt relationships—words can too, and they bear this in mind when they consider how to deliver a message. Integrators place a high value on traditions, and this too reflects their sensitivity to the feelings of others. After all, where do traditions come from? People. And from the Integrator's perspective, things that are important to people deserve respect.

Whenever possible, Integrators prefer to avoid confrontation, and their desire to keep the peace is aided by their tendency to see things more in shades of grey than in black and white. From the Integrator's perspective both sides can be right, so why argue about it?

And yet, an Integrator will usually try to bring those with divergent views closer together. They consider it a worthy goal to reach consensus, getting everyone on the same page without leaving anyone out. An Integrator's not going to leave you on the side of the road just because you don't immediately agree on which freeway to take. They'll work with you to understand what's behind a disagreement and how it might be resolved. Sounds like a friend we'd like to have!

Integrators can also be defined by what they're not. Don't try to motivate them through competition or assume they want to be leading the charge—usually an Integrator isn't gunning for first place or jockeying for the baton. Instead, they're driven by a strong sense of duty and a desire to make a difference.

And numbers or technology? Not so much. Words, feelings, and relationships are the Integrator's domain.

There are two subtypes of Integrators. We call them Teamers and Dreamers. Teamers are more extroverted, and Dreamers more introverted.

Teamers

Teamers are outgoing, perhaps best defined by their relationships with others. Those personal connections with colleagues are even more important to Teamers than they are to Dreamers. And Teamers place a higher value on traditions and on loyalty in these relationships too—if you've got their back, they'll have yours. While Teamers go deep with their relationships, they also go broad, including a large swath of people in their extended network—all the better for getting lots of input and diverse perspectives.

Teamers are optimistic, energetic, and quite comfortable expressing their emotions. That makes them a lively presence. If there's a Teamer in the room, you'll probably know it.

Dreamers

Dreamers are typically defined more by what's happening in their head and their heart, which makes them a bit more elusive than the Teamer. Dreamers are reserved, particularly around new people, listening and observing more than talking. During that quiet time, Dreamers are processing what's happening in the moment and what it means, reviewing how things have happened in the past (particularly what's gone wrong), considering what might happen in the future, and tracking how others in the room are feeling and reacting. This tendency is perhaps related to the higher levels of stress that Dreamers report—that's a lot to think about! While they value relationships almost as much as their Teamer colleagues, Dreamers don't spread the love around quite so broadly. Instead, a smaller group of close colleagues is their comfort zone.

Even more so than Teamers, Dreamers' motivations come from within, rather than comparing themselves to or competing with others. They have a strong aversion to confrontation and aren't fond of making decisions that might be unpopular. After all, doing so could lead to a conflict! Dreamers openly admit they aren't always terribly disciplined or realistic about things. Instead they prefer to embrace their quiet creativity as they travel their own winding path.

———

Overall, Integrators are gestalt thinkers who excel at seeing how individual pieces fit into a larger context. They're natural mediators who understand diverse perspectives, without needing to prove that one is better than another. They value a positive, inclusive, and respectful environment and strong relationships with others.

And yet, while Integrators are befriending and helping everyone, people are complaining about them, just as they do about all the other types. (Is no one safe from criticism?)

Which brings us to...

The issues with Integrators

JUST SAY WHAT YOU MEAN

One of the most common criticisms of Integrators is that their diplomatic style makes it difficult to know where they stand—do you love my idea or hate it? I can't tell. Others complain that they have to flex their interpretation muscles, doing extra reps just to understand an Integrator's meaning. Some go so far as to say that the Integrator's indirectness causes a trust issue. Or sometimes the problem is in following a conversation that occurs in a roundabout way because an Integrator is trying to spare someone's feelings. So many loop-the-loops can lead to motion sickness and leave listeners wishing that the Integrator would just be straight with them. What's the real deal?

TOUGHEN UP

While Integrators are busy considering everyone else's feelings, they don't always get the same courtesy. Instead, they're accused of being overemotional and oversensitive. Apparently the touchy-feely stuff can make others uncomfortable. People complain they often have to worry about hurting an Integrator's feelings and that it's exhausting to have emotions in the mix at work. They don't want to have to wonder who's going to take offense next.

YOU CAN'T PLEASE EVERYONE

One of the reasons for the Integrator's indirect style is their aversion to conflict, and some people see this as a real problem. To hear others tell it, there might be a giant pink elephant sitting in the middle of the conference table and an Integrator wouldn't acknowledge it if they fear it may cause a conflict. Suppose someone else thinks the elephant is purple. Will it lead to an uncomfortable argument? Integrators are sometimes perceived as so intent on being liked and making everyone happy that they elevate these goals above making the best decision or getting work accomplished efficiently.

HOW MANY COOKS DO WE REALLY NEED?

And speaking of decisions, people sometimes also see Integrators as being overly inclusive and taking too long to make decisions because they're trying to make sure everyone is on board. While many see consensus as a nice-to-have, Integrators see it as a priority. If everyone agrees with a decision, then they're all more likely to push hard toward making things happen, right? But others sometimes complain that a decision everyone agrees with is necessarily a watered down or weaker decision. And it can take a long time to get there.

JUST DECIDE ALREADY

And once they've taken absolutely forever to make a decision that includes everyone's input, the Integrator is still prone to changing their mind! Other types complain endlessly about this tendency of Integrators. The Integrator is often considering new information, additional input, or shifting context, but to others it can seem like they're simply delaying things or causing rework because they're being wishy-washy.

But before you dismiss Integrators as fickle or flighty, consider...

The (social) intelligence of Integrators

Despite the complaints people have about Integrators, when asked which type is most enjoyable to work with, more people say Integrators than any other type. And there are lots of reasons people appreciate them.

COME A LITTLE CLOSER

If two people are standing on opposite banks of a river and need to accomplish something together, a bridge might be a good idea. Integrators often serve as that bridge. Their ability to see both sides of an issue, combined with their diplomatic skill, makes Integrators well suited to the roles of mediator, facilitator, and peacemaker. An Integrator can help two sides understand each other a little better and can illuminate the ways in which each might shift their position enough so that the chasm between them isn't so wide. In a time when teamwork is paramount, bringing people and teams together is perhaps the Integrator's greatest strength.

I HEAR YOU

One of the reasons Integrators are so skilled at their Integratory-magic is that they tend to be great question askers and listeners. When's the last time someone truly listened to you? The Integrator's specialty is asking people for their input, opinions, thoughts, suggestions, and reactions. The bottom line is, people feel understood when someone really listens, and they start to trust the listener. Once the Integrator gains that trust, they can lead a person toward understanding someone else, and pretty soon people are stepping into each other's shoes and taking a bit of a stroll together.

I FEEL YOU

While some would like to pretend we can all leave our emotions at home, in reality those pesky sentiments sometimes accompany us to work whether we'd like them to or not. And that can be a good thing. The ability to sense others' emotions gives the Integrator another tool to work with in their efforts to understand and harmonize. Their sense of compassion means many people are more comfortable sharing their thoughts or feelings with an Integrator than they might be with someone else, and this further aids the Integrator in identifying ways to bring people closer.

HAPPY TO HELP!

We've likely all experienced the difference between a colleague who is happy to help and one who does so begrudgingly, or even worse, stands in the way of what you need to get done. It's just darn pleasant to be around a helpful Integrator, and not only that, you can accomplish more, faster, when you have a helpful colleague contributing to your efforts.

WEB-WEAVERS

Integrators have an uncanny knack for connecting ideas that others might not connect, and for recognizing context others might not see. Say your newly formed team needs to complete a complex project but it's unclear who's in charge. An Integrator is likely to be the one to suggest that the solution might be found in how ants collaborate without a leader. Or, imagine a situation where various cost-cutting measures are being considered. An Integrator is likely to point out the domino effects of one option or the other, and to help envision the long-term implications each might have.

INTEGRATORS ARE...

- Empathic, diplomatic, and relationship oriented
- Attuned to nuance; they see shades of grey rather than black and white
- Inclined to weigh all the options and check with others prior to making decisions

INTEGRATOR MOTTO | Work with me, people!

"A house divided against itself cannot stand."

ABRAHAM LINCOLN

16th President of the United States

The 16th president of the United States, Abraham Lincoln, is known as The Great Emancipator. He paved the way to abolishing slavery while working tirelessly to preserve his country and ensure that "government of the people, by the people, for the people, shall not perish from the earth."

In addition to his height and his hat (in which he kept important documents), he's remembered for his character. He shared credit with others when things went well, and took his share of the blame when they didn't. He was known as being attentive, inclusive, empathic, and diplomatic.

These are characteristics of the **INTEGRATOR**.

Lincoln came from humble beginnings and taught himself how to read and write on his Kentucky family farm. With less than a year of formal education, he earned his certificate to practice law in Illinois, which in those days simply required one to exhibit good moral character.

Lincoln was a man who prioritized listening over expressing his own opinions. And he came by that listening habit honestly—prior to his career in law he was a bartender at Berry & Lincoln, a tavern he briefly co-owned. As a lawyer he preferred to help legal rivals find compromise and settlement, but if mediation failed, one of his greatest assets as an attorney was his ability to appeal to the jury through earnest and purpose-driven stories.

Lincoln's sincere and simple oratory style made him a man of the people and he used these attributes to develop a career in politics. Through a senate race (lost) and a presidential campaign (won) he gained a national reputation for his social responsibility and empathy. His presidential speeches moved people, sometimes to tears. Four months after the

Union defeated the Confederate Army, Lincoln delivered the Gettysburg Address. This compassionate president was sure to choose every word carefully. Recognizing the sacrifices made to preserve a free country, his speech, now engraved on the wall of the Lincoln Memorial, continues to inspire those who read it.

His sense of empathy extended to animals as well. When asked about whether Lincoln had any hobbies, his wife once replied, "Cats." Stories of his cat-scapades include his once letting a feline friend eat from the table during a formal White House dinner, and his rescue of a trio of orphaned kittens while visiting General Grant in Virginia. He was also the first president to pardon the White House turkey on Thanksgiving (a holiday he proclaimed), sparing its life because his son had grown attached to it.

As president, and as listener-in-chief, Lincoln held White House office hours, during which anyone could stop by to chat. He was an inclusive leader who valued the strengths and perspectives of others, even his rivals whom he chose to be part of his cabinet. He esteemed his younger constituents too. Once an 11-year-old girl wrote to Lincoln encouraging him to grow a beard, because he would "look a great deal better" and because "all the ladies like whiskers." Not only did he reply to her letter, but he sought further counsel, writing: "As to the whiskers, never having worn any, do you not think people would call it a piece of silly affectation if I were to begin it now?"

Lincoln was compelled by a strong sense of duty. He had a ceaseless desire to bring consensus and calm across the land, and also to seek freedom for all people. He's perhaps best known for his role in passing the 13th constitutional amendment, but his underlying and enduring goal was focused on the preservation of the union. Celebrated for his ability to bring people together, connect on a personal level, and build trust through listening, Abraham Lincoln led with an Integrator style, and he left big shoes for succeeding presidents to fill—size 14, in fact.

Pioneer

Outgoing
Detail-Averse
Spontaneous
Risk-Seeking
Adaptable
Imaginative

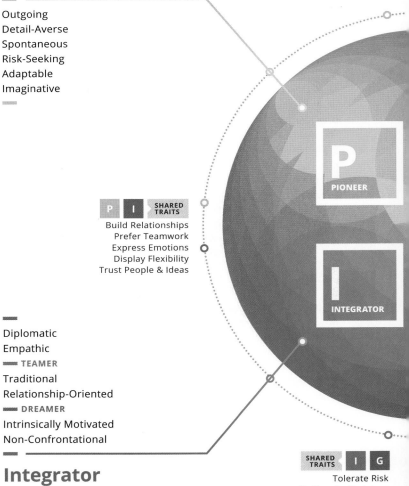

P **I** **SHARED TRAITS**
Build Relationships
Prefer Teamwork
Express Emotions
Display Flexibility
Trust People & Ideas

Diplomatic
Empathic
TEAMER
Traditional
Relationship-Oriented
DREAMER
Intrinsically Motivated
Non-Confrontational

Integrator

SHARED TRAITS **I** **G**
Tolerate Risk
Deliberate Decisions
Internalize Mistakes
Get It Done
Trust the Tried & True

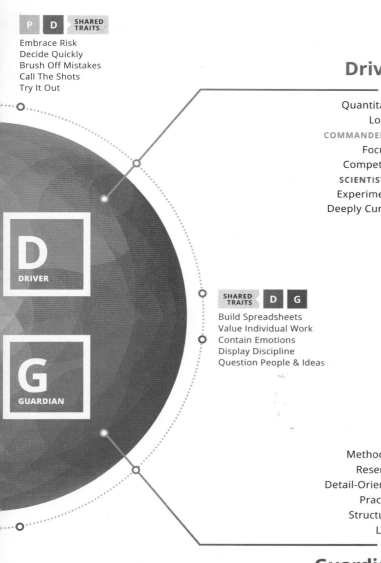

P **D** SHARED TRAITS

Embrace Risk
Decide Quickly
Brush Off Mistakes
Call The Shots
Try It Out

D DRIVER

G GUARDIAN

Driver

Quantitative
Logical
COMMANDER
Focused
Competitive
SCIENTIST
Experimental
Deeply Curious

SHARED TRAITS **D** **G**

Build Spreadsheets
Value Individual Work
Contain Emotions
Display Discipline
Question People & Ideas

Methodical
Reserved
Detail-Oriented
Practical
Structured
Loyal

Guardian

Recognizing Others Through Business Chemistry "Tells"

In poker, the best players learn to look for clues that provide reliable information about their opponent's hand. These "tells," as they're called, are helpful because they are *consistently linked* to a specific meaning. Players can deduce something about their opponent's game by observing their tells. Perhaps one person has an eye twitch whenever she's bluffing, or another person licks his lips when he has a strong hand. They may not always be right (people have been known to fake a tell to throw their opponent off), but overall a player's *probability of being right* is increased when he or she looks for, and acts upon, these indicators.

When it comes to working styles, similar principles apply. Certain observable behaviors are consistently linked to particular styles, and thus serve as useful clues as to a person's Business Chemistry type. In Chapters 3 through 6 we shared observable traits for each of the types; these can be key tells. Maybe you already feel confident you can spot a strong Pioneer by their spontaneous risk-taking, while an extreme Guardian will give themselves away with their meticulous and methodical approach.

We see this in action when we facilitate sessions with executives. Often we ask people to work with others of the same type to create a simple list of things they love at work and things that bug them. Over and over, the same themes emerge. Pioneers adore big ideas and abhor rules, while Guardians put structure on the good list and chaos on the bad. Drivers love winning and hate small talk, while Integrators embrace teaming and avoid conflict.

*

WHAT DO YOU LOVE? WHAT BUGS YOU?

Yet the most interesting thing about this "Loves and Bugs" exercise is not the lists the groups create, but the behaviors they demonstrate while creating them. Over thousands of sessions, the patterns are predictable. The Pioneers will be raucous, with many people talking and even writing at the same time, often using an assortment of colors or sketching pictures. The Guardians will be slow to start, often asking for clarification on the instructions and then writing a neatly ordered list in two straight columns. The Integrators will consult one another extensively, often struggling to come up with things in the bugs category, and they will frequently decorate their set of traits with emoticons. And the Drivers will start before the instructions have even been fully given, write down a short list of things (often captured, without discussion, by the first one to pick up the pen), and then stand around waiting impatiently for the others to finish. As a fly on the wall (or a facilitator), it's immediately clear that you can learn a lot about an individual's working style simply by observing them.

Of course this scenario is contrived, with people grouped according to type. That setup (by design) naturally amplifies certain behaviors, particularly if the group starts bonding over their commonalities. When you see a group of senior executives high-fiving about their mutual love of whiteboards, for instance, it's obvious what we mean. But even in a more natural setting you will see these patterns emerge.

So based on what you've learned so far about each of the types, it seems you should be good to go, right? To a point, yes. Looking for these obvious tells that hint at someone's type is a great place to begin, but you need a little bit more to be a Business Chemistry ninja.

The reality is that things are rarely so simple. To start, recall that people are a combination of all four types, so when you're looking at someone's behavior, you're seeing a mélange of traits, which you'll need to tease apart. Sometimes people are so aligned with one type that it jumps out at you, but other people's traits are less extreme, making their type more challenging to pinpoint. And primary–secondary type combinations can mean two people of the same primary type behave somewhat differently. So for instance a Pioneer with a good dose of Integrator might jump around between options, while a Pioneer with a concentration of Driver might be very decisive. And some of the most telling traits (pun intended) are actually shared between types instead of unique to a particular type. Add to this that Business Chemistry is relative rather than absolute, and you'll want to avoid jumping to conclusions.

So yes, things are a bit more complicated than they might initially seem, but this chapter will serve as your guide for how to quickly make sense of the information surrounding you.

When we look for clues about someone's Business Chemistry type, we call the process creating "a hunch." We call it that because a hunch is not a conclusion, but a starting point; it is an informed hypothesis about someone's type. The process is pretty straightforward.

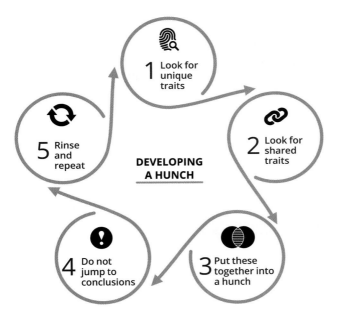

You start by looking for traits that are unique to a type and traits that are shared between types. Then you put these together into a hunch. In doing so you should consider primary–secondary type combinations and relativity, and then test and refine your hunch based on actual interactions with the person. This chapter will cover how to do all of that. In the next chapter we'll cover the remaining two steps, providing guidance for how to avoid jumping to conclusions and addressing why developing hunches should be an ongoing, rather than one-time, process.

So let's get into it!

Look for traits unique to a type

We've spent a lot of time in previous chapters talking about the unique characteristics of the four types. And sometimes a person's Business Chemistry type is so obvious that you can be reasonably confident about creating a hunch in absence of any further information. When someone is an extreme Integrator, for example, their strong focus on relationships, and their careful, diplomatic way of speaking can give them away pretty quickly. To start developing a hunch, it might be easiest to take a look at the following four lists and determine which one best fits the person whose working style you're trying to suss out.

Pioneer	Guardian	Driver	Integrator
Outgoing	Methodical	Quantitative	Diplomatic
Detail-averse	Reserved	Logical	Empathic
Spontaneous	Detail-oriented	Focused	Traditional
Risk-seeking	Practical	Competitive	Relationship-oriented
Adaptable	Structured	Experimental	Intrinsically motived
Imaginative	Loyal	Deeply curious	Non-confrontational

© 2018. Deloitte Touche Tohmatsu Limited

Look for traits shared between types

If you're not very confident about your hunch after the first step (or even if you are), we'd recommend you try this second step. In addition to the traits that are unique to each type, there are also key traits that are shared between types. Sometimes these shared traits are even easier to observe than those that are unique to a specific type, and thus can be helpful in developing a hunch.

To get what we mean by shared traits, it's helpful to think of the universe of traits as exactly that—a universe. Picture a vast space filled with characteristics like adaptable, empathic, practical, and competitive, represented as individual stars. These stars are attracted to, or repelled from, other stars, creating little clusters, or constellations, of associated traits. In the Business Chemistry universe there are four major trait constellations. These are the four primary types. (This metaphor is a more poetic representation of the Eigen analysis we'll describe in the appendix.)

In this universe, while the constellations are discernible, they're not completely isolated from one another. There are stars (traits) at their edges that overlap with neighboring constellations. For simplicity's sake, we've flattened this universe into two dimensions in the diagram below, to indicate the connection points between the types.

Business Chemistry Traits Universe

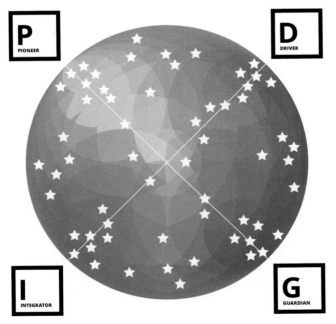

© 2018. Deloitte Touche Tohmatsu Limited

Looking at this flattened chart, you'll see that the extreme ends of the diagonals represent opposite terminals on a spectrum. One diagonal is anchored by Pioneer traits at one end and Guardian traits at the other. The other diagonal has Driver on one end and Integrator on the other. These types at either end of the diagonals are diametrically opposed to one another and thus do not share traits between them. (We'll have more to say on that dynamic in later chapters.) But each type also has two adjacent types or "neighboring constellations" located to either side. If you split the chart into hemispheres—top:bottom and left:right—you'll see that the types within each hemisphere have traits in common that can be useful in refining your hunch.

___

SHARED TRAITS:
PIONEERS & DRIVERS, GUARDIANS & INTEGRATORS

When you split the universe graph horizontally, you can see that Pioneers and Drivers share several traits on the top of the circle, and Guardians and Integrators share several on the bottom. Being in opposite hemispheres, the Pioneer-Driver

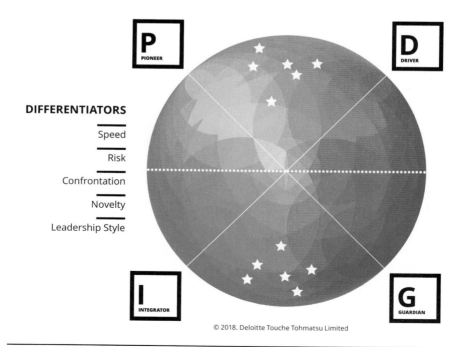

shared traits are the inverse of the Guardian-Integrator shared traits, as one might expect. The main distinguishing traits between these pairings relate to: 1) speed, 2) risk, 3) confrontation, 4) novelty and 5) leadership style. When you're trying to get a sense of what someone's working style might be, start by looking for where people fall in terms these five things to home in on a hemisphere. Are they more like the Pioneer and Driver pairing or are they more like the Guardian and Integrator one?

Speed. Pioneers and Drivers both make decisions quickly, though how they get there looks different. Pioneers tend to go with their gut and take a leap (sometimes literally not just figuratively), whereas Drivers are more likely to evaluate options, but rapidly, by eliminating extraneous data. (Or anything else they consider extraneous.)

Guardians and Integrators, in contrast, are both slower to make decisions, but likely for different reasons. Guardians because they're checking all the details, ensuring all the i's are dotted and the t's are crossed. Integrators because they're thinking through all the possible scenarios and long-term implications, or because they're connecting with a network of stakeholders, seeking input and alignment.

Pioneers and Drivers also tend to speak more rapidly than Guardians and Integrators, and they're quick to jump in with the "gift" of filling the silence if they perceive there's too much of a pause in discussion.

Risk. Pioneers and Drivers are both more likely to seek out risk than Guardians and Integrators. Pioneers are often acting intuitively. The opportunity just *feels* like it's worth the risk. (*Woohoo, I've always wanted to jump out of a plane!*) Whereas Drivers have likely *calculated* that it's worth it. (*The probability is extremely low that my chute won't open and I'll plummet to my death.*)

For Guardians, risk is somewhat alarming by its very nature, as it threatens stability. (*Is the plane crashing? No? Then why would I throw myself out of a perfectly functioning aircraft?*) Integrators, too, sometimes feel apprehensive about risk, but their aversion may stem more from a fear of unintended consequences and negative impacts to individuals. (*I know Paul doesn't really want to jump and I don't want to make him feel bad by leaving him behind.*)

Confrontation. Pioneers and Drivers are more comfortable with confrontation than Guardians and Integrators. For Pioneers this is likely because they don't internalize incidents or people's reactions to them, and they're able to move on quickly from a tense moment. They're also used to butting up against resistance in their quest to move beyond the status quo. For Drivers, confrontation can actually be fun, playing into their love of challenge and a good argument. You got a problem with that?

In contrast, Guardians dislike rocking the boat, and can be particularly sensitive to negative interactions as they tend to mull things over well after the interaction is in the past. Integrators dislike confrontation as they don't want to risk damaging relationships, and they hate to hurt other people's feelings. They're also prone to taking things to heart themselves. Both of these types are more likely to follow a path of subtler resistance—dragging their feet or gradually chipping away at an undesirable position—rather than addressing it head on.

Novelty. Both Pioneers and Drivers gravitate toward what's original or novel, while Guardians and Integrators are more oriented toward what's existing or traditional. This manifests in interesting ways according to type.

With ideas for instance, Pioneers love fresh, blue-sky thinking, whereas Drivers like to define new realms of thought through experimentation. Both tend to be faster to adopt new technology and innovations.

On the other side, Guardians like ideas that are proven, tried and true, while Integrators often take tried and true concepts and combine them in imaginative ways, making an effort to recognize and promote other people's contributions to the idea.

With tradition, Pioneers and Drivers will be quicker to dismiss established practice, Pioneers typically because they're thirsty for something new, and Drivers often because they don't consider traditions necessary or worth the effort to maintain. (And if they're rejecting traditions like the rock-hard fruitcake of a dear auntie, we don't blame them.)

Guardians and Integrators on the other hand value tradition more highly. Guardians perhaps because traditions are integral to the way society is structured and operates, and Integrators likely out of respect and appreciation for culture, and an understanding that traditions help people get along better. (And it sure does make Auntie happy when we eat her cake.)

These differences are consistent with the shared tendency of Guardians and Integrators overall to value loyalty more than the Pioneers and Drivers sitting on the other side of the universe.

Leadership style. Pioneers and Drivers (particularly Commanders) describe themselves as being more likely to "take charge" than Guardians and Integrators. This corresponds to the classic, somewhat stereotypical model of a leader who steps up, seizes control, and makes sure the right things are happening.

Guardians and Integrators arguably tend to practice a more nuanced approach to leadership. For instance, Guardians might take leadership based on some specific expertise versus universally grabbing the reins. And Integrators might lead through influence, or by composing and orchestrating a team of contributors. Or, either might prefer to contribute by playing a more behind the scenes, individual contributor, or supporting role.

By considering their approach to speed, risk, confrontation, novelty, and leadership, we hope you can determine whether a person's style is more similar to the Pioneer and Driver hemisphere, or the Guardian and Integrator one. Once you've done that, you can refine your hypothesis by splitting the sphere in the other direction.

SHARED TRAITS:
PIONEERS & INTEGRATORS, DRIVERS & GUARDIANS

Now we dive into the other view of shared traits, splitting the universe graph vertically. In this orientation you see that Pioneers and Integrators share several traits on the left side of the circle, and Drivers and Guardians share the inverse traits on the right. The distinguishing traits between these pairings relate to: 1) information, 2) flexibility, 3) attitude, and 4) people. Again, the point is to figure out which side better characterizes a person's style—the Pioneer and Integrator side, or the Driver and Guardian side.

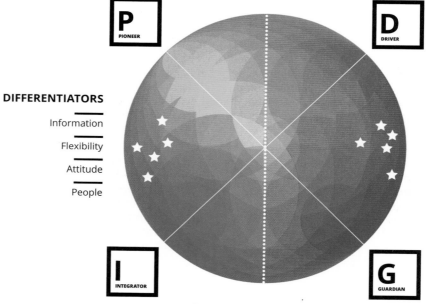

DIFFERENTIATORS

Information

Flexibility

Attitude

People

© 2018. Deloitte Touche Tohmatsu Limited

Information. The two vertical sides of the circle are different both in terms of what kinds of information their associated types like, as well as how they process information.

Pioneers and Integrators tend to be very visual and don't necessarily seek numbers or stats. Pioneers, often described as "big picture thinkers," tend to like actual pictures, and bigger and bolder is often better. Integrators, with their interest in relationships and people, are particularly drawn to stories, and they love rich descriptions that help them imagine the situation or circumstance.

Drivers and Guardians, in contrast, are more quantitatively oriented, and love facts and figures. For them, data is essential. But Drivers, likely motivated by their urge to quickly achieve their objectives, will usually seek just enough information to feel confident in their conclusions. Guardians are much more likely to immerse themselves in a comprehensive level of detail to ensure that everything is just right and nothing has been overlooked.

When it comes to processing information, Pioneers and Integrators are non-linear thinkers, highly contextual and guided by intuition. Drivers and Guardians are logical and disciplined, tending to take a more linear approach and looking for data to back them up.

Flexibility. Pioneers and Integrators tend to be very comfortable with ambiguity and nuance, and they typically follow a fluid thought process. Whereas Drivers and Guardians like clarity and precision, and are more methodical.

Pioneers and Integrators tend to change their minds more frequently than Drivers and Guardians. For Pioneers, that might be simply because something more interesting comes along. For Integrators, it could be because they're open to options and can often see the pros and cons of various perspectives.

Drivers are more likely to make rational decisions based on facts, and are therefore unlikely to change their minds unless there are new facts available or their logic is proven faulty (a possibility they would claim is highly unlikely, though they'd welcome a well-prepared dispute). Similarly, Guardians have likely done the math (literally) to arrive at their decision, not to mention probably having triple checked their work, so there would have to be a pretty big change in the underlying variables to change their mind.

Attitude. Pioneers and Integrators are, in general, more optimistic and trusting than the other types. This correlation makes sense given that Pioneers would arguably be less eager to venture into unknown territory if they thought it wasn't likely to end well. And Integrators' strong relationship orientation likely requires a faith in others.

In contrast, Drivers and Guardians are more skeptical and exacting. Drivers likely because they need a verifiable reason to believe in something, and they have little tolerance for excuses when people can't meet the high standards they set. Guardians probably because if they haven't personally checked and confirmed something, there's a risk that it might not be correct.

Pioneers and Integrators also tend to be expressive, sharing their emotions freely. For Pioneers, this is probably more of an expression of their own emotions (often *joie de vivre*), without really tuning into other people's, whereas Integrators might genuinely reveal their own full spectrum of emotions, but might also encourage others to express their emotions as a means to form a bond with them.

Both Drivers and Guardians tend to keep their feelings in check. Some might say for Drivers that's because they don't have any, although we'd argue that it's more likely because they believe emotions are irrelevant and/or a distraction to the work at hand. And you can see where a Guardian might avoid unfettered emotions—after all, how can you have things under control if your own emotions aren't?

People. Pioneers and Integrators are both relationship oriented. They're collaborative, and value teamwork and diverse perspectives. Integrators tend to be perceptive, paying attention to and understanding human dynamics, whereas Pioneers tend to play to people—as an audience or as potential compadres in the pursuit of fun. Both are also generous, though perhaps in different ways. An Integrator is likely to be found spending time coaching junior members of the team, while the Pioneer might be spontaneously buying a round of drinks at the bar.

Drivers and Guardians are more inclined to work independently, or at least to enjoy it more when the opportunity arises. They're not as motivated to maintain large networks and don't prioritize extensive social connections. But both are happy to have the Pioneer buy drinks.

By combining the previous view of shared traits with this one—focused on a person's approach to information, flexibility, attitude, and people—you should be able to narrow your hunch even more.

Put together a hunch

Developing a hunch about someone's type is a bit like being teleported to an unfamiliar area in space and trying to figure out where you are based on the few stars you see around you. You try to get a general sense of your location first, by looking for both unique and shared traits. When you see them, you ask yourself, "In which hemisphere are these traits located?" Then you investigate further to confirm or adjust your assessment.

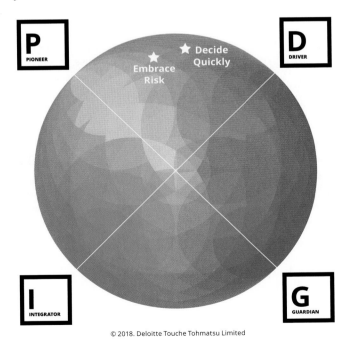

© 2018. Deloitte Touche Tohmatsu Limited

To see how this works in practice, let's imagine that you have a new boss. You've interacted a few times but you don't know her very well. You've maybe tried to get a sense of her style by considering the unique traits associated with each type, but you're not feeling confident about your hunch so you look around some more. Let's say that you've noticed two really visible tells: Your boss makes fast decisions and she seems to embrace risk. When you check your universe map, you can see that puts her in the top hemisphere—the Pioneer-Driver zone. But is she more of a Pioneer or a Driver?

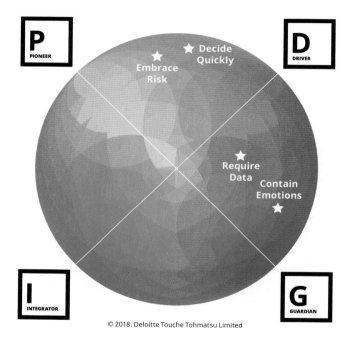

© 2018. Deloitte Touche Tohmatsu Limited

Now you look around some more. Let's say there are another two traits: Your boss is not very expressive and she insists on having data to inform a decision. That puts her in the right hemisphere—the Driver-Guardian zone of your universe map. In both cuts of the universe diagram, she has traits aligned with the Driver type, so your educated guess would be that she's a Driver. So far, so good. Even if you stopped at this point, you'd have a solid start for connecting with her more effectively.

But to be really confident about this hunch there are a few more things to consider: 1) People don't have only primary types, but also secondary types and these can be important. 2) Business Chemistry is relative, which matters as well. 3) Since situations impact people's behavior, it's best to observe them over time in a variety of situations to see their most consistent behaviors.

SECONDARY TYPES MATTER

Let's start with secondary types. People's working styles aren't characterized purely by one type, so let's continue with the example of your new boss to see if we can glean even more information about her. Since her primary type seems to be Driver, her secondary type would have to be either Pioneer or Guardian. Wait, how would you know that? Because Business Chemistry runs along dimensions, and unlike comic books or quantum physics, where things can be in opposing positions at the same time, when it comes to Business Chemistry people can be at one end of a dimension or the other, or anywhere in between, but they can't be at both ends at once. Those two dimensions are the diagonals in the model: Pioneer to Guardian, and Driver to Integrator. So if your boss is a strong Driver, by definition she can't also be a strong Integrator.

You've narrowed down the options to Driver-Pioneer or Driver-Guardian. This is worth trying to get a bead on, because these combinations have different ways of thinking and interacting. To do so, it's perhaps easiest to go back to the unique traits: Does your boss love details or abhor them? Is she outgoing or reserved? If you consistently answer yes to the traits associated with one or the other, chances are she has a strong secondary type. If not, or if she has traits of both, then perhaps she's mostly defined by Driver and she has a less extreme secondary type.

IT'S ALL RELATIVE

As you start looking for tells in the people around you, it's helpful to remember that Business Chemistry is relative. While people's working styles and preferences tend to be more or less consistent across most situations (a bit more on that in the coming pages), the way they come across can depend on the company in which they find themselves.

Have you ever had the dubious pleasure of painting your house? You know how it works then. You walk into the store and look at row upon row of little squares with tiny variations in color. They have names that are meant to be evocative, but aren't really that helpful—like Misty Mountain or Chilled Sangria. You pick a few and bring them home.

In Kim's house the process goes something like this: Kim says, "What do you think of this one, honey?" Her husband replies, "It looks white to me."

And then Kim proceeds to run around the house holding the swatch up to different colors to see how it looks a little green against the light wall, but more blue when she holds it in the corner. (It never looks white, by the way, despite her husband's claims.) The color of the swatch does not in fact change, but it seems more green or more blue, depending on the backdrop.

The same thing happens with working styles. A person might seem like a Pioneer in a typical business setting, but how does he appear beside a CEO who launches a new venture by rappelling from the top of an airplane hangar? Does he still seem like a Pioneer in comparison? Or what if he's in a meeting with a traditional company in Asia, where the culture itself emphasizes many Guardian-like traits?

Another thing to consider is that people sometimes change their behavior deliberately, based on who they're interacting with. Suppose a person who is generally quite empathic, diplomatic, and relationship oriented finds herself on a team full of very strong Integrators. She might embrace more of a direct, goal-focused approach on purpose, to balance out the majority type in the group. Alternatively, she might double-down on her Integrator tendencies to fit in.

We all have a natural hue, but the way we come across depends on our context, so it's important to consider that when you're trying to get a sense of someone's type. If you'd like more details about how Business Chemistry takes relativity into account, see the appendix.

THE EXCEPTION OR THE NORM?

Once you've considered unique traits, shared traits, secondary type, and relativity, you should have a pretty reasonable hunch about someone's type. But your next mission is to test that hypothesis through actual interactions with the person. Because it's clear that the situation someone is in has great potential to influence how they think, feel, and behave. It's quite likely, for example, that a person who usually speaks loudly will speak more softly in a quiet office if they notice that everyone else is whispering.

While you shouldn't expect anyone to act exactly the same in every situation, Business Chemistry is about how someone *prefers* to work, and how they think, feel, and behave in professional settings *most of the time*. The instructions for our online Business Chemistry assessment (which we'll tell you more about in the appendix) ask people how they'd describe themselves generally in a business context. Likewise, when you attempt to develop a hunch about someone's type you should do so within this same context, looking for how someone behaves most often.

Ideally you'd observe someone across a variety of situations and interactions. And as you work with them further, you'll take your understanding of their working style from a general zone on the universe map to a particular collection of stars that are uniquely their own.

E: NONE OF THE ABOVE

Most of the time, you will have enough clues to develop a reasonable hunch about someone's primary and/or secondary types. But some people aren't extreme on any of the dimensions, so you will likely pick up tells from each of the patterns. Or perhaps you will identify one trait, but you won't find the other things with which that trait is normally correlated. These people can be valuable team players because of their flexibility, but they can also be difficult to get a read on. That's OK, it just means you might need to base your hypotheses more on situations (she is very Pioneer when we're in a situation where idea generation is needed, but very Guardian when it's time to execute) or context (he is comfortable taking risks within his own team, but uncomfortable when he's with a new group). And whether you're dealing with someone who defies all hunching attempts, or someone who epitomizes the extreme of a type, it's essential that you try hard to avoid jumping to conclusions. That's just what we'll address in the next chapter.

Using Business Chemistry Responsibly

At its most basic, Business Chemistry is a framework for identifying and categorizing people's working styles. Doing so can provide important clues to another's perspective and is one practical way to deepen understanding, cultivate empathy, and create chemistry. It simplifies an otherwise complex and sometimes mystifying endeavor—crafting powerful work relationships.

But we feel it's time to interject a warning here. With great (hunching) power comes great responsibility. It can be easy to make judgements about someone based on incorrect assumptions or biases, and doing so is no better than assuming (incorrectly) that everyone is just like you. Indeed, it's worse; you not only miss the actual insights that Business Chemistry can provide, but you also layer on the negative consequences of typecasting. In this chapter we'll address how to avoid these negative consequences and use Business Chemistry responsibly.

Avoid jumping to conclusions

We sometimes get asked whether categorizing people into Business Chemistry types is really just stereotyping. And it could be seen that way. Another view is that such conscious categorization is preferable to the unconscious biases that often plague us in the workplace and beyond. Let us explain.

While stereotyping can sometimes be harmful, it's pretty natural. Humans are prone to preconceptions and stereotypes. These biases come from the brain's attempt to cope with the overwhelming amount of information it has to process every day. It simply can't handle the data points rushing at it from every direction, so it simplifies the world by categorizing just about everything—including people. Essentially, our brains engage in stereotyping automatically.

In their 2013 book, *Blindspot: The Hidden Biases of Good People,* Mahzarin Banaji and Anthony Greenwald reveal some surprising statistics about how many of us have biases associated with race, gender, age, and other characteristics of people. We're often unaware of these biases, and in fact, our conscious or stated attitudes may conflict with them.[1]

We suspect that most people would prefer not to operate under the influence of unconscious biases and likewise prefer that others don't. For example, when Suzanne is speaking with a group of leaders, she'd prefer that their brains aren't homing in on the fact that she's a woman, or that she has a slight Midwestern accent, or that she has blond hair. Those characteristics should be irrelevant in that situation. But the research suggests that their brains likely *are* focused on these things and, further more, that they're forming an impression of Suzanne based on the associations they have with those categories. Without knowing it, her audience members are likely deciding that she's emotional (a trait commonly assumed of women), that she's "Minnesota-nice," and if they've heard too many blond jokes, well ... it's not good.

So let's get down to brass tacks. If we'd rather not be judging each other in this way, why are we encouraging you to categorize people based on Business Chemistry? The thing is, interventions designed to reduce the amount of stereotyping we do have met with limited success.[2][3] But we'd suggest that one way to mitigate the impact of our brain's unconscious biases based on workplace-irrelevant factors is by encouraging conscious categorization based on workplace-relevant factors. In other words, we're proposing that in a work setting, categorizing based on Business Chemistry might be better than categorizing based on other factors, especially if you're aware that you're doing it and you take some particular precautions, which we'll describe below.

This strategy is akin to taking away a pair of scissors that a toddler has gotten a hold of. You can snatch the scissors away, or you can try to reason with her, but replacing the scissors with a hand-mirror is probably a better bet.

Rather than simply trying to overcome our unconscious biases, one of the simplest solutions may be to meet our brain's fundamental need for categorization with a different way of categorizing—one we *choose* and are fully aware of.

> ✱ **MEET YOUR BRAIN'S FUNDAMENTAL NEED FOR CATEGORIZATION WITH A WAY OF CATEGORIZING YOU CHOOSE AND ARE FULLY AWARE OF.**

There's evidence that this type of replacement strategy works when we're trying to break a habit. Take for example, that donut you might be eating each day as a mid-afternoon snack. Instead of just trying to resist the donut, it's more effective to create a new routine that replaces the habit, like taking an afternoon walk.[4] If stereotyping or unconscious categorization can be seen as a habit we'd like to break, then replacing it with a new routine, like focusing in on one's Business Chemistry type, should help.

So if the leaders Suzanne is speaking with focus in on the fact that her Business Chemistry type is Guardian (rather than the fact that she is a blond, Midwestern woman), the associations their brains are making will likely be more relevant to the situation. Their impression of her now may be that she's detail-oriented, meticulous, practical, and maybe a bit inflexible.

Is this the perfect solution to unconscious bias in the workplace? No, it's not perfect. By definition, categorizing anything means simplifying, and that means overlooking some nuance. Maybe Suzanne is a Guardian who is *not* inflexible and now her audience will mistakenly think that she is. (No worries here, as Suzanne can be *quite* inflexible at times.) You might suggest it would be better to get to know each and every person we encounter individually, and it probably would. But most of us encounter far too many people in a given week, or even in a given day, to get to know them all personally. It might help to identify those individuals for whom it's critical you get beyond categories to learn about their unique characteristics—maybe your boss, those who report to you, and anyone about whom you are making highly impactful decisions, such as whether to hire or promote them, or how to rate their performance.

But we won't deny that, used carelessly, categorizing people based on Business Chemistry could have some detrimental effects. We don't recommend you view Business Chemistry as the last word on how someone might prefer to interact, receive information, or make a decision. Nor should you use it as a predictor of someone's success in general, or in a particular role or industry, or as the basis for determining whether to offer someone a job or a promotion. One's Business Chemistry type is not a statement on what they can or cannot do, nor is it the sum total of who a person is.

Instead we recommend using Business Chemistry to make an initial prediction about how someone might prefer to interact, receive information, or make a decision. After determining that, try to find out more. Additionally, you can use Business Chemistry as a common language for talking about differences in perspectives; or as a starting point for considering why a particular work relationship is challenging and how you can turn it around; or as a basis for exploring whether your team's ways of working enable the success of all types of people. In the chapters that follow we'll provide more guidance on why and how you might use Business Chemistry in all of these practical ways.

But for now, to help you use this replacement approach responsibly, we've rounded up a "Least Wanted" list of the usual suspects that can cause problems, so hopefully you'll know them when you see them.

BUSINESS CARD BIASES

Yes, it's true that titles can tell you a lot about someone's function in an organization, but titles are not necessarily reliable predictors of an individual's working style (nor is function, for that matter). In our experience, people sometimes mistakenly map a role to a particular Business Chemistry type.

Take for example, the chief financial officer (CFO) role. We often hear things like "He must be a Guardian, because he's a CFO." Indeed, as one might expect, CFOs as a group are often seen as detail-focused pragmatists who deliberate before taking a risk. But as you'll learn in Chapter 11, our own research with the C-suite found that CFOs were most commonly Drivers, with Guardians coming in second. And this role had healthy representation across the other types as well. Indeed, in one of our *Business Chemistry Confessions* podcast episodes, we interviewed Mark Buthman, CFO Emeritus at Kimberly-Clark Corporation, and an Integrator. In that discussion he acknowledged that his style might not seem like the standard CFO profile, but that his ability to bring people together and build teams was in fact key to his success.

✳

CREATING A HUNCH IS AN EXERCISE IN PROBABILITIES.

When you assume that a person *must* be a certain type because of the role they're in, you're basing your hunch on a generic data set, versus looking for tells from the actual person. Developing a hunch is an exercise in probabilities, so if you stop at generic assumptions, you're stacking the odds against yourself.

Remember, your Business Chemistry type is your most comfortable zone to play in, but that by no means implies you can't venture outside of it. Accordingly, just because a role requires a certain approach, doesn't mean it's only open to certain types. To use our CFO example, you don't need to be a Driver or Guardian to be able to work with numbers. An interesting question to consider is how far and how often you need to venture out of your comfort zone in order to fulfill a role, and is that sustainable? For many roles these days, there is so much flexibility in how you approach the position and who you team with in order to drive success, it's possible for a wider range of styles to play to their strengths while still meeting the role objectives.

So next time you get that business card that says "Systems Analyst" or "Marketing Specialist" or "Controller", check yourself before you rush to a conclusion about their type. (But if their card says "Chief Troublemaker," you can venture, with some confidence, that they're probably a strong Pioneer.)

ALL-OR-NOTHING ASSUMPTIONS

Picture this. You have a person who is always spouting off crazy ideas in meetings, who changes her facts every time she tells a story, and whose laughter can be heard five offices down every time she takes a conference call. Such a Pioneer in every way. Or is she? This person, it turns out, also really values tradition (unlike most Pioneers) and was appalled when you suggested eliminating the annual Founders' Feast because you thought it was "unnecessary kowtowing to the past." Oops.

It's tempting to assume that because a person has most of the traits associated with a type that they have all of them. Remember, everyone has a unique mix of traits, even if they strongly associate with a particular type.

There's a certain popular magazine that Kim admits to occasionally picking up while waiting in the dentist's office or the grocery store checkout line. At the very end of the issue they always have two pictures which appear, at first glance, to be identical, but that in fact have subtle differences.

Your mission when you encounter people that seem to clearly fit a type is to treat them like those picture challenges. Don't just say, "Yup, they look like that type" and then brush your hands and move on. Remind yourself that categories are simplifications and must be taken with a grain of salt. Then look for the traits people have that don't match their type, which can be as important to understand, and appreciate, as the things that are more typical. One exercise that helps drive this home in our work with teams is for each member of the team to share and discuss one trait that is characteristic of their Business Chemistry type but does *not* apply to them personally.

> *****
> **WHAT CHARACTERISTIC TRAIT OF YOUR TYPE DOES *NOT* APPLY TO YOU PERSONALLY?**

PEJORATIVE PIGEONHOLING

We admit it can feel good to identify with others who share your Business Chemistry type. We often see a bonding effect in sessions as executives of the same type welcome one another as one of their own. One of the negative aspects of this tribalism though, is a tendency to negatively characterize those who are *not* like you, which is often most harshly directed at the type opposite yours. Instead of focusing on, and appreciating, all the positive aspects of other types, people can get fixated on the dark side traits—negative perceptions of types at their worst.

For instance, just to share a few of the things we hear:

- Pioneers lack substance.
- Guardians are rigid.
- Drivers are jerks.
- Integrators are flaky.

These negative labels obviously generalize in a way that is neither accurate nor helpful. Worse, this kind of mindset can prevent us from converting diversity into positive potential. After all, if you always think of Drivers as jerks, how likely is it that you're going to take advantage of all the positive things Drivers have to offer?

This effect can be exacerbated in groups dominated by a particular Business Chemistry type. These *mono-style* teams must make a concerted effort to not dismiss the value of other types, and rather actively seek, incorporate, and nurture diverse perspectives.

* WHAT IS THE UNIQUE VALUE OF YOUR OPPOSITE TYPE?

One exercise we like to do with teams is to ask them to brainstorm the unique value brought by other types, particularly their opposites. What follows is a typical list a team might produce.

WE GUARDIANS LOVE PIONEERS BECAUSE THEY...

- Bring energy and passion to every interaction
- Are optimistic and encourage us to take risks
- Are full of new and interesting ideas

WE PIONEERS LOVE GUARDIANS BECAUSE THEY...

- Help us keep track of the details
- Serve as a reality check
- Keep us out of trouble

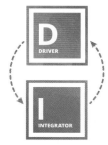

WE INTEGRATORS LOVE DRIVERS BECAUSE THEY...

- Keep us moving forward at a swift pace
- Are not afraid to ask challenging questions
- Encourage competition in a way that pushes us

WE DRIVERS LOVE INTEGRATORS BECAUSE THEY...

- Bring a collaborative spirit to the team
- Keep an eye on team morale
- Encourage us to include diverse views

Finally...rinse and repeat

At the end of the day, the purpose of creating a hunch is not to figure out a person's type as an absolute, abstract concept, but rather to determine how they actually show up at work, what they're likely to want and need, and how you can best interact with them. The point is not *categorization*, but rather *observation*, *recognition*, and *refinement*. Only then do we have a solid basis for *adaptation*, and if we're lucky, *appreciation*. We are not suggesting a one-and-done task, but rather an ongoing process for how you see and relate to the people around you.

The more you start looking for clues related to individual types, the more you'll notice not only the ways that people really *match* the different patterns, but the ways that they *don't match* as well. You will accelerate your ability to do in business what probably comes to you naturally in your personal life: You'll see, not types, but individuals—and that's a key ingredient for great chemistry.

REFERENCES

1. Banaji, Mahzarin R., and Anthony G. Greenwald. *Blindspot: Hidden Biases of Good People*. New York: Delacorte Press, 2013.

2. Paluck, Elizabeth Levy. "Interventions Aimed at the Reduction of Prejudice and Conflict." *The Oxford Handbook of Intergroup Conflict,* edited by Linda R. Troop. New York: Oxford University Press, 2012.

3. Hoffman, Adam. "Can Science Help People Unlearn Their Unconscious Biases?" Smithsonian.com. July 02, 2015. https://www.smithsonianmag.com/science-nature/can-science-help-people-unlearn-their-unconscious-biases-180955789/.

4. Duhigg, Charles. *Power of Habit: Why We Do What We Do in Life and Business*. New York: Penguin Random House, 2012.

Business
Chemistry
Electives

9

What about Introverts and Extroverts?

An Introvert and an Extrovert walk into a conference room. They sit across the table from each other. Then the Extrovert says...

Does it really matter what the Extrovert says? Maybe not according to Steve Schloss, CHRO and Chief People Officer of the United States Golf Association: "Even if what the Extrovert is saying is likely incorrect, this individual is likely to win the day in that given conversation because the Introvert chose to listen, process, observe, and maybe come back at a later point." Steve said this during one of our favorite *Business Chemistry Confessions* podcast episodes. And while it sounds a bit like a joke, it describes a scene we've witnessed in real life many times. An Introvert pauses before speaking, and then never gets a chance to speak at all as the conversation barrels ahead.

But Steve isn't advocating for an Extrovert style over an Introvert style. In fact, he says later in the same podcast episode, "If you want applause, you can speak all you want, but if you want results, you have to listen." We love the pairing of these two quotes together because it highlights the importance of having a balance between styles. If you pause too long before speaking up, you lose, but if you talk too much, you lose as well. Unless, of course, all you wanted was applause.

When it comes to personality differences, it seems people have always been particularly interested in the Introvert/Extrovert distinction. But in 2012 introversion burst into the spotlight with the publication of Susan Cain's book *Quiet: The Power of Introverts in a World that Can't Stop Talking*.[1] Through a meticulous compilation of research, Cain argues there are many ways in which society today is built for Extroverts, which means we lose out on much of the potential value Introverts can bring to our schools, our organizations, and our communities. She really struck a chord—her book has sold millions of copies and her accompanying TED Talk has been viewed more than 18 million times. But as Cain does, we'll suggest that we don't have to lose out on the value Introverts bring, and in the chapters that follow we suggest lots of practical ways that you can help create an environment on your own teams and in your own organization that will support the performance of both Introverts and Extroverts.

In Chapters 3 through 6 we touched on the ways in which the Business Chemistry types relate to introversion and extroversion. Guardians are generally more introverted and Pioneers more extroverted. But Integrators and Drivers are mixed, each having two subtypes that divide along these lines. Among Integrator subtypes, Dreamers are more introverted and Teamers more extroverted. Among Driver subtypes, Scientists are more introverted and Commanders more extroverted. As you'll see in the next chapter, this particular lens on the Business Chemistry types becomes particularly significant in relation to some of our research findings. Given that, we thought it would be helpful to devote a bit more attention to the Introvert-Extrovert distinction here.

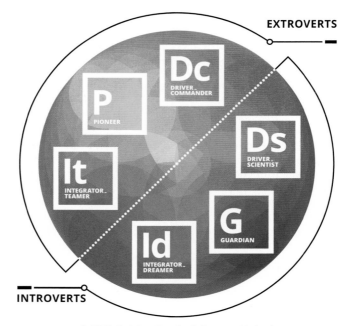

© 2018. Deloitte Touche Tohmatsu Limited

What's in a label?

To start, it seems to make sense to back up a bit and define what we mean by introversion and extroversion. While most of us likely have some sense of what is meant by these terms, there is no universally agreed upon definition of Introvert or Extrovert. Among the most highly researched definitions is one associated with the five-factor model of personality, which characterizes Extroverts as outgoing and energetic, and Introverts as solitary and reserved.[2][3] Other definitions highlight physiological differences in the sensitivity of Introverts' and Extroverts' neurological systems, particularly in relation to dopamine[4] and to base rates of arousal.[5] Extroverts are less sensitive to dopamine and naturally have lower levels of arousal, leading them to seek out stimulation in order to achieve optimal levels of both. Introverts are more sensitive to dopamine and have generally higher levels of arousal, leading them to avoid stimulation so as not to become overwhelmed. In line with that distinction, Cain describes Introverts as having a preference for quieter, less stimulating environments and Extroverts as preferring more stimulation.[6] Still other definitions highlight common distinctions between the primary focus of one's attention: a person's inner world versus the world around them; or their primary source of energy, time alone or with others.[7] And some definitions get even more specific, identifying multiple subtypes of Introverts or Extroverts.[8][9]

We're not going to tackle the challenge of arguing which of these definitions is superior. In fact we considered several of these lenses when we initially set out to understand how the Business Chemistry types relate to introversion and extroversion. And what we saw right away was that the distinction was clear for Pioneers, who seemed more extroverted, and Guardians, who seemed more introverted, but that wasn't the case for Drivers and Integrators. That is, it wasn't clear until we looked closely at the subtypes. When we did that, we noticed that both Dreamers and Scientists seemed to have more of the Introvert characteristics, while Teamers and Commanders had more of the Extrovert. So to develop our own working definitions of Introversion and Extroversion as they play out in the workplace, we analyzed all the Business

Chemistry traits and identified those showing a statistically significant difference between the three more introverted Business Chemistry types and the three more extroverted types. Our resulting definitions are as follows:

Extroverts are outgoing and energetic. They talk fast, make impulsive decisions, and adapt easily. They prioritize having lots of people in their networks and take charge in groups.

Introverts are reserved and unhurried. Their contributions to discussions are measured, and they deliberate before making decisions and adapt at a gradual pace. They maintain smaller networks and add value in supporting roles.

Trait differences between extroverted and introverted Business Chemistry types

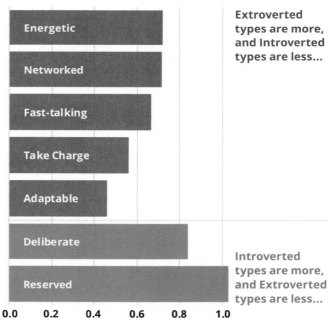

Size of the difference between Extroverts and Introverts

Not lunatics

Of course if you want to be really accurate about things, you should add "on average" to those descriptions, because these are of course generalizations. While we're at it, we should also note that people aren't wholly introverted or extroverted. In fact Carl Jung, who popularized these labels, once stated "There is no such thing as a pure Introvert or Extrovert. Such a person would be in the lunatic asylum."

In Chapter 7 we mentioned that people typically have both a primary Business Chemistry type and a secondary type, and these pairings are relevant here are well, because a person might have an introverted primary type and an introverted secondary type, extroverted primary and secondary types, or one of each. And these type combinations are a clue to just how introverted or extroverted a person is. Someone with introverted primary and secondary types may not be purely introverted, but they're likely to be more so than someone with mixed primary and secondary types. Likewise, someone with extroverted primary and secondary types is probably more extroverted than others.

Introverts   Extroverts

	Introverts	Extroverts
MATCHED	Guardian/Dreamer	Pioneer/Commander
	Dreamer/Guardian	Commander/Pioneer
	Guardian/Scientist	Pioneer/Teamer
	Scientist/Guardian	Teamer/Pioneer
MIXED	Guardian/Teamer	Pioneer/Scientist
	Guardian/Commander	Pioneer/Dreamer
	Dreamer/Pioneer	Teamer/Guardian
	Scientist/Pioneer	Commander/Guardian

We'll use ourselves as an illustration. Suzanne, as a Guardian-Dreamer, is quite firmly introverted, and may be even sneaking up on lunacy. But Kim, as a Pioneer-Scientist, is extroverted with a side dish of introversion. With this kind of mixed-type combination, she might also be thought of as an *Ambivert*.

Like Introverts and Extroverts, there is no universally agreed-upon definition of an Ambivert. We use the term to describe a person who quite easily moves back and forth between these Introvert and Extrovert orientations, similar to how an ambidextrous individual can fluidly switch between using their right or left hand. Chances are it's easier for someone with a mixed primary–secondary combination to move back and forth, but it's possible for anyone, particularly if their type is more moderate than extreme (we'll talk a bit more about that in the appendix).

While we do recognize this complexity, for the sake of our analyses throughout this book, we consider one's primary type to determine whether they're in the Introvert or Extrovert category—so Suzanne is considered an Introvert and Kim is considered an Extrovert, even though she has a mixed-type combination. And again, we'll acknowledge here that when we label people we're generalizing a bit for the sake of simplicity. Of course, all that you are cannot be captured in a single word. Not you and not anyone else.

___

More fraternal than identical

So generally we refer to all primary Guardians, Dreamers, and Scientists as Introverts, and to all primary Pioneers, Commanders, and Teamers as Extroverts. And yet, we're not suggesting that all Introverts are the same (nor are all Extroverts). Indeed, we see real differences between the Business Chemistry types within these Introvert/Extrovert categories. For example, Guardians, Dreamers, and Scientists all tend to be more reserved and deliberate than the extroverted types. However, Guardians are much more methodical and meticulous than the other two introverted types, while Dreamers are more empathic and relationship oriented than the others, and Scientists are more cerebral and technical.

Traits of introverted types

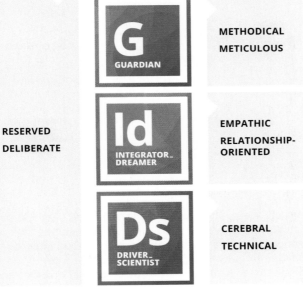

© 2018. Deloitte Touche Tohmatsu Limited

Similarly, Pioneers, Commanders, and Teamers are all more adaptable and energetic than the introverted types, but there are differences between them. Pioneers have a more fluid, less structured working style and they are more spontaneous than the other two extroverted types. Commanders, meanwhile, are more logical and disciplined than the others, and Teamers are more traditional and place more importance on reaching consensus.

Traits of extroverted types

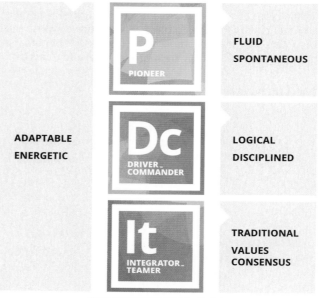

Despite these differences within the Introvert and Extrovert categories, as you'll soon see, we sometimes find the Introvert/Extrovert distinction to be clear and important in relation to our research findings. So as we move on to the next chapter we'll share with you when that division seems more useful and when it seems less so.

Who's better? Who's best?

Given that little bit of foreshadowing we bet you can't wait to get to the next chapter, but first, we want to address one more question. Is it better to be an Introvert or an Extrovert?

Well you probably know us well enough already to assume we're not going to argue that one is better than the other—they both make valuable contributions in most any situation. But we've already hinted that in today's business environment there are some ways in which being an Extrovert might be a bit easier or more rewarding than being an Introvert.

If that's a surprise to you, then you are probably an Extrovert and you probably haven't read Susan Cain's book *Quiet*, which we mentioned earlier.[10] We'll return to Cain's work here because it has direct relevance to creating work environments where all types thrive. She argues that society in general, and the typical workplace specifically, undervalues Introverts and all their strengths, leading to "a colossal waste of talent, energy, and happiness." She outlines how Western culture has transformed over time from a culture of character to a culture of personality in which an "extrovert ideal" dominates, and introversion is viewed as inferior. She goes on to highlight the ways in which institutions today are built for Extroverts and how that often contributes to the Introverts' talents remaining largely untapped. You can read Cain's book for yourself, so we won't belabor the point here, but we will mention that our research findings, which we'll outline in the next chapter, support Cain's perspective in multiple ways.

We'll close this chapter with a little thought experiment. Imagine an organization made up exclusively of strong Introverts. What would that be like? Is everyone waiting for everyone else to say what they think? Do opportunities expire because decisions take too long? Can teams keep up with the pace of change or do they lag behind? And who the heck is in charge around here?

Now what about an organization made up exclusively of extreme Extroverts? Are people fighting for control? Who will do the work that doesn't place them in the spotlight? If everyone adapts effortlessly to the latest trend, might teams lose track of their North Star, change course too often, and end up going in circles? And if everyone is talking at once, who is listening?

The point is obvious but we'll state it none the less. Great teams and organizations need Introverts and Extroverts to excel. The challenge is in creating an environment that supports their different needs, takes advantage of their unique strengths, and promotes their working effectively together. The next section of the book—Business Chemistry Applications—is all about that. But as a next step in this Business Chemistry Electives section, we'll spend some time considering the similarities and differences between the Business Chemistry types and factoring in this lens of introversion and extroversion.

REFERENCES

1. Cain, Susan. *Quiet: The Power of Introverts in a World That Can't Stop Talking*. New York: Broadway Books, 2013.

2. Peabody, Dean and Lewis R. Goldberg. "Some Determinants of Factor Structures from Personality-Trait Descriptors." *Journal of Personality and Social Psychology*, 57 (3) (1989): 552–567. doi:10.1037/0022-3514.57.3.552. PMID 2778639.

3. McCrae, Robert R. and Paul T. Costa. "Validation of the Five-Factor Model of Personality Across Instruments and Observers." *Journal of Personality and Social Psychology* 52 (1) (1987) 81–90. doi:10.1037/0022-3514.52.1.81. PMID 3820081.

4. Laney, Marti Olsen. *The Introvert Advantage: How Quiet People Can Thrive in an Extrovert World*. New York: Workman Publishing, 2002.

5. Eysenck, Hans Jürgen. *The Biological Basis of Personality*. Springfield, IL: Thomas, 1967.

6. See Note 1.

7. Jung, C. G. *Collected Works of C.G. Jung, Volume 6: Psychological Types*. Originally Translated by H.G. Baynes. Revised by R.F.C. Hull. Princeton, NJ: Princeton University Press, 2014.

8. Cheek, Jonathan M., Jennifer Grimes and Courtney Brown. *Personality Scales for Four Domains of Introversion: Social, Thinking, Anxious, and Restrained Introversion* (preliminary research manual). Wellesley, MA: Wellesley College Department of Psychology, September 2014.

9. See Note 7.

10. See Note 1.

Stress,
Career Aspirations,
and Other Headlines

10

We hope that so far we've described the Business Chemistry types in a way that allows you to see yourself in them, and also your colleague Joe, and maybe even your mom. We've aimed for colorful descriptions, attempting to paint pictures that make the types come alive (but hopefully not like those creepy pictures where the eyes seem to follow you around the room.) However, for those readers pining for more numbers and graphs, here they come. (If you don't want to look at graphs, no worries; we think you'll find the text interesting as well, so just focus on that and let those charts be a colorful blur in your peripheral vision).

Our initial research established the Business Chemistry types, the traits associated with them, and the key differences between them. Since then we've gained a deeper understanding of how the types are similar and different via a number of large-scale research studies we've conducted with professionals all over the world, and through in-person sessions with thousands of executives and their teams. We've looked for differences in relation to a number of factors, from reactions to stress, to career aspirations, to the conditions under which each type thrives, and we've found significant differences between the types every time. We'll focus here primarily on key findings, but for more detail on our research samples and methodologies, check out the appendix. (Maybe next we'll do a study on Business Chemistry differences in the likelihood of reading appendices.)

———

Stress!

There's a Randy Glasbergen cartoon from 1996 that shows one white-coated individual telling another: "According to the latest scientific research, the average human body is 20% water and 80% stress."[1] You may be thinking that sounds about right, even now, 20 years later. And if you were to do a quick Internet search on stress in the workplace, you might feel your own stress levels rise as you read all the dire warnings about the epidemic proportions and dangers of the stressed out workforce in the United States and elsewhere. And we're not going to suggest that stress isn't common or that it can't be dangerous (although there is evidence it can have positive effects too). However, we do feel compelled to say right off the bat that our research on stress—a study conducted with more than 23,000 professionals—suggests that not everyone is as stressed out all the time as we might be led to believe by the popularity of this topic in the media. When we asked people about their stress levels, just 28 percent said they're stressed often or almost always. Frankly, given the hype, this finding surprised us a little bit.

But it didn't surprise us that we found significant Business Chemistry differences in how much stress people experience. Specifically, our study suggests that Guardians are most likely to experience stress, followed by Integrators. And given everything we've just shared about the types, that's what we might expect.

Who's stressed out?

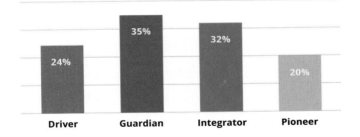

So what are Guardians and Integrators stressed about? We asked the same professionals about various potentially stressful situations and found that making an error topped the list, causing stress for more than 80% of all respondents. The other things we inquired about were experienced as stressful by roughly half of respondents. These included:

- a challenging workload, with long hours or juggling of multiple responsibilities

- moments of conflict, like getting reprimanded or delivering a difficult message

- situations that create urgency, like critical projects or time pressure

- face-to-face interactions, like delivering a presentation or meeting a new stakeholder.

We're getting a little stressed out just thinking about all of it. Are you?

Our next question was whether different Business Chemistry types are stressed out by different things, and the answer to that question is a pretty clear "no." The nature of the stressor didn't seem to impact which types experienced it as stressful. Guardians and Integrators indicated they experienced every situation to be significantly more stressful than did Pioneers and Drivers.

Spending a little time with us would illustrate this finding perhaps more clearly than anything else. In all kinds of situations Suzanne, a Guardian-Integrator, is often struggling to stem her mounting panic, while Kim, a Pioneer-Driver, is as cool as a cucumber. While writing this book, for example, Suzanne was constantly fretting about the timeline and whether we'd manage to get everything done, and Kim would reply, "I'm not worried, we're doing great!"

Findings from a second study we conducted with 17,000 different professionals suggest Guardians and Integrators are also less likely to feel they're effective under stress. But before you draw the conclusion that they can't take the heat, we should note that half of Guardians and Integrators reported they're most effective when moderately to very stressed, compared to around 60% of Drivers and Pioneers. So yes, we found a statistically significant difference, but all types have substantial portions of people who say they work well under stress (Suzanne just doesn't happen to be one of them).

Our research also suggests that introversion and extroversion play an important role in how much stress people experience. Among the Integrator subtypes, Dreamers, who tend to be introverted, reported stress levels similar to Guardians, while Teamers experienced more modest levels. On the flip side, among the Driver subtypes, Commanders, who tend to be extroverted, reported stress levels similar to Pioneers, while Scientists reported higher levels.

Who's stressed out?

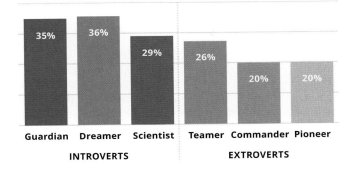

Why? Possibly due to physiological differences—there is evidence that Introverts have more sensitive neurological systems, which we talked about in the previous chapter. But it is also possibly due to differences in preferred ways of working and interacting with others, which may not always be aligned with typical work environments. It can be a tough world out there for Introverts, and it sometimes takes a toll.

So if some types—generally the more introverted ones—experience more stress than others, what do they do about it? We explored that question too in our second stress study. We found that when it comes to coping, jumping in and tackling the issue was the most common strategy overall, used by more than 80% of respondents. Other strategies that were almost as common were:

- cognitive coping strategies, like stepping back to look at the big picture, looking on the bright side, and thinking through possibilities

- groundwork strategies, like gathering more information or doing organizational tasks

Two other strategies were reported by less than half of respondents, fewer than we might have expected based on what outside research suggests about the ways people cope:

- interpersonal strategies like asking someone for help, talking with someone about how you're feeling, or bouncing ideas off of them

- time-out strategies, like doing something that energizes or relaxes you (e.g., yoga, going for a run), socializing, or blowing off steam.

And the Business Chemistry types reported using different strategies in varying degrees. While taking action was common among all types, it was reported most frequently by Drivers, with Pioneers close behind. This isn't surprising given the general bias of these types toward immediate action, with Guardians and Integrators being a bit more likely to think things through before jumping into action. Pioneers favored cognitive strategies more than other types did (after all, they love ideas!), and they used time-out strategies more than the other types. Pioneers also employed the most strategies overall, as you might expect from the most adaptable type. Guardians used groundwork strategies most often, which fits with their process- and detail-oriented natures. Integrators didn't show a strong preference for a particular coping strategy, using action, groundwork, and cognitive strategies to similar degrees. And while it was not their most common strategy, Integrators along with Pioneers, used interpersonal strategies more than other types. No doubt their relationship-orientation is a key factor here.

Use of coping strategies

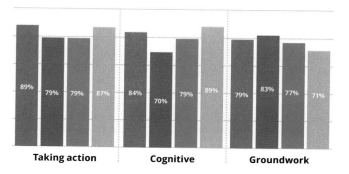

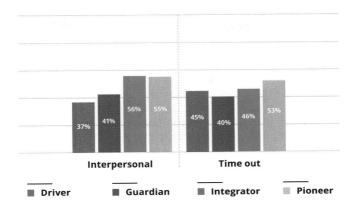

	Interpersonal				Time out		
37%	41%	56%	55%	45%	40%	46%	53%

■ Driver   ■ Guardian   ■ Integrator   ■ Pioneer

Psychological safety

You know that colleague of yours who seems to blurt out whatever they're thinking in a meeting, no matter how outlandish or potentially controversial the idea? Chances are, that person has a strong sense of *psychological safety*—the feeling that it's okay to share one's ideas and take some interpersonal risks. The concept of psychological safety has been in the media spotlight over the past couple of years, in part because of some research conducted by Google.[2] The general gist of their findings fits with what psychologists have previously found, that more successful teams tend to have a higher sense of psychological safety.[3] After all, if some of your people are holding back, your team is missing out.

After reading about that study we got pretty interested in psychological safety ourselves, so with 11,000 professionals we explored whether there are Business Chemistry differences in the extent to which people feel safe or unsafe, not only when it comes to idea-sharing, but also in relation to some other areas. And although we queried a different sample of professionals, the results look a lot like those from our stress study.

Overall, Guardians and Integrators were the most likely to report feeling unsafe, and we saw an introversion/extroversion effect similar to the one in the stress study. Not only did Guardians feel significantly more unsafe than Pioneers, but Dreamers felt more unsafe than Teamers, and Scientists more than Commanders. Here are some specifics.

Starting with the most typical definition of psychological safety, around 35% of Guardians and Dreamers in our sample indicated they feel unsafe, saying it's rarely or only sometimes true that they feel they can share their ideas freely without fear of judgement or rejection. For Pioneers and Commanders this number was less than 15%.

Feels unsafe sharing their ideas freely at work

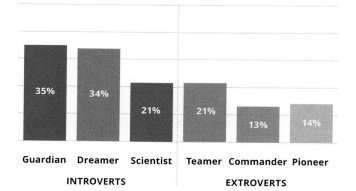

35%	34%	21%	21%	13%	14%
Guardian	Dreamer	Scientist	Teamer	Commander	Pioneer
INTROVERTS			**EXTROVERTS**		

INTROVERTS FEEL LESS SAFE THAN EXTROVERTS.

We've shared that in our definition a key difference between Introverts and Extroverts is that Introverts are quieter, particularly around new people. The findings from this study illuminate that distinction further, suggesting that part of the reason for this reserve may be a fear on the part of Introverts that what they have to say will be judged or rejected.

Extroverts, on the other hand, maybe can't fathom why anyone would judge or reject their ideas, or, possibly, they simply don't care. After all, as we discussed in the previous chapter, we're living in the time of the *Extrovert ideal*, characterized by Susan Cain as the higher societal value placed on charisma and outspokenness than on character and reserve.[4]

We also explored some other aspects of feeling unsafe at work. When it comes to honestly discussing how they're feeling when stressed, Guardians were most likely to feel unsafe, and again, there was a clear introversion/extroversion effect; Dreamers and Scientists joined Guardians in being more likely to indicate this is a challenge. Teamers and Commanders, like Pioneers, were less likely to think so. If you're paying attention, you might notice that our findings suggest those who feel most stressed also feel least safe discussing it. Would talking about it more help? Studies suggest it might.[5]

Feels unsafe discussing stress levels with their manager

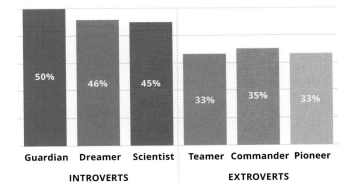

The pattern of results was almost identical in terms of whether people feel they can bring their whole selves to work, with more Guardians, Dreamers, and Scientists indicating they weren't so sure. Again, this may relate to the Extrovert ideal—if they're aware, consciously or unconsciously, that their way of being in the world is less valued, Introverts are likely to feel less comfortable being themselves. Can you blame them?

Feels unsafe bringing their whole self to work

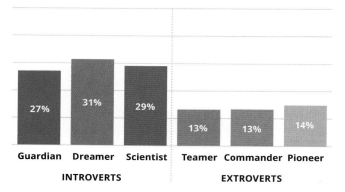

In terms of feeling they're able to take care of their physical health, Dreamers were particularly challenged, while Commanders were the least likely to say this is a problem. And it's Dreamers and Guardians that were most likely to indicate difficulties with creating work–life boundaries without fear or guilt. These results are particularly significant in light of our findings on career priorities described below. Spoiler alert: Guardians and Integrators prioritize work–life balance more than Drivers and Pioneers. This leads us to wonder, what's the impact for individuals and organizations when those who most value work–life balance feel least able to attain it?

Feels unsafe taking care of their physical health

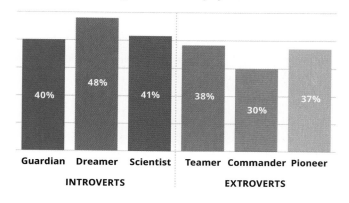

Feels unsafe creating work/life boundaries

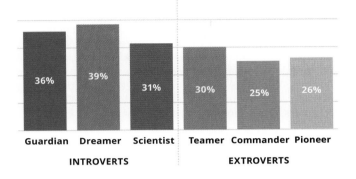

Guardian	Dreamer	Scientist	Teamer	Commander	Pioneer
36%	39%	31%	30%	25%	26%

INTROVERTS   EXTROVERTS

Locus of control

When we realized the parallels between our findings about stress and about psychological safety, we started wondering about chickens and eggs. Are Guardians and their introverted compatriots more stressed because they feel unsafe? Or do their feelings of discomfort spring from their higher stress levels? Or is something else going on? And while we were at it, we wondered what makes Pioneers, and their extroverted friends, so comparatively carefree and secure?

We looked into one psychological construct with potential to illuminate at least part of what's going on—good ol' locus of control. Remember that from your psychology 101 class? People with an internal locus of control believe what happens in their lives is primarily a result of their own actions, while those with an external locus of control believe outside factors ultimately determine their fate. For example, someone with a more internal locus of control would tend to believe that they'll be promoted if they work hard. On the other hand, someone with a more external locus of control might feel their own work ethic won't be enough if the boss likes the other candidate's style more, or if someone else is in the right place at the right time. Reality probably falls somewhere in between.

Prior research has shown relationships between a more external locus of control and both higher stress levels and lower psychological safety.[6] We wondered about the relationship of locus of control with Business Chemistry, so we asked 9,000 of the same professionals from the psychological safety study whether they feel in control of their destiny when it comes to work. All the types had a more internal than external locus of control, but we still found differences, and again a strong introversion/extroversion effect. The extroverted Pioneers, Commanders, and Teamers all showed a strong internal locus of control, while the Introverts—Guardians, Dreamers, and Scientists—all scored comparably lower.

Internal locus of control:
"I am in control of my destiny when it comes to work."

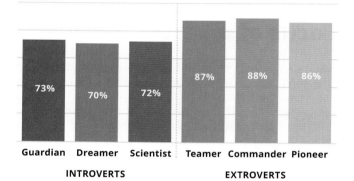

Guardian	Dreamer	Scientist	Teamer	Commander	Pioneer
73%	70%	72%	87%	88%	86%

INTROVERTS — EXTROVERTS

If their natural style is less valued, is it possible that Introverts have had more experiences that tell them they don't control their level of success, at least not as long as they're being themselves? Instead, societal or managerial preferences for Extroverts may be seen as having a strong impact on whether introverted types succeed.

Other research suggests there might be something to this. Studies have found that groups facing societal or institutional biases or incidents of prejudice, such as African Americans and LGBTQ individuals, have a higher external locus of control.[7][8]

And not to give anything away, but the extent to which the types feel they can control their destiny is particularly interesting in light of what we're about to tell you in relation to career aspirations and leadership. So let's get right to that.

Career aspirations

Did you know that not everyone aspires to be a leader? No really, it's true! Sometimes you'd never know it from the way leadership is talked about in organizations and in the media. Becoming a leader is often represented as the holy-grail we're all searching for... the brass ring we're all trying to grab. The assumption seems to be that we all want to lead, or at least those of us who have any ambition or talent do. But our research suggests that's not true. We asked almost 14,000 professionals across various organizational levels about their career aspirations, requesting they choose their top three aspirations out of a list of ten. We found there are lots of ways beyond traditional leadership that people of all Business Chemistry types want to contribute in their organizations. That said, let's go ahead and get the leadership stuff out of the way first, then we'll tell you about the other roles people aspire to.

The majority of Pioneers and Drivers (more than 65%) said that being a leader is a top career aspiration. In contrast, about half of Guardians and Integrators did. So there's a significant Business Chemistry difference here, but there are two important things we want to highlight. The first is that more than 30% of Drivers and Pioneers *did not* say they aspire to leadership. That, paired with the even larger number of Guardians and Integrators who didn't, clearly debunks the notion that everyone wants to be a leader. But the second key point is equally important. While their numbers were lower, *plenty* of Guardians and Integrators want to lead (and indeed plenty of them *do* lead, as you'll see in the next chapter).

Equally interesting is the role introversion and extroversion play here. When it comes to the Driver subtypes, we see a sizeable difference, with the more extroverted Commanders being the most likely of all types to have leadership aspirations, significantly more than even Pioneers. But the more introverted Scientists weren't quite as keen on the idea.

There are also differences between the Integrator subtypes, with the more introverted Dreamers being the least likely of all to set their sights on leadership, even less than Guardians, and the more extroverted Teamers looking a bit more like Scientists in this regard.

"When it comes to my career, I most aspire to be a *leader*."

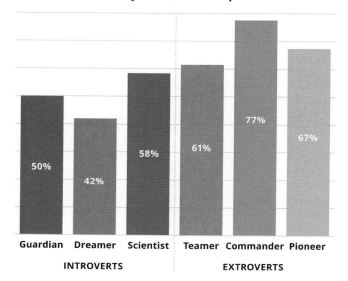

So the three more introverted types were less likely to aspire to leadership roles (on average half did) than the three more extroverted types (on average almost 70% did). This is particularly interesting in light of the other findings we just shared—that the introverted types are more stressed, feel less psychologically safe, and have less of an internal locus of control. Huh.

We can't help but wonder if there aren't some parallels between what we're seeing here and the so-called *ambition gap* that Sheryl Sandberg addresses in her book *Lean In: Women, Work, and the Will to Lead*.[9] Sandberg compiles research suggesting that women are less likely to aspire to leadership, at least in part, because of the bias and sexism that still exists in many of today's workplaces and in society as a whole. We'll address gender as it relates to Business

Chemistry in the next chapter, but at this point we'll simply suggest that Introverts' lower likelihood of aspiring to lead may be a reflection of similar ongoing experiences of bias against Introverts.

At the same time, it's also possible that many Introverts don't relish the thought of a leadership role for other reasons that we'll explore shortly. We're not suggesting everyone should *want* to lead, simply that the patterns in our findings suggest a powerful opportunity for future inquiry in this area.

But just when you might be starting to think all of our studies have essentially the same findings, we'll note that leadership is the only aspiration where we saw the types divided neatly along the lines of introversion and extroversion. When it comes to the other aspirations we asked about, we saw different patterns. In other words, if you've gotten a little lazy and are no longer paying close attention, time to perk back up!

So if leadership isn't the only game in town, what else are people aspiring to? For one thing, they want to be top performers. Around half of Guardians and Drivers indicated this, whereas fewer Pioneers and Integrators did.

**"When it comes to my career,
I most aspire to be a *top performer*."**

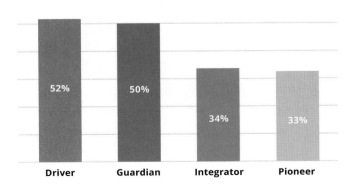

Driver	Guardian	Integrator	Pioneer
52%	50%	34%	33%

As they're the most competitive and focused type, we're not surprised to see Drivers in the lead here. And we think the relatively high Guardian number suggests their more modest emphasis on leading is less about any lack of ambition or willingness to work hard, and more about possibly preferring a role that's more behind the scenes. Not to suggest that Integrators and Pioneers don't work hard—but they may be a little less concerned about how their performance compares to others. Integrators tend to have more of an intrinsic versus competitive motivation and Pioneers, well, they like to color outside the lines.

We see a similar overall pattern when it comes to aspirations to be experts, but with some interesting subtype differences—overall around 35% of Guardians and Drivers saw the appeal of such a role, more than Pioneers or Integrators, who are closer to the 20% range. Between the Driver subtypes it was Scientists, in particular, whose goals lie here more than Commanders. This makes a lot of sense since Scientists are the most intensely curious of the types—they like to dive deep on a topic that interests them.

**"When it comes to my career,
  I most aspire to be an *expert*."**

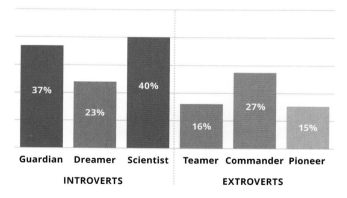

Guardian	Dreamer	Scientist	Teamer	Commander	Pioneer
37%	23%	40%	16%	27%	15%

INTROVERTS · EXTROVERTS

**"When it comes to my career,
I most aspire to be an *innovator.*"**

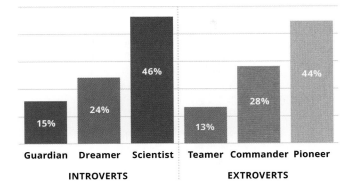

Guardian	Dreamer	Scientist	Teamer	Commander	Pioneer
15%	24%	46%	13%	28%	44%

INTROVERTS   **EXTROVERTS**

Scientists were also likely to aspire to be innovators (as were Pioneers), again showing a sizeable difference from Commanders, and also from Guardians and both types of Integrators. Since they're the most experimental of the types, we might expect this innovation to take the form of exploring various options, prototyping, and failing fast. (Hopefully with some successes mixed in!)

So while Scientists are less likely than their Commander colleagues to want to lead in the traditional sense, they have higher aspirations than Commanders when it comes to these other ways of leading in their fields, as experts and innovators.

Many people also aspire to roles that are more collaborative in nature—a greater percentage of Guardians and Integrators than Pioneers and Drivers said they aspire to be team players. And we see a similar division in relation to aspirations to mentor, with more Guardians and Integrators setting their sights here.

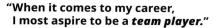

**"When it comes to my career,
I most aspire to be a *team player*."**

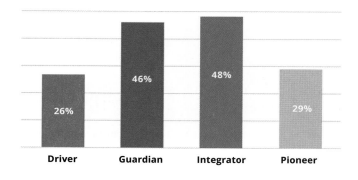

Driver	Guardian	Integrator	Pioneer
26%	46%	48%	29%

**"When it comes to my career,
I most aspire to be a *mentor*."**

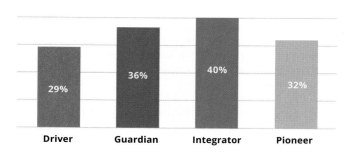

Driver	Guardian	Integrator	Pioneer
29%	36%	40%	32%

So this, then, is where some of the Guardians and Integrators who don't aspire to lead in a traditional manner are putting their focus—on contributing to their teams and enabling others in a different way. Sometimes it seems becoming a leader is elevated above all other goals, but shouldn't these other kinds of contributions be equally recognized for the value they bring?

We think so. After all, what would our teams be like if no one wanted to be a team player? If we were all competing to be out front and in control? If no one was interested in pitching in to do whatever it takes, without the promise of glory, or often even a thank you, so that the whole team can succeed together? Furthermore, what would our organizations be like without mentors? Without those who measure their own success, at least in part, by the success of those who they've reached a hand back to help?

————

Career priorities

If aspirations are about the future, priorities are more about the here and now, about living in the present. We asked the same group of professionals who told us about their career aspirations to choose their top three career priorities from a list of ten. Again we found plenty of interest.

One key difference is related to enjoyment. All the types placed a pretty strong emphasis on doing work they enjoy. After all, most of us spend an awful lot of time and energy at work, and it seems like a pretty grim existence not to enjoy it at all. But compared to the other types, Integrators placed the highest priority on enjoying both the work they do and the people they work with, while Drivers saw these things as less important. Perhaps this finding helps explain Integrators' stronger emphasis on the more collaborative aspirations of being team players and mentors—prioritizing who they work with and what they do more than what rung on the ladder they've reached. Dreamers, in particular, emphasized enjoying their work, while the Integrator subtypes were more similar to one another in regard to the importance of enjoying their colleagues.

"When it comes to my career, a top priority is *doing work I enjoy.*"

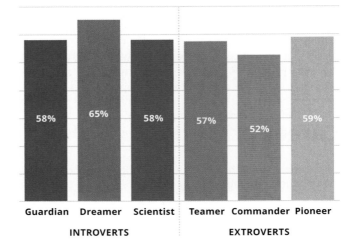

Guardian	Dreamer	Scientist	Teamer	Commander	Pioneer
58%	65%	58%	57%	52%	59%

INTROVERTS — EXTROVERTS

"When it comes to my career, a top priority is *working with people I enjoy.*"

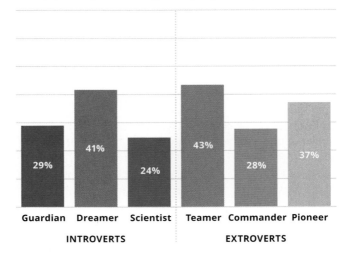

Guardian	Dreamer	Scientist	Teamer	Commander	Pioneer
29%	41%	24%	43%	28%	37%

INTROVERTS — EXTROVERTS

When it comes to making a difference in the world, Pioneers prioritized it the most, followed by Integrators. While we can't say for sure, we suspect that *making a difference* may mean something different to these two types. For Pioneers, who aspire to lead and to innovate, it's likely to mean making a dent in the universe—having an impact on how things are done that will be important and remembered, maybe resulting in a comet or asteroid named after them. (Did you know there are asteroids named after James Bond and Santa?) For Integrators, who also have higher aspirations to be team players and mentors, we speculate it may mean making a positive difference in other people's lives, whether on an individual or collective level, even without the asteroid.

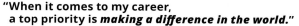

"When it comes to my career,
 a top priority is *making a difference in the world."*

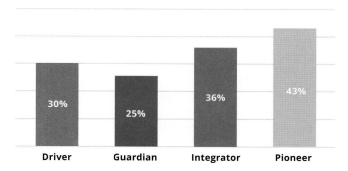

Now let's come back to work–life balance. We've already shared that Guardians and Integrators feel less able to set work–life boundaries than Pioneers and Drivers. Well it turns out, perhaps unfortunately, that when it comes to prioritizing work–life balance the pattern is the same—it was more important to Guardians and Integrators. Might this be because they're more likely to feel stressed more of the time? Regardless, it seems an unfortunate state of affairs that those who most value work–life balance feel least able to attain it. And again, we wonder, might this relate to those career aspirations? Leadership and work–life balance can be a tough mix, and this may be one reason that Guardians and Integrators place less emphasis on traditional leadership goals.

**"When it comes to my career,
a top priority is _maintaining work–life balance._"**

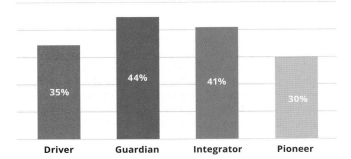

Driver	Guardian	Integrator	Pioneer
35%	44%	41%	30%

Advancement was a priority for Drivers more than the other types, and particularly for Commanders. This difference between the two Driver subtypes may reflect the Commander's more extroverted nature, with advancement representing a form of external acknowledgment for one's contributions, as well as upward movement toward the leadership roles Commanders desire. The comparatively lower scores of Scientists might reflect the fact that advancement often changes the nature of one's work, pulling them away from the more specialist kinds of roles (e.g., expert), which Scientists are more likely to value.

**"When it comes to my career,
a top priority is _advancement._"**

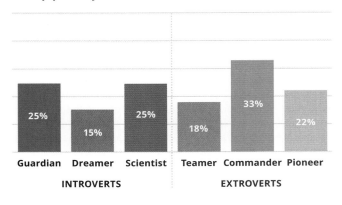

Guardian	Dreamer	Scientist	Teamer	Commander	Pioneer
25%	15%	25%	18%	33%	22%
INTROVERTS			EXTROVERTS		

Perhaps as interesting as the differences between types is where we don't see them. All the types put a high priority on a feeling of accomplishment—it was a top priority for around 60% of each type, with Teamers, Commanders, and Guardians emphasizing it slightly more than Dreamers, Scientists, and Pioneers. And maybe this isn't so surprising, because really, who would want to spend 40 hours a week (or 60) at a job where you never accomplish anything? But it's important because it provides a telling clue for where to find common ground across types. If you want to create an environment that meets the needs of everyone at once, a strong focus on accomplishment might be a good place to start.

✳

A FEELING OF ACCOMPLISHMENT IS A TOP PRIORITY FOR ALL TYPES.

Conditions for thriving

Speaking of getting stuff done, we were also curious about what the different Business Chemistry types need in order to feel like they're able to do their best work. So we asked the same group of people to select the top three (out of ten) conditions under which they're most likely to thrive. As usual, we found significant Business Chemistry differences.

Challenging tasks are what made Drivers tick. As the most competitive and goal-oriented type, Drivers likely relish knowing they've bested a particularly tough assignment. If the mountain isn't high or the river wide, why bother? And this fits right in with Drivers' desire to be high performers.

On the other hand, a sense that their work matters was most important to Integrators. This need may relate to Integrators' distinction as the type who feels the greatest duty to society and most wants to help others, as well as their aspirations to be team players and mentors. Maybe Integrators should adopt a variation of the unofficial U.S. Navy motto "Non sibi sed patriae" ("Not for self, but for country"), but the Integrator version might be "Not for self, but others."

"At work, I thrive when I have tasks *that are challenging*."

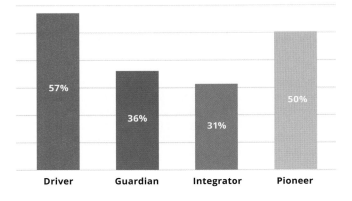

Driver	Guardian	Integrator	Pioneer
57%	36%	31%	50%

"At work, I thrive when I have *a sense my work matters*."

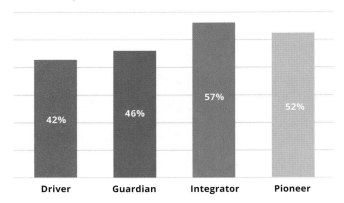

Driver	Guardian	Integrator	Pioneer
42%	46%	57%	52%

The chance to learn and try new things was most embraced by Pioneers. This finding fits right in with what we know about the types' orientations toward novelty (which Pioneers crave) and the tried and true (which is embraced by both Guardians and Teamers, who have lower scores here). Knowing this, would a Pioneer likely enjoy a role where they mostly do the same thing over and over? We think not.

"At work, I thrive when I have *opportunities to learn and try new things*."

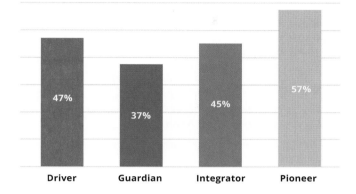

Driver	Guardian	Integrator	Pioneer
47%	37%	45%	57%

Clear expectations were more important for Guardians than for others (although it wasn't their top priority). As the type that most prefers structure and least tolerates ambiguity, Guardians likely appreciate clear expectations because they provide an explicit guide for how they should proceed. We've already learned that Guardians aspire to be top performers, and clear expectations help them know how to get there.

"At work, I thrive when I have *clear expectations*."

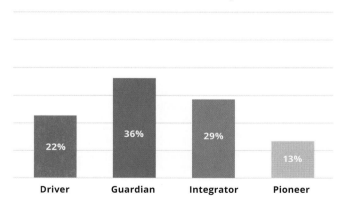

Driver	Guardian	Integrator	Pioneer
22%	36%	29%	13%

Is this everything there is to know about the differences between Business Chemistry types? Certainly not! Even if we're exhausted from trying to share so much in one chapter, our findings are not exhaustive. There are endless possibilities for future research which could help us understand the types even better. But we hope what we've shared here fills out those pictures of the types a bit more. Have you figured out your mom's type yet?

REFERENCES

1. Glasbergen, Randy. Cartoon. Glasbergen Cartoon Service. www.glasbergen.com.

2. Duhigg, Charles. "Group Study." *The New York Times Magazine*, February 28, 2016.

3. Edmondson, Amy C. and Zhike Lei. "Psychological Safety: The History, Renaissance, and Future of an Interpersonal Construct." *Annual Review of Organizational Psychology and Organizational Behavior*. (2014) 1: 23–43. doi:10.1146/annurev-orgpsych-031413-091305.

4. Cain, Susan. *Quiet: The Power of Introverts in a World That Can't Stop Talking*. New York: Broadway Books, 2013.

5. McGonigal, Kelly. *The Upside of Stress: Why Stress Is Good for You, and How to Get Good at It*. New York: Avery, 2015.

6. Triplett, Suellen M. and Jennifer M.I. Loh. "The Moderating Role of Trust in the Relationship Between Work Locus of Control and Psychological Safety in Organisational Work Teams." *Australian Journal of Psychology*. 2017. doi:10.1111/ajpy.12168.

7. Carter II, Larry W., Debra Mollen, and Nathan Grant Smith. "Locus of Control, Minority Stress, and Psychological Distress Among Lesbian, Gay, and Bisexual Individuals." *Journal of Counseling Psychology*. November 4, 2013. Advance online publication. doi: 10.1037/a0034593.

8. Becker, Brian E., and Frank J. Krzystofiak. "The Influence of Labor Market Discrimination on Locus of Control." *Journal of Vocational Behavior* 21, no. 1 (1982): 60-70. doi:10.1016/0001-8791(82)90053-7.

9. Sandberg, Sheryl, and Nell Scovell. *Lean In: Women, Work, and the Will to Lead*. New York: Alfred A. Knopf, 2013.

Nature or Nurture?
(And Other
Timeless Questions)

11

Phew, we've covered a lot since you first cracked open this book, so perhaps we should take a quick breather and review what we've learned before we add anything else to it.

There are four primary Business Chemistry types, as well as four subtypes, and each of them has defining and differentiating traits and preferences, which other types might alternately criticize and praise. You can get a sense of someone's Business Chemistry type by considering the traits unique to each type as well as those shared between types. When doing so it's important to consider context and to be aware that you're simplifying.

One important dimension along which the Business Chemistry types can be divided is introversion and extroversion, and yet not all Introverts are alike, nor are all Extroverts. There are key differences between the types that have to do with responses to stress, perceptions of psychological safety and locus of control, career aspirations and priorities, and the conditions under which each type thrives. Sometimes these differences show a strong introversion/extroversion divide, and sometimes they don't.

We hope you'll agree that together we've learned a lot of interesting stuff. But as with most interesting stuff, answering some questions often leads to more questions. And in this case, a key question is, *Why?* Where do these Business Chemistry types and differences come from? Are Integrators and Drivers born or made? Do Pioneers and Guardians develop via nature or nurture? How do demographic factors like gender fit in? And does one's type change over time, with age, life experience, and career advancement? These are the kinds of questions we'll explore in this chapter.

But before we jump in feet first with all of this, we'd like to take just a moment and pause (after all, one of us is a Guardian) to acknowledge that these topics have been and will be much discussed and debated in a variety of forums, from academic circles to social media ones. Therefore we choose the word *explore* on purpose, because our intent is not to advocate for a specific point of view on these topics. Rather we hope to share with you some interesting trends we see in the Business Chemistry data and consider possible theories that have been put forward that support those patterns.

So with that caveat, let's start with gender. Because what could possibly be controversial about that? ☺

Business Chemistry on Mars and Venus

If we were preparing for a meeting with a new important stakeholder and were given a choice between knowing their Business Chemistry type or their gender, we'd choose their Business Chemistry type, hands down. As we argued in Chapter 8, gaining some clues as to someone's working style is likely to be more valuable in a work setting than knowing someone's gender. And indeed we'll share in a moment some data that backs up this point.

And yet, people are often interested in knowing whether there's a relationship between Business Chemistry and gender, and we're happy to oblige. In our samples, on average women are more likely to be Integrators than Drivers, and men are more likely to be Drivers than Integrators. But we generally don't see significant gender differences in the likelihood of being a Pioneer or Guardian.

Business Chemistry and gender

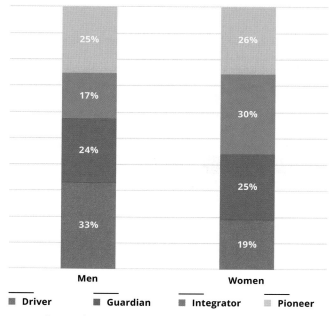

Men

Women

■ Driver ■ Guardian ■ Integrator ▨ Pioneer

Percent of group represented by each Business Chemistry type

We'll explore these differences in a bit more depth, but before we get to that, we want to point out right away that there are a substantial number of men who are Integrators and women who are Drivers. It's important to understand that the types are by no means proxies for gender even though we see some correlation between gender and the Integrator—Driver dimension. Viewing the types that way would be as meaningless as using height as a proxy for gender: On average men are taller than women, but that doesn't mean that a tall person is necessarily a man, or a short one a woman.

BUSINESS CHEMISTRY TYPES ARE NOT PROXIES FOR GENDER.

You may be wondering at this point why we see gender differences for two of the types but not the other two. Well, to start, many of the traits associated with the Integrator and Driver types are reflected in stereotypical gender roles. Whereas the traits more closely associated with the Pioneer and Guardian types are not usually seen as gendered in quite the same way. In our samples we do see statistically significant differences in the extent to which women and men indicate that some of these stereotypically gendered traits describe themselves;

women on average see themselves as more empathic, relationship focused, and non confrontational than men do, and men see themselves as more quantitative, logical, and competitive than women do.

How men and women differ

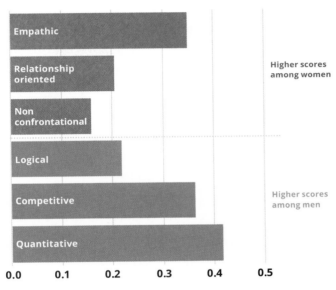

Size of difference between women and men

Before you decide to write us a nasty note, understand that of course we're not saying men aren't relationship focused or women aren't logical. Not at all! We're not saying anything about what men and women are or are supposed to be. What we *are* saying is that these are some of the traits that have historically been seen as, *on average*, more descriptive of one gender or the other, and that the professionals in our sample appear to see themselves, *on average*, in ways that are at least somewhat consistent with those stereotypes.

Now back to our original question: Does this mean one's Business Chemistry type is more likely to develop as a result of nature or nurture? Well, at this point we can't be sure—both are possible—but we'll go out on a pretty strong limb and suggest it's probably a bit of each.

One biological theory that was formative in the early stages of developing the Business Chemistry system is that people express varying levels of activity in a number of key neurochemical systems, and that each of these systems is associated with particular traits that characterize the Business Chemistry types. For example, estrogen and oxytocin correlate with the Integrator traits, and testosterone with the Driver traits.[1][2] Each of us has all of these systems and the corresponding neurochemicals; some are just more active than others, depending on the person. Likewise, we all have characteristics of each of the Business Chemistry types, but some are more dominant than others. This could contribute to the gender differences we see in trait prevalence. Indeed, research has found higher levels of estrogen and oxytocin, to be associated with relationship-building tendencies[3][4], and higher levels of testosterone, to be associated with traits like competitiveness.[5]

But environmental theories can also explain these patterns, generally suggesting that the experiences we have throughout our lives shape who we become and how we're likely to see ourselves, think, and behave. For example, theories of socialization suggest that we learn how we should behave based on what our parents, peers, and society expect of us and reward us for.[6][7] In the case of gender socialization, girls often learn that they're expected to pay attention to people's feelings, whereas boys often learn that their focus should be on winning. Both genders are rewarded for fulfilling these expectations. In this way, more girls would grow up to see themselves reflected in the stereotypically female Integrator traits, including empathy, and boys in the stereotypically male Driver traits, including competitiveness.

These theories don't conflict with one another—they can simultaneously be true and each can represent part of the explanation. And let's not forget that the particular situation we're in at any given moment can also impact how we think and behave. So, at this point we'd suggest that Integrators and Drivers, like Pioneers and Guardians, likely develop from a combination of biology and environment, which is influential both in the long and short terms.

We think it's also noteworthy that we've found other kinds of gender differences in many of our studies, but the Business Chemistry differences almost always outweigh the differences between genders. For example, as other research has suggested, we've found that more men than women aspire to be leaders.[8] However, we've also found that this difference is smaller than the difference between Drivers and Pioneers, who have higher leadership aspirations, and Guardians and Integrators, who have lower ones. In other words, women who are Drivers or Pioneers have higher leadership aspirations than men who are Guardians or Integrators. Likewise, we've found more women than men thrive when they have opportunities to learn and try new things, but this gender difference is much smaller than the difference between Pioneers and Guardians.

"When it comes to my career, I most aspire to be a leader."

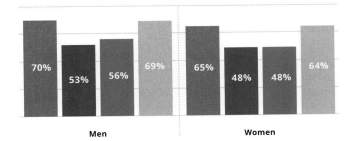

"I thrive when I have opportunities to learn and try new things."

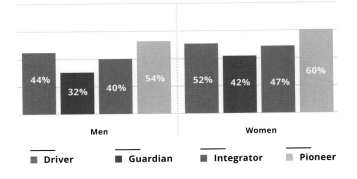

These patterns suggest that although we see an overlap between Business Chemistry types and gender, there are Business Chemistry differences in relation to these variables that are independent of gender. Statistical analyses (i.e., binary logistical regressions) confirm this is the case. In other words, it's not *because* more Integrators are women that Integrators are less likely than Drivers to aspire to lead, for example. (We discussed in the previous chapter some of the other reasons that Integrators may not aspire to lead.) Furthermore, these patterns suggest, as we have proposed, that when it comes to anticipating someone's preferences and behaviors, it's probably more useful to know their Business Chemistry type than to know their gender.

Talkin' 'bout my generation's Business Chemistry

Quick, before you look at the following graph, answer this question: Which Business Chemistry type do you think Millennials are most likely to be? When it comes to generation, surprise, surprise, we also see Business Chemistry differences. Even if that's not a shock, some people are a little surprised by the patterns we see in our samples. This is especially true when they learn that Millennials are the least likely of the generations to be Pioneers and the most likely to be Guardians. Baby Boomers, on the other hand, are most likely to be Pioneers or Integrators, while Gen X-ers fall pretty neatly in the middle.

Business Chemistry and generation

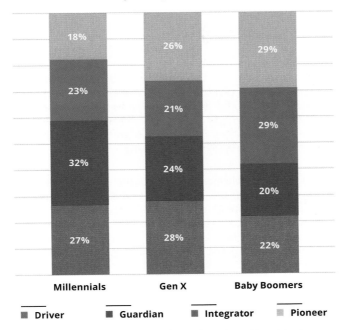

	Driver	Guardian	Integrator	Pioneer

Percent of group represented by each Business Chemistry type

Again, our findings lead to more questions. Why are we seeing these patterns? One explanation is a purely generational one—that there's something about the Millennial generation and the time during which they've come of age that makes them more reserved, more methodical, and less risk seeking. Perhaps 9/11, the subsequent financial crisis, the recession, and the collapsing job market, along with a slew of corporate corruption scandals have something to do with it?

Baby Boomers matured in a different time, and may have adopted a more novelty-seeking and relationship-focused orientation. Thomas Friedman, in his latest book *Thank You for Being Late,* describes growing up in an era that left him and others with "an optimism bias and with an expectation that this kind of broadly shared prosperity should and would continue. It was a virtual cycle of ascension. You felt the wind at your back—not in your face."[9] It would be no surprise if such different experiences during a foundational life stage led to differing worldviews and working styles between Baby Boomers and Millennials.

It's also possible that these patterns are more reflective of life-stage and career-stage differences. On the one hand, Millennials are in earlier stages of their lives and careers, so they may be more cautious in part because their roles require such an approach. Baby Boomers, on the other hand, are more likely to be experienced and established in their careers. They have many decades of experience learning the importance of relating to others, and are more likely in positions that allow, and reward, risk-taking.

As with our possible explanations for the gender differences in Business Chemistry types, both of these explanations may be contributing to the generational differences we see. A key question raised by our findings is whether, over time, we'll see Millennials develop to look more like Baby Boomers, or alternatively, if we'll see organizations change as the more Guardian-like Millennials move up the ranks. We can't wait to find out.

Chemistry in the corner office

Speaking of moving up the ranks, one of the most common questions we're asked concerns how Business Chemistry relates to leadership. The most obvious pattern we see in our samples is that leaders are significantly more likely to be Pioneers and less likely to be Guardians than are staff or managers.

It's telling that the pattern of results here is similar to, but not the same as, the pattern of results for generation. This suggests that the differences between generations are not totally explained by career stage or organizational level, although it doesn't rule out some influence of these factors.

Business Chemistry and organizational level

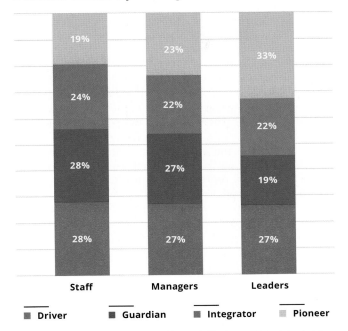

Percent of group represented by each Business Chemistry type

Most significantly, while we see more Integrators among Baby Boomers than the younger generations, we don't see the same pattern when leaders are compared to those at lower organizational levels. And of course, not all Baby Boomers are leaders and not all leaders are Baby Boomers. (In fact, even more of them are Gen Xers in our samples.)

Similar to generation, the big question that arises here is whether Pioneers are more likely to become leaders, or whether people change to become more Pioneer-like as they move up into the leadership ranks. Before we discuss that further (and we will), it's helpful to look at another analysis we've done, homing in on a larger sample of individuals at the highest levels of leadership.

While the leaders in the sample we just looked at included directors, SVPs, EVPs, and C-suite executives, we were curious about the C-suite specifically, and decided to dive deeper into an exploration of this group. After all, these days the public interest in some members of the c-suite has elevated them to somewhere in the realm of rock-star status. Our CxO sample includes more than 850 executives with C-suite titles, including chief information officers (CIOs), chief financial officers (CFOs), chief executive officers (CEOs), chief human resources officers (CHROs) and chief marketing officers (CMOs), among many other C-suite roles.

First, and maybe most important, is that like the other organizational levels we've considered, every Business Chemistry type is represented in the C-suite—no one is shut out. Yet, overall, like our broader sample of leaders, a greater proportion of these CxOs are Pioneers than Drivers, Guardians, or Integrators.

Business Chemistry among CxOs

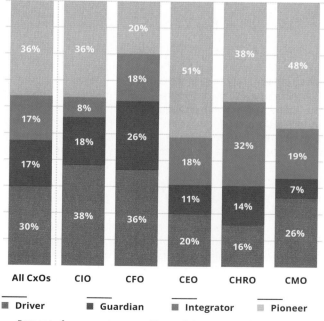

Percent of group represented by each Business Chemistry type

WHILE THE C-SUITE IS MORE HEAVILY PIONEER THAN ANY OTHER SINGLE TYPE, THE MAJORITY OF CxOS ARE NOT PIONEERS.

But this means the majority of CxOs, 64%, are *not* Pioneers. We really want to emphasize this because we know people sometimes rush to the conclusion that you can't make it to the top if you're not a Pioneer, or that Pioneers are better leaders than everyone else. We're not saying that at all. In fact, we didn't even measure the quality of leadership or the success of leaders; we considered only whether or not someone *is* a top-level leader.

THE PROPORTION OF BUSINESS CHEMISTRY TYPES AMONG CxOS DIFFERS BY FUNCTION, ORGANIZATION SIZE, AND GENDER.

Our results also suggest the prevalence of the Business Chemistry types in C-suite roles is influenced by factors such as function, organization size, and gender. For example, in our study Pioneers were more prevalent in the C-suite overall, but Drivers and Guardians were the two top types in the CFO role, while the CIO role comprised relatively similar proportions of Drivers and Pioneers. And the CHRO role had by far the most Integrators of the roles we analyzed, although Pioneers were still more common in that role. We'll note here that our sample sizes are smaller for some functions, particularly CHROs and CMOs, which means margins of error are higher (see the appendix for more details). But the differences are large enough that we have confidence in the overall patterns , which are somewhat predictable. CFOs often need a bit more of a detailed, quantitative approach (in addition to an overall strategic view), which Guardians and Drivers tend to have. The CIO role may be a bit more technical than some other CxO roles, and Drivers are the most technical type. And the CHRO role is focused on people, which is probably why we see more Integrators there than in any other C-suite role.

We love it when our results turn out as we'd expect! (Said Suzanne) But surprises can be fun too. (Said Kim)

We further found that in the largest organizations in our sample, those with more than 100,000 employees, the proportion of C-suite executives who are Drivers (35%) outpaces the proportion of Pioneers (29%), although Pioneers are more common in the other organization sizes we analyzed. Perhaps leading in the largest organizations requires a somewhat different approach than leading in an organization of more modest size. The more logical, focused, and competitive tendencies of the Driver are possibly more valued in these organizations than the adaptable, imaginative, and risk-seeking tendencies of the Pioneer.

While our sample of CxOs includes more men (69%) than women (31%) we still have a pretty good representation of both groups and we see gender differences too, as we do with our general business population. Both women and men in our CxO sample are most likely to be Pioneers, but a higher proportion of female executives are Integrators (26%) than Drivers (21%). By contrast, a higher proportion of male executives are Drivers (34%) than Integrators (13%). So even at the highest levels of leadership we see a tendency for different styles, on average, between women and men. This patterns raises the question of whether we'll see CxOs as a group change over time, assuming women continue to make headway into these ranks as they have over the past decades.

✱

TWO-THIRDS OF CxOs ARE EXTROVERTS.

We also found an effect for introversion and extroversion here. In addition to Pioneers being more common than Guardians, the Drivers in our CxO sample are more likely to be Commanders (about 60%) than Scientists (about 40%) and Integrators show a similar split, with more Teamers (about 60%) than Dreamers (about 40%). In all, just one-third of the executives in our sample are Introverts. This number is quite low in comparison to the other organizational levels we've analyzed—half of the managers and more than half of the staff in our sample are Introverts. This pattern didn't surprise us, given all that we've already discussed about some of the key differences between Introverts and Extroverts, including Extroverts' higher aspirations to lead.

While we were exploring Business Chemistry types among CxOs we went ahead and dug a little deeper, looking for individual traits that characterize them differently than the typical professional. We found that in lots of ways they're actually *not* so different. Our research suggests those in C-suite roles are not more (or less) disciplined, punctual, or practical. They don't place a different level of priority on relationships or building a network, or feel a different level of duty to society. They're not more or less imaginative, interested in exploring new things, or fond of experimenting with novel ideas. And they don't have differing comfort levels with expressing emotions, nor do they place different levels of value on composure.

How CxOs differ from the typical professional (and how they don't)

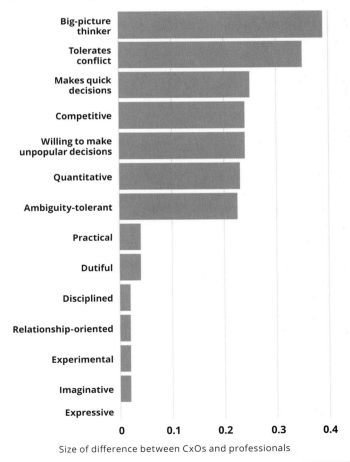

Size of difference between CxOs and professionals

But then there are ways in which CxOs *are* different. Our findings suggest they're more likely to be energetic, big-picture thinkers who are comfortable with ambiguity, and at the same time, they tend to take more quantitative approaches to things. They're also more competitive and willing to address conflict, and they tend to make decisions more quickly, without worrying about the popularity of those decisions. There seems to be a sort of toughness about these CxOs, and they have a tendency to not sweat the small stuff.

———

WHAT'S BEHIND THESE FINDINGS?

As always, we wondered why we were seeing these results.

Self-selection factors

Well, we've already discussed some of the self-selection factors that are likely at play. We've shared that Guardians and Integrators generally have a less robust internal locus of control and are less likely to aspire to leadership. And if they don't set their sights there, it's not surprising that they're less likely to end up there. There are also various aspects of Guardians' and Integrators' styles that may make the C-suite less appealing to them. Guardians' natural reserve, discomfort with ambiguity, and less adaptable natures can make certain leadership roles an uncomfortable stretch. Integrators' emphasis on consensus and diplomacy, as well as their distaste for confrontation and making unpopular decisions, may make the C-suite an unappealing place to be. Likewise the importance both of these types place on work–life balance may be influencing the types of roles they pursue (or don't).

Add in that Guardians and Integrators are less likely to feel psychologically safe, and more likely to experience stress and to feel less effective under stress. The C-suite can be a stressful place to be, and these types may feel they can make a contribution in other ways that are less hard on them. (Remember from the previous chapter that they often aspire to be team players, mentors, top performers and experts?)

External selection factors

But we don't really think that this is all about personal choice. There are also a number of external selection factors that may lead to Pioneers being most common in the C-suite, with Drivers close behind. These factors include various elements of today's business environment, the Extrovert ideal we've already mentioned, the tendency for like types to attract, and the nature of the work Guardians and Integrators are often drawn to.

Today's business environment. Leading in today's fast-paced business environment often means moving at a brisk pace, being willing to embrace a significant level of risk, and making decisions quickly. On the one hand, both Pioneers and Drivers are particularly well-suited to working in this way, and it's likely that this is part of the reason we see both of these types strongly represented in the C-suite. On the other hand, Guardians and Integrators are typically less comfortable with a faster pace or higher levels of risk.

In addition to things moving fast, and in part because of the pace, today's environment is also quite uncertain. Predicting what will happen even in the short term can be challenging. This requires from leaders a certain level of adaptability, agility, and a facility for moving forward, despite having incomplete information. Again, the Pioneer's style is a good fit for these conditions, but the Driver's, a little less so. Compared to Pioneers, Drivers tend to be less comfortable using intuition and have a stronger need to verify information and to know the right answer. They also see things in more black-and-white terms than Pioneers do. Guardians are similar to Drivers in these ways, and while Integrators look a little more like Pioneers in regard to these traits, they're not quite as strong as Pioneers on any of them.

Team-based work seems to be the way of the world these days, which means leaders must be strong in leading both individuals and teams. Pioneers are the most likely type to say they prefer to work in a team rather than alone, that they value working with others who have diverse strengths, and that they take charge when in a group. They're also the least likely type to say they're quiet around people they don't know. Of course the other types work with teams too, but Guardians tend to be more reserved and less out front.

Integrators prioritize connections but, like Guardians, are less likely to take charge of the group. Drivers tend toward taking charge, but often in a less collaborative way than Pioneers, sometimes seriously ruffling feathers with a directive style that can be seen as results at all costs.

The Extrovert ideal. We've already referenced Susan Cain's work on Introverts and how it identifies a shift over time, from an American culture of character to a culture of personality—from valuing discipline, honor, and seriousness to valuing those who are "bold and entertaining."[10] Of the Business Chemistry types, Pioneers are perhaps those best described as bold and entertaining. They are also the only type that overwhelmingly tends toward extroversion. Guardians are usually more introverted, and Drivers and Integrators split the difference, having both more introverted and more extroverted subtypes. As a result of this extrovert ideal, the Pioneer's style is likely to be valued and rewarded. As one Guardian in our own research said:

 "PIONEERS ARE MOST VALUED BECAUSE THE BIG, SHINY IDEAS AND THE OUTGOING PERSONALITIES TEND TO GET THE MOST ATTENTION AND ARE SEEN AS DESIRABLE IN TODAY'S 'INNOVATOR-DRIVEN' SOCIETY"

Like promotes like. Classical psychology research by Donn Byrne, Theodore Newcombe, and others suggests we're attracted to people who are similar to us.[11] [12] And this tendency isn't limited to interpersonal relationships; there's evidence that managers are most likely to hire and promote those who are similar to them.[13] So more Pioneer leaders likely means more Pioneer promotions into leadership.

Our own research reflects the attraction between Pioneers. Here are some of the things Pioneers have said about their love of working with other Pioneers:

- "They keep me engaged and have a lot of ideas to stimulate my own brainstorming and problem solving."

- "It's easy to work with similar types—there's energy and building on ideas."

- "They're able to follow my thought process—we have energizing conversations about the art of the possible without worrying about reality."

- "We just explore and say yes to each other."

- "Creativity has no limitations. Every idea is explored and discussed. We try new things and don't worry as much about 'What will they think?'"

Unrecognized value. Some of the most unique strengths of Guardians and Integrators often play out behind the scenes or are difficult to quantify, which may make the value they bring less obvious. And if their value isn't immediately apparent, they may be less likely to be promoted.

Again our own research reflects this. Here are just some of the ways in which Guardians and Integrators are sometimes underappreciated for their unique contributions:

- "Work done by Guardians is often background—stuff that supports a decision, strategy, etc. They're integral in making sure decisions are well thought out, but rarely does that research and information get distributed."

- "Guardians are often seen as too focused on the details and not able to see the big picture. While those details can kill an implementation strategy if not addressed, they're not exciting and usually not remembered in a big win."

- "Guardians bring a lot of great ideas to the table, but because they're reserved and less likely to call attention to their contributions, someone else with a more outgoing personality often gets the credit for their success."

- "Group cohesion and collaboration don't necessarily line up with performance metrics, even though they're critical to team success."

- "Integrators' strengths are written-off as 'soft skills' and taken for granted."

■ "I feel that Integrators and their ability to create lasting relationships can become lost in the results-driven nature of business."

The power of power

We've danced a bit around the question of whether or how much people change over time, and the issue deserves a bit more of the spotlight. We've established that Pioneers are more likely than other types to be leaders and we've suggested a number of possible reasons for this. But suppose those self-selection or external selection factors aren't driving this difference. Might people become more Pioneer-like as they move up the ranks?

We've already shared that we see generational differences in Business Chemistry types that could be due to change over time (but might also be due to true generation effects). Personality research suggests that people do indeed evolve throughout their lives, well into older age. Among the traits studies have found to increase with age are conscientiousness, self-control, emotional stability, self-confidence, social dominance, agreeableness, and warmth.[14] [15] [16] But that's at a general level. What we're wondering is whether people change over time due to a specific role that they've achieved, like a leadership role.

Psychological research has plenty to say about this in support of the stance that people do change as they gain power. Indeed, experiments show that people change even when they're temporarily made to feel powerful.[17,] [18,] [19] They're more likely to take a big-picture approach and decisive action, paying less attention to constraints. They're also more able to flexibly adapt to change, and are more impulsive and less aware of risk. They even have lower levels of stress hormones. Sound like anyone you've gotten to know throughout these chapters?

REFERENCES

1. Brown, Lucy L., Bianca Acevedo, and Helen E. Fisher. "Neural Correlates of Four Broad Temperament Dimensions: Testing Predictions for a Novel Construct of Personality." *PLoS ONE* 8 (11) (2013): e78734. doi:10.1371/journal.pone.0078734.

2. Fisher, Helen E., Heide D. Island, Jonathan Rich, Daniel Marchalik and Lucy L. Brown. "Four Broad Temperament Dimensions: Description, Convergent Validation Correlations, and Comparison with the Big Five." *Frontiers in Psychology* 6 (2015): 1098. doi: 10.3389/fpsyg.2015.01098.

3. Taylor, S. E., L.C. Klein, B.P. Lewis, T.L. Gruenewald, R. A. R. Gurung, and J.A. Updegraff. "Biobehavioral Responses to Stress in Females: Tend-and-befriend, Not Fight-or-flight." *Psychological Review* 107 (2000): 441-429.

4. Nyborg, Helmuth. "Human Evolution, Behavior, and Intelligence." *Hormones, Sex, and Society: The Science of Physicology.* Westport, CT: Praeger/Greenwood. 1994.

5. Casto, K.V., Edwards, D.A. "Testosterone, Cortisol, and Human Competition." *Hormones and Behavior* 82 (2016): 21-37.

6. Grusec, Joan E., and Paul D. Hastings, eds. *Handbook of Socialization, Second Edition: Theory and Research.* New York: The Guilford Press, 2015.

7. Helgeson, Vicki S. *Psychology of Gender: Fifth Edition.* New York: Routledge, 2016.

8. Sandberg, Sheryl, and Nell Scovell. *Lean In: Women, Work, and the Will to Lead.* New York: Alfred A. Knopf, 2013.

9. Friedman, Thomas L. *Thank You For Being Late: An Optimist's Guide to Thriving in the Age of Accelerations.* New York: Farrar, Straus and Giroux, 2016.

10. Cain, Susan. *Quiet: The Power of Introverts in a World That Can't Stop Talking.* New York: Broadway Books, 2013.

11. Byrne, D. *The Attraction Paradigm.* New York: Academic Press. 1971.

12. Newcombe, T. *The Acquaintance Process*. New York: Holt, Rinehart and Winston. 1961.

13. Rivera, L. "Hiring as Cultural Matching: The Case of Elite Professional Service Firms." *American Sociological Review* 77 (2012): 999-1022.

14. Roberts, Brent W., and Daniel Mroczek. "Personality Trait Change in Adulthood." *Current Directions in Psychological Science* 17, no. 1 (2008): 31-35. doi:10.1111/j.1467-8721.2008.00543.x.

15. Roberts, Brent W., Kate E. Walton, and Wolfgang Viechtbauer. "Patterns of Mean-Level Change in Personality Traits Across the Life Course: A Meta-Analysis of Longitudinal Studies." *Psychological Bulletin* 132, no. 1 (2006): 1-25. doi:10.1037/0033-2909.132.1.1.

16. Srivastava, Sanjay, Oliver P. John, Samuel D. Gosling, and Jeff Potter. "Development of Personality in Early and Middle Adulthood: Set Like Plaster or Persistent Change?" *Journal of Personality and Social Psychology* 84, no. 5 (2003): 1041-053. doi:10.1037/0022-3514.84.5.1041.

17. Galinsky, Adam D., Joe C. Magee, Deborah H. Gruenfeld, Jennifer A. Whitson, and Katie A. Liljenquist. "Power Reduces the Press of the Situation: Implications for Creativity, Conformity, and Dissonance." *Journal of Personality and Social Psychology* 95, no. 6 (2008): 1450-466. doi:10.1037/a0012633.

18. Resnick, Brian. "How Power Corrupts the Mind." *The Atlantic*. July 09, 2013. https://www.theatlantic.com/health/archive/2013/07/how-power-corrupts-the-mind/277638/.

19. Whitson, Jennifer A., Katie A. Liljenquist, Deborah H. Gruenfeld, and Brian Cadena. "The Blind Leading: Power Reduces Awareness of Constraints." *Journal of Experimental Social Psychology*. May 2013. https://www.sciencedirect.com/science/article/pii/S0022103112002132.

Business
Chemistry
Applications

12

**Pioneers in Hell:
How to Stop Killing
Their Potential**

Last year, a Pioneer—let's call him Jack—was being lauded by his company for boldly departing from convention and leading his business unit to new heights of innovation. Shortly thereafter, Jack got a new boss. Before their first in-person meeting, his boss asked him to put together a plan for the upcoming year. And populate a detailed template. In a spreadsheet. With multiple pivot tables and complex macros.

Jack, a consummate Pioneer, put off completing it as long as he could; he didn't have a particular aversion to numbers, but he felt they missed the bigger point of his ideas. Not to mention how his eyes would cross and his mind would wander every time he looked at row upon row of inputs and outputs and compounding variables. If he could have used a tool to visualize the data that would have helped. He finally got it done just in time for the meeting, but the process sucked the life out of him.

On the day of the meeting, Jack entered his boss's office relieved to have the whole spreadsheet ordeal behind him and ready to brainstorm possibilities for the year. But he barely began to wax enthusiastically when his boss shut him down with the words, "Let's just walk through the template, shall we?" And they did. Line by line. Cell. By. Cell. And at every stop his boss would question the numbers, the assumptions, the formatting. Every time Jack would ask her to "imagine this" or "picture that" she would simply sit there with a grim expression, whereas she positively lit up when she found a rounding error!

> **✳**
> "LET'S JUST WALK THROUGH THE TEMPLATE, SHALL WE?" AND THEY DID. LINE BY LINE. CELL. BY. CELL.

That meeting was just the start of a series of agonizing "interrogations," as Jack called them, where the intent seemed to be to have him confess to the crime of impracticality with intent to harm. Jack had always thrived under laissez-faire leaders who liked him precisely because he was a bold thinker who didn't let today's reality get in the way of tomorrow's opportunities. He kept trying to bring up some of his ideas in different ways. Maybe if she could just visualize it she would see the potential? Or maybe if he came up with more novel options for her to consider she would become interested? But the bigger and bolder he got, the more his boss tightened in on the questioning. His new boss's scrutiny impacted him like kryptonite. He felt like he couldn't flex his creative muscles, while at the same time he was being tortured with a forced march through granular details.

After a few months, came the final straw. HR implemented **MEMO #104: REGARDING THE MATTER OF WORKING ARRANGEMENTS AND OFFICE UTILIZATION**, requiring leadership, including Jack, to be present in their assigned offices during business hours. Up until that point, he'd had the freedom to more or less work where he wanted, when he wanted. His favorite spot was a bistro table outside the local coffee shop, but he also loved the main conference room with the giant whiteboard, and of course some of his best ideas often came to him during his afternoon run. His euphemistically named "office", in contrast, was a cramped closet with white file cabinets (never used), white walls (poorly lit), and NO whiteboards. After pacing restlessly in his office cage for a week, Jack gave his notice.

Last we heard, he was trekking in the Himalayas, spending some of the signing bonus he got from joining a venture-backed start-up as their "chief disruptor in residence."

Let's talk about it

Remember we said in Chapter 2 that we were going to share some of our conversations with you? We're going to do so here and in the next three chapters. It might help to remember as you go along that Kim is a Pioneer-Driver (specifically a Scientist) and Suzanne is a Guardian-Integrator (specifically a Dreamer).

KIM: This story highlights a classic conflict we see all the time: Opposite types clashing because they approach things from completely different perspectives. In this case it's our Pioneer Jack interacting with his new boss, who is likely at the more extreme end of the Guardian spectrum.

There's an expression that constraint breeds creativity but that's definitely not the case here. Here you have a guy brimming with ideas who is constrained at every turn—first in how he's asked to think about his ideas, then in how he has to communicate his ideas, and finally in where he needs to work. He has no outlet in which to express his creativity and vision—the things he's best at—and instead he is tortured doing things that clearly are not strengths for him. It's like watching a race horse get harnessed to a plow. The thing is, for Pioneers, being held back from exploring possibilities can indeed feel like a physical restraint that weighs on them. Pioneers are high-energy types, but that energy feeds on the rapid generation of concepts and *what if's*. If you take that away, or worse, like in Jack's case, go further and force them to do something completely contrary to their nature, it depletes them.

■ **SUZANNE:** One of the unfortunate things about this story is that, while Jack seems to experience his Guardian boss as a bit of a wicked step-monster, she's probably not really trying to ruin his life. She's simply getting the work done in the style that's most comfortable for her. She either hasn't made the effort to get to know Jack and how he's different from her, or she gets that part, but not how she might need to adjust her approach in order to get the best from him. We often see this when people report to someone that's their opposite type, regardless of which party is which type. In this case it cost the organization an enthusiastic and imaginative leader who had been thriving under his previous boss. That's really a shame.

■ **KIM:** You're right, it's unlikely his boss is trying to be malicious, but people who are "the boss" often have an expectation (consciously or not) that others should bend to them. After all, they're the ones in charge. And perhaps they believe they owe their leadership positions in large part to the success of their particular approaches and thus are unwilling, or unaware, that they should modify them. For Jack, it sounds like his previous leader was more similar in style to him, or at least explicitly valued his contributions, so the contrast with this role change is even starker.

■ **SUZANNE:** I think the "I'm the boss so we'll do it my way" approach is pretty typical, regardless of the boss's type, and if you're the boss, then maybe you do feel it's your prerogative. The thing is, it doesn't usually bring out the best in your people (at least those who are different from you), because it can mean their needs are unmet. So it's often counterproductive.

KIM: Yes, counterproductive but common. And there are common mistakes people tend to make in response. A mistake Jack makes in this situation is one we see with all types—when he's not successful in making a connection, he doubles down on what's made him successful in the past, and what he feels he's great at. He gives his boss more, even grander possibilities—exactly *not* what she's looking for. And although this doubling down is a normal reaction for all types, it's amplified in a sense for Jack because, as a Pioneer, he's naturally optimistic. His assumption is going to be that *of course* she will ultimately come around; he just needs to keep trying. He's looking for that classic, validating *yes, and...* response from her, and all he's getting is a series of *buts* and *nos*.

SUZANNE: I think that's a great point to keep in mind when working with a Pioneer—even if you can't say *yes*, can you avoid saying *no*, especially right away? Because nothing dampens a Pioneer's enthusiasm faster than the word "*no*." I'm not suggesting anyone go ahead and do everything a Pioneer suggests (actually I'd pretty strongly recommend you *don't* do that!), just that you demonstrate you have an open mind and are eager to hear and consider the Pioneer's creative ideas. We'll make some suggestions in the next chapter for how Guardians might do this, because they're often seen as most likely to burst bubbles, but these strategies work for any type. One of these suggestions is to try something more like, "How might we?" or "I like/I wish," as in "How might we test your idea in a low-risk way?" or "I like the vision of the future you're painting. I wish I had a clearer idea about how we'd overcome the barriers that exist."

KIM: At the risk of piling on here, the word *no* is more than just a buzzkill for a Pioneer (though it is that). For a Pioneer, your *no* is like a neon sign over your head flashing "closed for business." Because Pioneers love the contributions of others in the brainstorming process—it fuels their thinking—so if you're not even open to discussing possibilities, in a Pioneer's mind, you might as well have your lights off with no one home.

Now, I get it, some Pioneer ideas are a little out there, maybe just plain...well, bad. And it can be hard to say nice things about ideas that you believe are obviously terrible.

So if you can't in good faith say something like, "I really like the way you're thinking," try a question instead. Not "Why the heck did you think that was a good idea?" Rather something like, "Have you ever seen something like that before?" "How do you think our customers would react if we did that?" or the old but good standard, "What would [insert respected name here] do in this situation?"

SUZANNE: Another idea for making a situation like this work a little better is to explicitly acknowledge the differences in perspective and the flexing on both sides that will likely be needed to make it work. This can be helpful in any opposite-type pair, but in this case Jack's boss might admit that she is less likely to latch on to big, grand ideas right away, and ask for Jack's help in getting her there by providing her what she needs—answers to her specific questions. Then she might promise that in return she'll try hard to be a problem-solving thought-partner, rather than a party-pooping killjoy.

KIM: If they're comfortable having that type of conversation it could help, but it seems even harder here because this is a new relationship. Jack's boss might be willing to give him a little more latitude *if* they had a strong foundation of trust, but trust takes time to build, particularly for a Guardian. You and I have worked together for years and I think one of the reasons you tolerate some of my crazy ideas and quick decisions is that you know that ultimately I will come through and not leave you hanging. That knowledge is based on a long history of interactions, so you're basing your trust on evidence, not wishful thinking.

SUZANNE: True. I've had lots of opportunities over time to see, not only that you won't leave me hanging, but also that your crazy ideas are a much needed balance for my sometimes overly practical ones (not that there's anything wrong with practicality in the right dosage).

KIM: But unlike you and I, Jack's boss probably doesn't know much about Jack other than that he's got a reputation for doing things outside of the norm (which doesn't necessarily sound like a good thing to a Guardian). But is he a man who keeps his word? Who follows through? Who brings something more substantial than flash in-the-pan ideas? She's essentially putting Jack through his paces until he proves himself to her. And yes, there are ways she can make that process more palatable to him, as you point out. But Jack could also have been less miserable, I suspect, if he used one of the Pioneer super powers of looking at things from a whole new perspective. Instead of seeing the situation as a worthless set of interrogations he could have changed the lens for himself, and approached it as a chance for him to build trust and rapport.

■ **SUZANNE:** Speaking of trust, I'd like to bring us back to Memo #104: Regarding the matter of working arrangements and office utilization. Kim, you hinted before that constraints rankle Pioneers particularly, and this memo (and the policy behind it) is such a good example of how to create the exact opposite of an engaging work environment for a Pioneer. Not only does it force everyone to work in a physical setting that sounds quite uninspiring, but just the idea that people are being told what they *have* to do is likely to set teeth on edge. And a Pioneer's teeth are likely to be extra sensitive to such a thing.

Instead of just announcing a (quite unimaginative) solution to a perceived problem, a better way to handle such a situation, especially if you've got some Pioneers hanging around, might be to present people with the problem itself. Suppose the issue is that people have been complaining they don't ever know where to find anyone when they need to get in touch. Go ahead and pose that problem to a Pioneer or two. Not only are you likely to end up with some much more creative solutions to the problem, but they are likely to be solutions that engage, rather than offend your Pioneers—and probably others too!

■ **KIM:** I love the idea of getting others involved in addressing the perceived issue versus putting out solutions that are unlikely to suit anyone. That approach is particularly appealing to the Pioneers as they love creative problem solving. Unfortunately because Jack didn't feel he could truly contribute to his full potential, he solved that problem by leaving the company.

It's important to note that, as a Pioneer, Jack probably didn't agonize over the decision to leave. He probably didn't review and question everything he did and reflect on whether he could have done things differently. Chances are he didn't even consider for a moment that maybe the problem was with him. He might have felt it was unfortunate that he couldn't continue his work, and streak of success, but the point is he didn't take it personally. He decided the overall environment didn't suit him, and so he moved on to the next thing. This means that this is much more of a loss for the company than it is for Jack.

SUZANNE: Given that a Pioneer probably *won't* agonize over the decision to leave, it seems even more important for leaders to focus on creating environments that make them want to stay. And not just stay, but bring that typical Pioneer passion to bear on whatever the goals of the organization are. One powerful way to do that is to make sure Pioneers are well positioned to do what they most want to do—tackle tough problems by innovating. Now this doesn't mean you should let Pioneers totally off the hook when it comes to doing some of the more mundane tasks that we all need to do—that wouldn't be fair to others. (I'm speaking as a Guardian here, since we're the ones who tend to end up with all that mundane stuff if Pioneers get the impression they don't have to do any of it.)

KIM: This is a fine line, because I know that many Pioneers (myself at the head of that chaotic throng), would leap at any opportunity to avoid what we think of as day-to-day drudgery. So while I do think it's important to give Pioneers things they love, it can help to follow a little Mary Poppins advice: "A spoonful of sugar helps the medicine go down." Break up the unpalatable tasks into more bite-sized chunks, interspersed amongst more Pioneer-friendly activities.

SUZANNE: And it's not just about giving them "fun" things to do. We know Pioneers are the most likely type to say they thrive when they have opportunities to learn and try new things. We know that they aspire, not only to lead, but also to innovate, and that making a difference is important to them. So to keep a Pioneer engaged for the long term (or probably even the short term) it's critical that some good percentage of a Pioneer's time can be dedicated to doing what they're great at or what they're excited about. After all, we all want that! And the organization benefits when people are able to play to their strengths.

KIM: I would take that a step further and say that organizations benefit not only when people can exercise their unique strengths, but also when they are put in environments that actually *give* them strength. So for our Pioneers, don't just give them an assignment to innovate something. Also provide sources of inspiration—place them on cross-disciplinary working groups, send them on research field trips, encourage them to spend time in a public co-working space on days they don't need to be in the office. Environment is not just a physical reality, although that plays a role. Rather it's a mix of factors that contribute to an overall experience.

Creating optimal environments can be a tall order for leaders, because it isn't a single thing and it's different for each of the types. And of course you can't cater to everyone all the time. That being said, many leaders overestimate the amount of effort it takes to flex, and underestimate the degree of positive impact. Like a chef in a kitchen who takes the time to sear the meat and steam the vegetables versus throwing everything in a pot of boiling water, the leader who understands what is required for different people and proceeds accordingly will get much better results.

SUZANNE: Boiled meat. Yuck. But it's true—meeting everyone's needs at the same time can seem tough, especially when people's needs sometimes conflict. And that's why providing options works so well. A Driver might think field trips feel like a waste of time. A Guardian would possibly think a public co-working space was even worse than an uninspiring office. The idea is not to make everyone do the same things, but to give everyone the same level of opportunity to choose what they do (or at least where they do it).

I think this is more important than ever when people need to do some of those tasks that are particularly hard for them. So for example, most of us have to do some level of required stuff related to performance management, security, technology, and such things. These kinds of tasks might be particularly painful for a Pioneer—so couldn't we at least give them some freedom in when, where, or how they get it done?

KIM: I'd vote for that. The question for leaders though becomes: How do you give them some freedom while keeping guardrails in place to mitigate risk? Because, perhaps not coincidentally, some of the things that Pioneers hate to do are usually required to manage risk in some way.

Your problem as a leader here is two fold. First, Pioneers likely do not want to follow the process you've put in place to deal with the risk (please, no more three-hour instructional videos on employee policies). Second, they tend to downplay or even dismiss the risk itself, saying things like "Come on, is it really that big a deal? What's the worst that can happen?" or "How likely is this anyway?" For these situations you need to paint a picture of the threat. Bring it to life for them in a visceral way that lets them envision the grim possibilities. And then maybe you can get them more onboard with a process (hopefully tailored to better suit the ways they engage).

SUZANNE: I have this picture in mind of a devastated and desolate landscape, and it's quite depressing! Another likelihood is that Pioneers might say (or at least think) something along the lines of "All truly great innovations have been realized because someone ignored the potential risks that others feared," or "Only great risks bring great rewards." But that's actually not the case, and you can engage in a bit of myth-busting by sharing some pretty compelling evidence to help Pioneers (and others) see this. Both Malcolm Gladwell[1] and Adam Grant[2] have written about very interesting research exploring our (faulty) associations of risk taking with entrepreneurship. One of the key points they highlight is that, generally speaking, entrepreneurs *do* tend to take lots of risks, but also, generally-speaking, entrepreneurs tend to fail. Further more, the reasons for these failures often revolve around poor or even absent analysis, a lack of foresight, and a failure to properly prepare (all things Pioneers are accused of). The entrepreneurs who succeed, far from chasing blindly after a dream, tend to hedge their bets in several different ways, by keeping their day jobs even after launching a successful start-up, for example.

Taking great risks *can* sometimes lead to great things, but share with your Pioneers the idea that such risks should be engaged in as you would a well-balanced stock portfolio; you protect yourself with some relatively safe investments so you can make some risky ones too. In this case, the safe investments are all those policy-related processes, and it's adhering to these closely and thoroughly that enables us to go ahead and take some of those other risks.

KIM: Spoken like a true Guardian—but I get your point. There's another aspect here that's important to address, particularly for Pioneers but really for all types, and that's overconfidence bias. There's been lots of research showing that people tend to overestimate their degree of certainty, and probability of success, even in the face of tempering data.[3] The classic example I've seen quite a bit living in the Silicon Valley is the entrepreneur who is *convinced* that their venture will be successful, even though the success rate in general is abysmal. But enough ventures do succeed that the myth persists, largely due to base-rate fallacy, essentially the concept that people will put more weight on specific examples than general information.[4] These biases are part of being human and thus plague all types, but I suspect that Pioneers might be particularly at risk because of their optimism and inherent confidence (arrogance?), which is not helped of course by their overall tendency to trust their gut over statistics and probabilities.

That's a wrap

We just shared a whole lot of tips for how to create an environment where Pioneers excel, and we thought a summary of those points might be helpful. While focusing on the needs of Pioneers, you'll want to watch out for turning off the other types. After all, you want everyone to excel, not just Pioneers. So we've added to our summary some ideas for how to keep things palatable for Guardians, the Pioneer's opposite.

To meet the needs of Pioneers	To make it palatable for Guardians
Allow time for free-flowing discussion and idea generation.	Timebox discussion so it doesn't carry on too long.
Brainstorm and white-board on the spot.	When possible provide an option to prepare in advance, or at least take a few moments for quiet idea-generation before opening the floor.
Keep an open mind. Even if you can't say yes, try to avoid saying no.	Let Guardians know there will be a time for critique, it just isn't now. Coach them on less soul-crushing ways to share concerns, such as saying "I like/I wish" and similar techniques.
Provide options for where, when, and how to work.	Guardians likely want these options too!
Position them to do what they love and explain how more mundane tasks enable them to do so.	Don't let Pioneers off the hook on some of the more mundane tasks.

> ## If you are a Pioneer

We know that as a Pioneer you're probably pretty good at coming up with imaginative solutions on your own. However, we thought you'd still appreciate a few suggestions from us regarding how you might flex to fit just a bit better into an environment where people might not seem to acknowledge the full extent of your creative genius.

STICK WITH IT

Einstein famously once said, "It's not that I'm so smart. It's that I stay with problems longer." Executing on a visionary idea, and seeing it through to fruition, takes a certain amount of stick-to-it-ness. Visions don't typically become reality all on their own. And while Pioneers are often thought of as visionaries, people sometimes complain that they struggle to stick with an idea long enough to make it a reality. And there's research suggesting that when the going gets tough—like when a problem gets really difficult to solve—Extroverts give up more quickly than Introverts do.[5] And as we know, most Pioneers probably lean more toward extroversion than introversion. One of the reasons for this lack of follow-through is that Pioneers, more than any other type, like to tackle what's new. That's great, except for the fact that what feels bright and shiny new now will eventually feel old and a bit tarnished, and that often happens before something is actually finished.

If you're a Pioneer, try breaking your idea into smaller execution chunks and celebrate the achievement of each one (Pioneers love a good party) before launching into the next "new" phase. In addition to keeping up the enthusiasm, this also gives you a way to evolve your plan as you go (let's face it, you know you will), while still getting things done!

MAKE THE NEW SEEM OLD

In the early 1800s, the first automobiles were often referred to as horseless carriages. Why? Because people understood what that meant. They were used to carriages pulled by horses, so it wasn't a very big leap to imagine a carriage without a horse. Calling an automobile a horseless carriage made it seem familiar. While it may seem counterintuitive to novelty-embracing Pioneers, when trying to sell something quite revolutionary to ordinary people, the familiar can be a good thing.

It's important for you to remember, Pioneers, that your love of novelty isn't equally shared by everyone. Indeed, some people are quite suspicious of ideas that seem totally new or foreign. Instead, they're more comfortable with what's familiar. They respond more positively to change that's incremental rather than disruptive. So when you're hoping to get people on board with your innovative idea, emphasizing just how new and different it is may be the wrong move. To reach these people, emphasize what's *not* new. This will likely feel counterintuitive to you, but it can get people comfortable with your idea more quickly.

SAY IT AGAIN... AND AGAIN...

You may be a brilliant visionary who can paint a picture of a new future that will make people swoon. You may be such a great communicator that communication experts ask for your advice. But chances are, you're still under-communicating about your ideas. Because here's the thing: As we suggested earlier, for many people, the more familiar they are with something, the better. This is called the *exposure effect*.[6] So even when your idea is quite new, if people keep hearing about it over and over, it will start to seem familiar. Management guru John Kotter has suggested that most change agents under-communicate their vision by a power of 10, so just an extra mention or two isn't likely to do it.[7] If you really want to get others behind your idea, be ready to tell them about it repeatedly, and preferably in multiple ways. It's also best to leave a bit of time in between when you first present an idea and when you ask people to tell you what they think about it. Pioneers tend to process things quickly and go with their gut, but many others don't work this way. For the best response, give the idea time to marinate.

TAKE A BREATHER

Yes, Pioneers (and anyone wanting their ideas to stick) should overcommunicate their vision. But that doesn't mean they should be the only ones communicating. A common complaint about Pioneers is that their high-energy, put-it-all-out-there, talk-to-think style can be overwhelming, and can crowd out other voices. Pioneers often aren't even aware of their verbal steamrolling, so simply making a conscious effort to let others get a word in edgewise can help. But Pioneers, don't include others in the conversation just to be nice (although it never hurts to have good manners). You should include others because they might have something to say that would make your idea even better, help it see the light of day, or spark another idea.

If you're a Pioneer, amp up your inquiry. When you get on a roll, pause occasionally to ask a question—and not just the rhetorical kind. Give people a chance to share their thoughts and when they do, actually listen. You never know where that can lead.

SEEK FIRST TO UNDERSTAND

Pioneers often describe themselves as uninterested in details and process. At least that's how they say it when they're being polite. Sometimes Pioneers even use the phrase "unnecessary details," which to a Guardian sounds like an oxymoron. If you're one of those Pioneers, think twice before you ignore the details or process, or before you "improve" something by stripping everything away. Take a moment to find out why the detail or process is important to others. Ask: "Why does this matter? What would be the consequence of skipping this step, ignoring, this detail, etc.?" If you think you have a better way to do something, that's awesome! But proposing a better way without thoroughly understanding why things are the way they currently are will not only annoy others, it might also result in your messing things up. Start by getting a lay of the land. Once you've done that, you'll be better positioned to offer ideas that might actually be helpful.

RED FLAG: CAGES, CLIPPED WINGS, AND COAL MINES

As we've said before, Pioneers tend to be very adaptable, which means in theory they can make themselves comfortable in most work situations—particularly since many of their core characteristics map so well with established leadership stereotypes. That said, if Pioneers are constantly being caged in and not given room to roam and grow, or they are consistently kept from letting their ideas take flight, chances are they won't be very happy. And if you're an unhappy Pioneer, you're also unlikely to stay that way for long. Pioneers rate loyalty lower on the scale of importance than other types and will be off to other opportunities. So in other words if you're a Pioneer, most of the time you'll probably know when it's time to go.

We think the bigger red flags to look out for, as Pioneers, are not those obvious threats but the more insidious ones. There's been an interesting discussion in the business literature about the role of so-called deviants.[8][9][10] These are people willing to step outside the box and question the status quo—often a natural role for Pioneers. Deviants are invaluable to organizations because they help them evolve and break new ground. But they also shoulder personal risk in so doing. After all, if the train is chugging along fine and you're the lone voice who insists on taking a different track, you might expect some upset people if the train then derails.

In an organization with strong leadership support, this may not be a big problem, but some organizations use their deviants like canaries in the coal mines. They send them out into uncharted, risky environments. If the canary chirps away and shows it's safe, they come charging in to mine the riches. But if the canary stops chirping because it's not safe, they figure they can always get another canary. Such fair-weather organizations might seem like they're giving you great opportunities, but make sure you know what you're signing up for. And if you get the sense that they're out for their own success at the expense of yours, you might want to flex those wings and fly to more welcoming climes.

REFERENCES

1. Gladwell, Malcolm. "The Sure Thing." *The New Yorker*, January 18, 2010.

2. Grant, Adam M. *Originals: How Non-Conformists Move the World*. New York: Viking, 2016.

3. Kahneman, Daniel. *Thinking, Fast and Slow*. New York: Farrar, Straus and Giroux, 2015.

4. Ibid.

5. Howard, Rick, and Maeve Mckillen. "Extraversion and Performance in the Perceptual Maze Test." *Personality and Individual Differences* 11, no. 4 (1990): 391-96. doi:10.1016/0191-8869(90)90221-c.

6. Zajonc, Robert B. "Attitudinal Effects of Mere Exposure." *Journal of Personality and Social Psychology*, 9 (2, Pt.2 (1968): 1-27.

7. Kotter, John P. *Leading Change*. Boston, MA: Harvard Business Review Press, 2012.

8. Gino, Francesca. "Let Your Workers Rebel." *Harvard Business Review*. June 08, 2017. https://hbr.org/cover-story/2016/10/let-your-workers-rebel.

9. Pascale, Richard, Jerry Sternin, and Monique Sternin. *The Power of Positive Deviance: How Unlikely Innovators Solve the World's Toughest Problems*. Brighton, MA: Harvard Business Review Press, 2010.

10. Vadera, Abhijeet K., Michael G. Pratt, and Pooja Mishra. "Constructive Deviance in Organizations." *Journal of Management* 39, no. 5 (February 26, 2013): 1221-276.

**Guardians in Hell:
How to Stop Killing
Their Potential**

13

Once a Guardian named Gwendolyn was given one month to coordinate the creation of a website illustrating her organization's vision and how they were living it. This was a high-profile project dreamt up by the board, and one that lots of stakeholders deeply cared about. Was Gwen an expert on websites with a deep understanding of the vision? Did she have a broad network of connections to draw upon? Did she thrive in the role of herding cats? Not at all. She was highly skilled in other areas, but she got this particular project because she happened to be standing nearby when it was assigned. From her Guardian lens, this wasn't a fairytale about being handed a golden opportunity. It was a horror story.

The good news was that because of the tight time frame, there were lots of resources (also known as people) assigned to the project. This was also bad news—lots of people to coordinate, and every one of them with strong opinions, hell-bent on expressing them energetically, and all at the same time. Everyone was looking to her to make quick decisions but Gwen could barely think straight in their presence. And they seemed to be present *all the time*.

Gwen and her team were provided the "gift" of a dedicated section of their open-space work environment in which to collaborate. Because so many important people had a stake in the project, the team was expected to be visibly working together on site as much as possible. But that meant constant interruptions and no quiet place to think or to focus on the heads-down, detailed work that she, as a Guardian, typically excelled at. When she pointed this out to leadership they told her to stop being so inflexible—this is how innovative work gets done.

✳

THE WHOLE THING WAS TOTALLY OPEN-ENDED, WITH NO STRUCTURE OR PLAN.

And the necessity of face time was the *only* expectation of the project that was clear. Beyond that the whole thing was totally open-ended, with no structure or plan, and no definition of success, except that it was imperative it get done on time and that it be brilliant. But what did that even mean? Whenever she tried to get more clarity she felt pushed aside, the underlying message being that she should be able to figure it out for herself. When she pointed out inconsistencies, errors, or potentially problematic future implications of current decisions, she was answered with eye-rolls and the suggestion that she stop nit-picking.

And the vision? Well that wasn't quite set in stone yet either. Every other day it seemed that the language around the vision was changed, sometimes a little and sometimes a lot. It represented a moving target, and yet the deadline didn't move along with it, and no one seemed to understand that each time the vision was tweaked, there was a domino effect on all the other detailed elements of the project. At the same time, various members of the board and the leadership team kept dropping in spontaneously and expecting updates, which Gwen was never given time to prepare for. When they asked her to present at the leadership meeting, without prior notice, she balked, but they couldn't understand the problem.

It wasn't long before Gwen started to feel that her strengths and her way of working weren't valued by her organization. She had started the project with a commitment to give it her all and produce a stellar product, but soon she was just hoping that this whole thing was some kind of nightmare that she'd wake up from. As her level of engagement started to wane, she gradually pulled back from actively working to make the project the best it could be. She overlooked inconsistencies and let them stand. She let little errors slip by. She stopped pointing out potential risks. She let go of the idea that she'd feel pride in her work and in the end, her goal became just to get through the project.

Let's talk about it

As we begin our conversations, remember that Kim is a Pioneer-Driver (specifically a Scientist) and Suzanne is a Guardian-Integrator (specifically a Dreamer).

■ **SUZANNE:** As a Guardian I *definitely* relate to this story, particularly the part about her being able to see the domino effect that will result from a small change in one part of the project, and knowing that others aren't worrying about it, or maybe can't even see it. I've often felt that way while we've been writing this book!

I think this is one of the places where the Guardian's strengths can cause them some real challenges. If I'm the person focused on all the details, who understands how all the small things fit together and impact each other, and if I've created a detailed plan around all of that, I may be less than open to any changes because I see how even a small change can lead to a huge amount of rework. Adding to that, Guardians are the type most likely to get stressed out, so suddenly I will get upset and argue against a change that looks very minor to someone else. Because that someone else is often focused at a much higher level, they don't see the problem and they're just wondering what the heck I'm panicking about and why I'm so resistant. And indeed I *am* resistant, even if the change would ultimately be for the better. So, Kim, now you know why it takes me awhile to come around sometimes. ☺

KIM: Yes, but thank goodness you eventually do. ☺ In all seriousness though (and excluding you, I hope, Suzanne), I think sometimes Guardians do "come around" but not because they actually agree with the changes. Instead, like Gwen, they've just given up trying to do the right thing. Not only is that dissatisfying for the Guardian, but it's a loss for the organization because that Guardian is the one specifically on the lookout for things that could trip up the plan, things that other people would probably overlook. It's a balance though, because no plan is likely to persist in the face of constant change like we see in business today, and so Guardians will often need to adjust, even if that's not their preference. But they can still play to their strengths and add value by injecting perspective as to the direction and degree of change needed rather than reflecting universal resistance.

SUZANNE: You know, one of the ways leaders can help Guardians move through this is by acknowledging that they understand the change is going to cause a domino effect and some amount of rework. That they recognize that the plan was a good one, and they appreciate all the work that went into it, but because x, y, and z factors have changed, the plan needs to change too. Sometimes I think it's the sense that no one else is paying attention to the details that makes a Guardian hold on really tightly, and then eventually get frustrated and give up, wondering, "If no one else cares enough, why should I?"

KIM: Yes, that makes sense. Gwen is in a particularly tough situation though, because the domino effect you describe isn't the only thing that's going against her natural grain. In addition to that she is: 1) managing an ill-defined project where she lacks expertise, 2) coordinating with what sounds like a group of over-caffeinated Extroverts, and 3) needing to work in an environment ill-suited to her needs. Not exactly a recipe for Guardian success!

SUZANNE: Right. More than any other type, Guardians appreciate clarity in terms of expectations and definitions of success. While some of the other types might feel constrained by too much clarity, for Guardians, knowing exactly what's expected and what a raging success would look like, serves as a North Star that illuminates the possible paths forward. Instead of trying to figure out *where* to go, it helps them focus their energy on charting the most advantageous course, identifying the best footholds and spotting potential pitfalls. It allows them to properly prepare for the trip, removing some of the stress that uncertainty can cause for a Guardian. I mean, why the heck would anyone want to wander around in the dark when light is available?

And furthermore, it's one thing to do something in the dark that you're an expert at doing, but if they haven't got the necessary expertise, that's an extra layer of challenge for Guardians. It makes me think of my last camping trip with my kids. We got a late start and arrived at the campground after dark, which would not have been a big deal—we've set up our tent so many times we can do it with our eyes closed—but I failed to factor in that I had bought a new tent! So now here I am flailing around in the dark with two kids and a tent with lots of pieces we don't recognize, and we can't really see the instructions or even the picture of what the darn thing is supposed to look like once we've put it up, so I don't know how to do it the right way.

KIM: Ah yes, the joys of camping. I've been in a situation like that as well, but of course my Pioneer self never bothered to read the instructions. My boys and I just put the tent up in a way that looked good, but then endured the consequences the next day as the weather took a turn for the worse and our rain tarp wasn't adequately secured. That's when I wished I didn't suffer from hypo-Guardian syndrome!

SUZANNE: I can imagine! As for being trapped with those over-caffeinated Extroverts in an ill-suited work environment, this is a reality for many Guardians, I think. In fact, it's a reality for many non-Guardians too these days. Open office work environments have become more common, but studies increasingly show people dislike working in such environments and experience higher levels of stress as a result.[1][2] And what's stressful for people in general is often even more stressful for people who are Guardians.

KIM: I know what you mean. Although I'm a primary Pioneer (which is more extroverted), I'm a secondary Driver with a Scientist leaning (which is more introverted). I love open, collaborative spaces for brainstorming, but for pretty much everything else I like to be away from people in order to focus. In Gwen's case, she's such a strong Guardian that she clearly aligns with Introvert preferences universally, but for many people (like me), these extroversion/introversion affiliations can be more context dependent.

In some ways though, Gwen's challenges go beyond the particular context of the tasks she's tackling to a more pervasive cultural norm. She's working in a company that seems to have a strong working style of its own, and that style sounds like a combination of Pioneer and Integrator. Her company's culture emphasizes innovation, adaptation, collaboration, and other defining characteristics of Pioneers and Integrators. It's perhaps not surprising then that these traits are highly valued, and that she in turn feels undervalued since her orientation is quite different.

SUZANNE: And Gwen's not the only one! Our research has shown that Guardians are the most underappreciated type. And it's not only Guardians who say that; the other types also acknowledge that while the perspective and type of work typically done by Guardians is critical, it's not always recognized or highly valued. What if leaders could find more ways to acknowledge the importance of the work that keeps the trains running on time and prevents disasters large and small, rather than putting quite so much focus on those dreaming up the next kind of new train?

KIM: Great point. To be clear, I'm certainly not saying that there's no hope for a Guardian like Gwen in an organization like this, but I do think it takes transparency and active role-engineering to flip this kind of situation from a potential de-motivator (as it was for Gwen) to a distinct advantage. I worked with one company who did this quite well. They had a leadership team dominated by Pioneers and Integrators, a reasonable mirror of the company culture overall. As they were beginning to compete in highly regulated markets, they recognized that their organization's shoot-from-the-hip attitude might not serve them well into the future. They looked around their group and noticed that one of their peers was a solid Guardian. They recalled that he had stepped in a number of times over the past few years to keep them from stumbling into holes or blundering into dead ends. He always had a thorough grasp of the details underpinning any decision, and was known for his well-considered perspectives.

They made him their chief operating officer, and then they went one step further. They asked him what he needed to be successful. His answer, not surprisingly, was: clear objectives, a voice at the table (which meant other voices sometimes had to be silent and actually listen), and the authority to make decisions that might slow growth in the near term but would be essential for sustainable success.

SUZANNE: Oh, yes… if only more leaders would simply ask people, "What do you need to be successful?" or, "What can we do to make it easier for you to contribute?" Not only do others need to sometimes be silent and listen, but Guardians might ask also for the opportunity to prepare, in advance, for meetings, brainstorming sessions, and decisions. Guardians often prefer to process information alone, in a quiet setting, where they can take their time considering all the relevant information, data, and details. They tend to percolate ideas gradually, and if they're provided with the opportunity to do so, they likely *will* do the prework (unlike some of the types who like to be more spontaneous), and they'll come prepared to offer a thoughtful perspective. *Then,* they need the space to offer that perspective, which sometimes means others need to pipe down a bit.

All of this is sometimes easier said than done. For one thing, some of the other types don't always do things that far in advance. They may have to make an extra effort to get materials ready prior to a session where a decision needs to be made, or to share an agenda or at least a topic before a meeting or brainstorming session. But it's worth it, because it's going to bring some of the quieter voices to the table.

KIM: It does take conscious effort to accommodate different types. I confess that it pains me a bit to have to do the kind of preparation necessary for my Guardian colleagues, but that's where Business Chemistry diversity can be a boon. Instead of me trying to "be a Guardian" and think through all the details that my opposite types will need to be successful, I call on the Guardians themselves to define a process they think will work, and to schedule out key preparation milestones in addition to actual meetings. Having that time set aside explicitly on my calendar forces me to think through materials, agendas, or other specifics they need, in a timeline that works for them, but it spares me needing to track the overall process. It essentially parses out what is usually a very fluid and (from the outside at least) obscure approach, into predictable and digestible chunks.

Now some might argue that I'm making extra work for the Guardians, but in my experience the whole point is that Guardians don't see this as extra work; they see it as necessary work that they are uniquely well suited to provide. Furthermore, they seem to appreciate having a chance to spell out what they need and when they need it, with the reassurance of seeing that train of progress moving along the track.

SUZANNE: That's kind of how we divided up responsibilities for this book. I've been the one to own the timeline and determine when we're going to write what, and to keep track of the various pieces that need to be incorporated into which part of each chapter. I haven't minded playing this role at all; in fact, I have *needed* to be the one doing it!

One of the important side effects of asking a Guardian to do some of the work they're well suited for, and that increases the chances they'll get what they need to succeed, is that it's a great way to reinforce for a Guardian that what they do and who they are is valued. I've already mentioned that Guardians sometimes feel underappreciated, but it's not only that. Our research tells us they're also the least likely of the types to feel safe sharing their ideas and bringing their *whole selves to work*. Part of this may just be due to their natural reserve—they tend to be Introverts after all. But research has shown that people who feel they need to cover up aspects of who they are tend to be less committed to their organizations.[3] So if something about the work environment is making them feel uneasy, this can pose a real challenge for organizations.

KIM: Precisely, and without that commitment, you're likely to miss out on the unique contributions that Guardians (and each type in their own way) can provide.

SUZANNE: Yes, I think organizations often miss out on the potential contributions of Guardians, for all of the reasons we discussed above, but also because of their desire to get practical, when others are being theoretical. One Guardian told us she resented the role of always having to burst everyone's bubble by pointing out that their ideas were totally impractical for a multitude of reasons. While Guardians themselves may need to work on their sense of timing and the way in which they deliver this message, which we'll discuss later in this chapter, leaders can also guide Guardians to make these important contributions in ways that are even more helpful (and palatable to others). Suppose a Guardian was asked to identify only the one most critical potential problem (rather than the endless list they likely have) and then to help *solve it*. Wouldn't that benefit everyone?

That's a wrap

We just shared a slew of ideas for how to create an environment where Guardians excel, and we thought a summary of those points might be helpful. But beware of turning off the other types while focusing on the needs of Guardians, because you want everyone else to excel too. So our summary includes some suggestions for how to keep things palatable for Pioneers, the Guardian's opposite.

To meet the needs of Guardians	To make it palatable for Pioneers
Provide pre-work, data, and information in advance of a discussion or decision.	Make it optional, not required, to review materials in advance.
Share an agenda prior to meetings.	Make agendas flexible with some space for open discussions and options should a change of course be called for.
When a change is required, acknowledge the potential domino effect on the details Guardians care about and explain why the change is needed.	Pioneers like change so that shouldn't be a problem in and of itself, but don't go through the entire domino effect, just address the fact that it exists.
Provide clear expectations including what success looks like.	Allow flexibility in how to reach success.
Offer workspaces that provide permission to be alone, control over the environment, sensory balance, and psychological safety.	Mix quiet workspaces with other kinds that are likely to appeal to Pioneers, and allow people to choose where they work, at least some of the time.

Acknowledge the value of the Guardians' work, which often involves more invisible tasks that keep the trains running on time.	Pioneers get a lot of love; they can probably stand to share some.
Pipe down and listen up so Guardians have a chance to process and don't need to fight to enter the discussion.	Consider identifying certain points in a meeting to make space for quiet voices and other times where a free-for-all is okay.
Ask Guardians to help solve any potential problems they identify.	Ask Guardians to wait a beat before identifying potential problems.

▶ If you are a Guardian

If you're a Guardian or even another type who sees a bit of yourself in Gwen's story or the conversation we've been having, you don't have to sit around waiting for someone to fix the situation for you—there is plenty you can do yourself.

DIP A TOE IN

Among the many profound sayings attributed to Plato is this one: "Wise men talk because they have something to say, fools because they have to say something." We'd bet most Guardians would agree with that sentiment and are very busy being wise men and women, holding back on sharing their thoughts until they're perfectly formed. But not everyone is quite so wise, nor do they all ascribe to this principle. Instead, some people will assume that if you don't share your thoughts, you have no thoughts. They'll judge you as disengaged, not leadership material, or even as being not too bright. Meanwhile, the conversation will go barreling ahead, leaving your partially formed, but potentially brilliant thoughts in the dust. Executive coach Ephraim

Schachter suggests that such reluctance to contribute to discussions negatively impacts how people, and particularly Introverts, are viewed. Among the reasons he identifies for Introverts' reluctance to weigh in during meetings are that they haven't formed an opinion yet, they feel their opinion has already been shared by someone else, or they don't feel it's safe to share their opinion. Our own research backs up this point. In a blog post titled "The #1 Mistake Introverted VPs Make in Meetings" Schachter suggests there are ways to counter each of these barriers without going too terribly far out of your comfort zone.[4] For example, if you're not yet ready to share an opinion, you can still contribute to the conversation by asking a question. Or, if you feel someone else has already shared your thought, you might agree and then expand on it. The point is, there are many different ways to contribute to a discussion that won't make Plato roll over in his grave, and your professional reputation may depend upon your doing so.

ASK FOR IT

One strategy that might make it easier for you to speak up in a meeting is to prepare in advance. Spending a little bit of time thinking through the topic to be discussed or the decisions to be made—even jotting some notes down about your thoughts—can make a huge difference in your readiness to speak once the conversation gets going. But of course you can only do this if you know in advance what the discussion topics will be. So *ask*. Ask whoever is running the meeting for as much information in advance as possible. Ask what the topic will be, but also ask whether there will be a brainstorming session and for what purpose. Then spend a little time thinking and brainstorming alone before the meeting. Is there relevant data that you can review? Do so. Are there particular expectations for how the meeting will run? Since Guardians typically value clear expectations more than other types do, don't wait for someone else to offer—ask.

We've found that Guardians are more likely than others to experience stress and less likely to say they're effective when stressed. If you're experiencing a lot of stress, it can be helpful to understand why your experience might be different from those around you, and then to ask for what you might need to manage it. In addition to requesting additional information so you can be better prepared for meetings, other requests that might help you reduce or manage stress may be a quieter or more private work environment (at least some of the time), limits on the amount of face time you need to put in, flexible deadlines so you don't feel rushed, or fewer team-based projects and more individual work time.

SHIFT YOUR MINDSET

While it's sometimes possible to reduce stress levels by altering working conditions or responsibilities, it's often not. But there's still something you can do to make stress more palatable, and that's to shift your mindset. There's evidence that changing your mindset about stress may be even more helpful than efforts to reduce that stress.[5] Particularly for Guardians, who as Introverts may experience the physical symptoms of stress more intensely than others, one helpful exercise may be to relabel the physical feelings of stress as something else, like excitement. One classic research study showed that people both felt better and performed better in a public speaking exercise when they labeled the butterflies they were feeling as excitement, rather than nervousness or fear.[6] Another way to shift your mindset around stress is to use your strong values to your advantage. When you're in the midst of a stressful time, spend 15 minutes writing about your core values. Doing so is likely to have several effects on you, from making you feel more in control, to reminding you that the stress is likely to be temporary, to nudging you to take more positive action. In her book *The Upside of Stress*, Kelly McGonigal states that "writing about your values is one of the most effective psychological interventions ever studied."[7] And the research McGonigal outlines suggests that writing about your values even once can have positive effects months and years later, long after you've forgotten about the writing task itself.

BE A POSITIVE FORCE

Guardians are great at spotting mistakes, identifying the cracks that make an idea impractical, and foreseeing what might go wrong with a plan. Indeed, many Guardians can't help pointing such things out. This is a valuable role to play, but people won't always love you for it, because it feels like a downer. You may be practicing what's called defensive pessimism—spotting everything that could go wrong so that you can plan for it—and this can be an effective way to tame your anxieties.[8] The problem is, this approach can sometimes sap the energy and enthusiasm of others. If you're committed to this practice, you might continue with it, but privately. Alternatively, you could try strategic optimism on for size. This practice involves envisioning the best possible outcome and then planning up a storm to make *that* happen. Both involve planning—the Guardian's specialty—but the tone is quite different and is likely to impact those around you differently.

Likewise, you might attempt to alter the timing and tone of your critiques. A free-ranging brainstorm session is not the time to point out the holes in someone's idea. There's a reason that one of the fundamental rules of brainstorming is to withhold judgment; fear of judgment can squash creativity. When innovation is the goal, as it often is, people need space to get expansive first. Once that's happened and many ideas are on the table, there should be some time for narrowing the focus to the best ideas and considering their feasibility. Even then, it can be useful to think about how you can expand or build on an idea rather than tearing it apart. In their book *Creative Confidence*, David and Tom Kelley give this advice:

> When we disagree with someone else's idea we push ourselves to ask, 'What could make it better?' 'What could I add to make it a great idea?' Or 'What new idea does that spur?' By doing so we keep the creative momentum going instead of cutting off the flow of ideas.[9]

They also favor the language of "How might we...?" as an optimistic way of seeking improvements rather than discarding a creative idea; for instance, "How might we make this idea a bit more feasible?" Another option is practicing I like/I wish, as in: "I like how creative the idea is... I wish we could find a way to make it less expensive to implement." Give it a try.

OPEN UP JUST A LITTLE

People sometimes feel that Guardians are closed off and hard to get to know. While everyone has a right to privacy, keeping to yourself can make others feel like you're not interested in them. Plus, it reinforces the stereotype that Guardians are boring. If people never have a chance to learn the interesting things about you, what other conclusions can they draw? We're not suggesting that you have to start sharing your most intimate hopes and dreams with your colleagues, but talking a bit more about your favorite hobbies might not be a bad thing. And while you're at it, you might consider asking someone else about their hobbies too.

RED FLAG: ALL EYES ARE LOOKING UP

Many people move through their careers looking upward, to the next rung on the ladder. There's nothing inherently wrong with that. Lots of organizations expect this kind of upward focus and are designed to enable and reward it. In fact, in some organizations, the set-up is more like an escalator than a ladder; as long as you're doing a relatively good job there's a natural momentum that will automatically carry you up, at least to a point. But when you're looking for the environment that best suits *you*, where you can make your greatest contribution doing work you're fully engaged in, that place is not always at the top of the ladder. This knowledge is reflected in our finding that Guardians (along with Integrators) are less likely than Pioneers or Drivers to say they aspire to be leaders. Of course Guardians can and often do make great leaders, but it's important to recognize that if you'd prefer to contribute in other ways, you may have to actively search for such an opportunity.

You might ask yourself whether the best fit for you is in your current role, on your current team, or even in your current organization. As one example, we know Guardians, in particular, often aspire to be in an expert role. Are you in an organization that values and rewards that type of role? Guardians also value work–life balance more than the other types do. Does your current situation allow you to maintain the type of balance you want? If not, you might want to evaluate whether you should attempt to flex to improve your fit within an environment that doesn't suit you, or whether you're better off searching for one that will suit you better.

REFERENCES

1. Kim, Jungsoo, and Richard De Dear. "Workspace Satisfaction: The Privacy-Communication Trade-Off in Open-Plan Offices." *Journal of Environmental Psychology* 36 (December 2013): 18-26. doi:10.1016/j.jenvp.2013.06.007.

2. Zeiger, Mimi. "Steelcase And Susan Cain Design Offices For Introverts." Fastcodesign.com. June 13, 2014.

3. Yoshino, Kenji and Christie Smith. "Uncovering Talent: A New Model of Inclusion" (report). The Leadership Center for Inclusion, Deloitte University. New York: Deloitte Development LLC, 2013.

4. Schachter, Ephraim. "The #1 Mistake Introverted VPs Make in Meetings | LinkedIn." *CSuite Accelerator.* March 2016. http://csuiteaccelerator.com/.

5. McGonigal, Kelly. *The Upside of Stress: Why Stress Is Good for You, and How to Get Good at It.* New York: Avery, 2015.

6. Brooks, Alison Wood. "Get Excited: Reappraising Pre-performance Anxiety as Excitement with Minimal Cues." *Journal of Experimental Psychology* 143 (June 2014): 1144-58. doi:10.1037/e578192014-321.

7. See Note 5.

8. Norem, Julie K., and Nancy Cantor. "Defensive Pessimism: Harnessing Anxiety as Motivation." *Journal of Personality and Social Psychology* 51, no. 6 (1986): 1208-217. doi:10.1037//0022-3514.51.6.1208.

9. Kelley, Tom, and David Kelley. *Creative Confidence: Unleashing the Creative Potential Within Us All.* New York: Crown Business, 2013.

**Drivers in Hell:
How to Stop Killing
Their Potential**

14

Picture if you will a Driver, we'll call her Dana, who worked in a building filled with row after row of glass-fronted offices. The desk in her own fishbowl office was installed in such a way that she couldn't help but face the hallway. She hated that setup. People would casually walk by, and if they happened to make eye contact with her they seemed to see that as an open invitation to come in and interrupt her with small talk, even though she was clearly busy. She tried to keep her head down as people trolled outside, but sadly that didn't seem to be a sufficient deterrent.

Dana's work was complex, and she felt like every time she began to get traction on the challenge at hand, she'd be interrupted. Often it was someone from another business group who "just wanted to say hi" but who would then proceed to say far more, hoping Dana would join in the gossiping. Dana just wanted to get back to her work. She couldn't believe people didn't notice her total lack of interest in the topic, and in further conversation. Other times her direct reports might pop in to talk about some trouble or another. In these situations, Dana was happy to provide her opinion; the issue was that even after she gave them explicit advice, they often kept waffling between options and repeating the same litany of concerns. If they disagreed, why didn't they just come right out and say so? Or if they didn't really want a solution to their problems, why were they bothering to ask for her help?

Given this history of disruptions to her productivity, Dana was particularly irritated when she was asked to join an impromptu team meeting. Her group met *all* the time, ostensibly with an agenda though no one seemed to stick to it. They rarely had what Dana would consider to be a real discussion. Everyone was polite, and softened each message so that no one would have hurt feelings. When Dana, in contrast, said anything direct or even mildly confrontational, the group would look at her as if she'd just kicked a puppy. And it killed her that they'd talk and talk to the brink of a decision but never actually make one.

✳ IT KILLED HER THAT THEY'D TALK AND TALK TO THE BRINK OF A DECISION BUT NEVER ACTUALLY MAKE ONE.

This particular meeting started out no differently. Late of course, because half the team didn't get there on time. And then even later because the first five minutes were spent oohing and ahhing over a colleagues' vacation photos. Dana had nothing against spectacular scenery, but she had other things she needed to be doing with her time. When they finally started the meeting though she perked up, because the topic was a meaty one: the rollout of a customer engagement system.

Unfortunately, her brief spark of interest quickly turned to disbelief, then disdain. The new system was intended to support each customer's unique needs; that meant that the teams supporting each customer would have no standard metrics or targets. Rather, each team would receive a high level "progress report" (a name Dana found euphemistic since without targets, how would they know if they were progressing?) based on a self-evaluation generated by the team members themselves. The new system had no rigorous process, no consideration of how the system might be gamed, no comparative scores to rank oneself by, and no logic for how the "progress reports" would translate into individual compensation and promotion decisions. Dana was appalled. Worse yet, her colleagues seemed delighted. They were talking about how refreshing it was to focus on customers as individuals rather than numbers, and on how this system provided so much flexibility for the team. When Dana pointed out some of the obvious flaws in the system, they accused her of not being a team player. Dana had had enough. She went back to her office, and wrote a scathing blog post about idiot leadership under her anonymized handle Domin8. Then she wrote an email to her team leader regarding the new customer system, saying her customer had a "unique need" to have her online and available at all times (after all, if you have to join them, beat them). She began multi-tasking in every meeting from then on.

Let's talk about it

As we begin our conversation, remember that Kim is a Pioneer-Driver (specifically a Scientist) and Suzanne is a Guardian-Integrator (specifically a Dreamer).

KIM: Here's a woman who clearly just wants to get her work done, and who also clearly defines her work objectives as the specific tasks on her list to complete. As a Driver she's going to be put off by anything standing in the way of her objectives, but these interruptions she experiences are particularly annoying because, from Dana's perspective, they're pointless. She doesn't see the value in hobnobbing with officemates. She doesn't see the value in playing desk-chair therapist to her reports. She doesn't see the value in kumbaya-ing with the team. What she does see is an accumulation of wasted time that could have been put to better use.

SUZANNE: Yes I think you're right that Dana doesn't see the value of these things, but that doesn't mean they're not valuable. What Dana is missing is the fact that doing a little bit of hobnobbing and so on, could actually help her get her work done and meet her objectives—at least assuming she needs anyone else's participation in the process. Playing therapist and singing a bit of kumbaya with people builds connection, trust, and loyalty.

But putting that aside for a minute, it still makes Dana feel like she's not able to accomplish what she needs to and this obviously frustrates her tremendously. When there's a Driver on a team it becomes particularly important for a leader to be thoughtful about how time is spent when people are brought together. That doesn't mean there should never be time for socializing or a bit of water-cooler talk, but maybe the first 10 minutes of a 2:00 meeting could be used for gathering and optional catching up, with the official business at hand commencing promptly at 2:10. Alternatively, a leader could discuss with a Driver the objectives being addressed during that socializing time, such as "building connection, trust, and loyalty so that our team works together more efficiently and effectively."

KIM: Your point is a good one. Often people (of all types) feel like the benefits of certain activities are so obvious that they should go without saying, but the fact is those benefits might not be obvious to people of differing Business Chemistry types. It helps to explicitly state the intent, ideally in a way to which the other types can relate.

A direct mapping of "we're going to do x" to the desired outcome of "y" creates a sort of Rosetta Stone for people. In this case it's being explicit with the Driver about the importance of bonding to create more integrated teams. In another situation, it could be telling a Pioneer that it's important to have a quantifiable business case in order to secure stakeholder support for the big idea, or telling a Guardian that it's essential to change course in order to mitigate greater risk in the future, or telling an Integrator that tough decisions have to be made in the near term to support desirable long-term outcomes.

SUZANNE: I think this is a perfect example of how a leader can sometimes respond to the diverse needs of various types with one universal strategy—in this case, communicating about *why* things are happening, with a specific focus on the kinds of outcomes that type is likely to care most about.

KIM: Exactly. For Drivers this translation can be particularly important because the ability to walk in someone else's shoes and see things from another's point of view may not come naturally. Dana herself doesn't need to talk things out when she has a problem, and so she doesn't recognize that need when it's in front of her with her direct reports, for instance. She assumes people are looking for answers to their problems (which is what she would want), versus desiring to dissect the situation itself. She's probably not picking up on some of the subtle signals, both verbal and non-verbal, that would help clue her in. Her direct report could have been more explicit and said, "I'd really like to talk through this with you to better understand the situation. I'm not looking for a solution yet, I just want to use you as a sounding board for my thinking." Dana still might not have enjoyed that type of dialogue, but at least she wouldn't have had the added frustration of not understanding the purpose of the conversation.

SUZANNE: That's a really helpful suggestion. Dana is clearly a bit baffled by what her people want and need, and she's not alone in that. As you suggest, Kim, taking a walk in someone else's shoes isn't always natural for Drivers. In fact, the criticisms of this type go so far as to accuse them of having a touch of *mindblindness* (an inability to understand the thoughts and feelings of others). While Drivers typically don't like to think there's anything they're not good at, those who work with them might find the Drivers' style more palatable if they chalk it up to not *understanding* others, as opposed to not *caring about* others. By all means, if there's something that might be helpful for a Driver to know about what you think or feel, go ahead and tell them. Just keep it short, because Drivers appreciate brevity.

KIM: We've been discussing the importance of being clear with Drivers in the context of understanding other people's needs, but clarity is important to Drivers in general. You see with Dana's situation the frustration she feels about having a new customer engagement system that doesn't have explicit goals and metrics. It's a subjective, qualitative solution for a situation she clearly feels needs to be more cut and dry. She finds this particularly problematic in part because it seems illogical to her. But more importantly, it's not clear to her how the system will relate to her individual goals and performance.

Drivers in particular need to have clear goals to shoot for. As we shared in Chapter 10, Drivers, more than any other type, aspire to be high performers. For a Driver being in that category either means: 1) hitting all the criteria laid out for what it takes to be in the category labeled high performing, or 2) performing better than others on a relative scale, thus ending up in the high portion of the curve. From a Driver's perspective, if you don't have either of these things, how do you know you're doing well? Further more, having explicit goals to strive for, and a field in which to compete, is *motivating* for Drivers. It spurs them to push for their best. It's not surprising therefore that when there was ambiguity and squishiness inherent in the new system, it not only drove Dana crazy, but also compelled her to establish her own metric for success: being able to game the system.

SUZANNE: I think it's a very interesting question to ponder—how do you know you're the best if you don't have a measurement or an objective way to compare your performance to others? Some of the other types care less, but for Drivers, with their competitive natures, this kind of thing matters. So, in this kind of environment, what's a leader to do to keep a Driver engaged? For one thing, there's no reason there can't still be very clear (and challenging) goals set and progress against them explicitly measured. Furthermore, there might still be some element of competition or comparative metrics of a kind integrated into particular tasks and processes, even if it's not part of the overall performance management system. Small contests over time could give Drivers even more opportunities to best each other and everyone else.

KIM: This reminds me of a team I worked with, comprised largely of Drivers. The top-level managers were siloed by geography and had a history of competing with one another, each trying to maximize their individual territories. Unfortunately, this was suboptimal for the group as a whole. In order to try to get them to work together more effectively, their leader had implemented a new performance system that emphasized collaboration and shared goals. At first it was chaos; the managers didn't understand what they were shooting for and how to show that they were "the best". To address this, the leader and I established a way to harness their competitive spirit but re-orient it in a productive direction. For the things the managers directly controlled, we set Goldilocks-style ranges; they needed to hit right in the middle, not too much, not too little, but just right. For these we measured them against their personal best, so the competition was with themselves versus against other people in the group. For the group-level metrics to which they contributed, we set an industry benchmark, so as a team they were striving to beat the external competition rather than undermining one another.

SUZANNE: The other beautiful thing about this kind of solution is that the variety in it increases that chance that it will work for more of the other types as well, not only the Drivers. Guardians and Integrators, particularly Dreamers, tend to be more intrinsically motivated, so the measurement against a personal best may work even better for them. This directly hits the target for our definition of a great solution—one that meets the needs of several types without turning any of the others off.

KIM: Yes, the consistent problem we see is that leaders optimize for one type, either inadvertently (usually doing whatever suits themselves best), or explicitly (catering to a narrow set of traits that have been labeled valuable). Neither approach really unlocks the full potential of a leader's human resources, however. As you say, the best approach is one that can draw in all the styles and position them to their best advantage.

We should also come back to the point about the office setup since, as we've mentioned, poorly designed work spaces can be a problem for all types. For one reason, what's considered essential in a space will vary dramatically by type. And since people's working style preferences can be a mix of introversion and extroversion, designing space to suit one or the other is an over simplification. Drivers, for instance, tend to care less about the aesthetics of a space and more about its practicality. I worked with one Driver CTO whose favorite place to work at home was a nook he had carved out under the stairs (his wife teasingly called it his hobbit hole). It was cramped and cluttered, but he didn't care. It was perfect for him because it allowed him to immerse himself fully in the challenge at hand, free of interruption.

SUZANNE: In any office with either an open-space setup or the glass-fishbowl situation, interruptions are a pretty common occurrence, so a leader might want to check in to understand how people (of any type) are being impacted by them. Interruptions clearly bother Dana, not because she's antisocial (okay maybe she is a little bit, at least in the office ☺), but because it keeps her from focusing on her complex work. Must Dana have this particular office, or might there be one better suited for her working style and the type of work she's doing? Might a system be put in place where a red sign on the door means "busy—please walk right on by" and a green one means "still busy, but stop in if you must"? Maybe Dana could agree to keep the green sign up for at least one or two hours a day so people feel she's available? Alternatively, Dana might enjoy the gift of a giant fern, which could be strategically placed as to screen her a bit from the outside world.

KIM: I don't know if I would go so far as to recommend hiding behind plants, but I do agree that a clear signal like the red and green signs could help. Obviously, having a signal has the direct benefit of indicating a person's state and giving them some control over interruptions and interactions. The additional benefit is that it validates the need. If Dana were hiding behind a fern to avoid talking to people, it would be easy for others to start thinking of her as unfriendly, antisocial, and not a team player. People will label the behavior as undesirable and unproductive, whereas the contrary is true in Dana's case!

If instead you establish a system of some sort (like the red and green indicators), you publicly acknowledge that people have different needs. People know that when Dana has the red signal on, it's because she's really cranking on something. It's a sign of productivity, not reclusiveness.

SUZANNE: Not that there's anything wrong with reclusiveness some of the time (said the Guardian-Dreamer who works almost exclusively from home), but I get your point. Now I want to steer us toward another aspect of the Driver's style that people often misinterpret—their directness. We once asked people for a list of words that describe this aspect of the Driver's style and people didn't hold back (which seems fair, since Drivers rarely do). Among the many descriptors were these: rude, abrasive, harsh, brusque, cutting, cold, and mean. People who are hurt or offended by a Driver's behavior often interpret their approach through this lens. Drivers, however, often explain their direct style by saying they're just trying to be clear and efficient.

If we're going to expect Drivers to try harder to understand how others think and feel, then we should all be doing the same. It might help to think of your typical Driver as a porcupine—cute right? But also sometimes a bit frightening. The next time you feel the sting of a Driver-launched barb, take a minute to ask yourself about their intent. While injuring you may have been the outcome, was it really the goal? While the Drivers can work on trying to launch fewer barbs, others should realize that they're working against their porcupine nature. So can you maybe also work on growing a slightly thicker skin? Or perhaps don a suit of armor?

KIM: Absolutely. In order to tap into the full power of Business Chemistry, there needs to be movement on both sides. An individual can only flex so far, for so long.

As a visual (for you Pioneers and Integrators in particular), imagine a small table with a post at either end. You're trying to bridge the distance between them using a rubber band wrapped around each post. It's really hard to pull one rubber band all the way across to the other post. Even if you managed to get there, you'd be putting such strain on the band that it would easily snap. If instead you pulled each rubber band to the middle and connected them, you'd still achieve the desired result, but with less of a burden on each of the rubber bands. To your point, the Driver needs to be careful about the barbs, but that can only get us halfway there. The other parties need to meet them in the middle.

SUZANNE: Getting back to those spiky porcupines, have you ever read one of those articles about how to survive an attack from various wild animals? With some you should curl into a ball, with others you should make yourself big and yell, and with still others you just don't have a shot at all. (I just read one such article which suggested you have "zero options" if a crocodile ambushes you from a riverbank.) Incidentally, it turns out that porcupines are actually herbivores and unlikely to attack humans unless they feel threatened, whew. But when it comes to the species we call the Driver, there are some useful survival techniques you can try. And really I don't mean to suggest that Drivers are always on the attack—but flexing to their style and communicating a bit differently is likely to make your working relationship with them more effective in any kind of situation. The magic strategies of which I speak are essentially to be clear, concise, and confident. Drivers don't want to wade through a bunch of convoluted or indirect statements; they like to move fast, and they can smell fear a mile away.

KIM: Since I'm married to a Driver, and that's my secondary style, I'm entertained by your idea of treating them like wild animals, and plan to apply that philosophy in our household immediately ☺. But in all seriousness, the survival strategies you suggest can each be effective with Drivers, but the different approaches will yield different results. If you're just trying to survive and not be mauled, curling into a ball is definitely the safest path forward. I've seen plenty of senior executives placating difficult

Drivers, just to avoid a battle. And they live to fight (or curl up), another day. Indeed, if you're an innocuous enough ball, you might even trigger the protective instinct of a Driver and become part of their territory. They'll move on to other prey and leave you more or less alone, but you're definitely considered a notch below them on the power structure at that point.

If instead you want respect, the best strategy in my experience is the *hold-your-ground-and-be-fierce* path. You can be fierce through strong a commitment to your fact-based position, by the way, it's not just sound and fury, signifying nothing. Be like a honey badger. Just remember, honey badgers can take as well as they give, so be prepared to earn some scars. The good news is, those zero-options situations are rare. If you do end up in one, go out fighting. A Driver will respect you for that.

———

That's a wrap

We just offered a number of ideas for creating an environment where Drivers excel, and we thought a summary might be useful. But be careful not to turn off others while focusing on the needs of Drivers. Surely you want all the types to thrive. Our summary includes some ideas for how to keep things palatable for Integrators, the Driver's opposite.

To meet the needs of Drivers	To make it palatable for Integrators
Timebox socializing time, make it optional, or explain why it's valuable.	Do provide time for socializing!
Explain what you and others want and why you want it. (Drivers may miss subtleties.)	Coach Drivers in how to ask empathetic questions.
Provide ways for Drivers to measure their success.	Make systems flexible, not all about competing with others.
Offer practical workspaces where Drivers won't be disturbed more than necessary.	Create systems and signals that indicate the best times to disturb a Driver.
Don't overact to the Driver's brusque style.	Encourage Integrators to focus on likely intent rather than style.
Be clear, concise, and confident.	Ask Integrators to consider how they can be clear and concise while also being diplomatic, to display confidence without bravado.

If you are a Driver

Alright Drivers, so maybe you feel frustrated about some of the ways in which your work environment or the people on your team seem to be interfering with your progress. Here are some things you can do about it.

BE NICE

If you're really a Driver, chances are your eyes might roll a bit at that advice. We'd wager that being nice is probably not at the top of your list of goals, but just stick with us for a moment. Have you ever gotten feedback that people think you're overly direct, too brusque, or even kind of mean? Perhaps no one's been brave enough to give you that feedback, but you've noticed that people scatter when they sense your approach? Drivers aren't always aware of how their style impacts people, or they don't understand why others respond in a particular way. They sometimes think others are overly sensitive and should grow a thicker skin.

If you work with people who aren't Drivers (and who doesn't?) a little bit of nice can go a long way toward getting what you need from them. We're not saying that you should avoid telling the truth. Rather, spend a moment thinking about how what you're about to say might make someone else feel, and whether there's a way to say it that would make it easier for that person to receive. Maybe take a note from Isaac Newton, who once said, "Tact is the art of making a point without making an enemy."

Try adopting some small habits to start and then branch out from there. For example, before pressing send on an email, go back up to the top and add a more personal greeting or question. Something like, "I hope you had a great weekend" or "How was your fishing trip?" at the beginning of a message can shift the tone quite a bit. Then, go to the end of the email and do the same; add a thank you or maybe something slightly more, like "I really appreciate the effort" or "Thanks in advance. Your contribution always makes our work better." It doesn't take much to have a significant effect.

GET A SECOND OPINION

We've worked with a number of Drivers who've been surprised when they got negative feedback about their style. They just weren't tuned in to how they were impacting people (in spite of several occasions when another person ended up in tears), and they weren't aware that how they were actually coming across was different from what they thought they were projecting. If you're baffled by how people respond to you, it might be a good idea to ask someone for help.

We suggested one CIO work with an executive coach after receiving poor reviews from his team. While the CIO believed that he was providing clear direction and feedback, his reports felt that he was criticizing them and undermining their credibility. The coach asked the CIO to re-enact a typical interaction on film. When he watched himself, the CIO was shocked. "I'm making such an angry face," he said, "I had no idea." The coach also pointed out that the specific words he used made him sound accusatory and judgmental. They practiced communicating the same message substituting different words.

Perhaps you don't have the benefit of an executive coach, and you probably don't want someone following you around all the time filming what you do and say, but it can help to occasionally ask someone (who is not a Driver) for their perception of a specific interaction, or their suggestions for how to adapt. Just remember: If you're going to ask, *do not* immediately argue with what someone tells you!

WALK IN THEIR SHOES

Now we're going to take this "be nice" thing to a whole new level. We're talking about empathy. Empathy is a powerful tool to engage more effectively. It may not come as naturally to Drivers, but it can be learned. The first step is to figure out where someone else is coming from. As a Driver, you probably aren't as prone to introspection as some of the other types. Since you're not spending time evaluating your own feelings, you're even less likely to spend time evaluating others', which means you might need to dig deeper to really understand what's going on with them. If you're struggling to understand people's feelings and motivations, try what we call "The Toddler Challenge." Ask the question "Why?" five times in a row. **RULES OF ENGAGEMENT:** *you cannot respond to the why question with anything in the vein of, "Because it/they are stupid." Instead you need to play the sleuth and assume there is a logical explanation for what's happening; you just need to discover it.*

For example, using Dana's situation:

DANA: "I'm annoyed."
Why? #1

DANA: "I keep getting interrupted and it's not even for anything useful."
Why? #2

DANA: "Because people are always complaining to me about their problems but they don't seem to want solutions."
Why? #3

DANA: "Because they want to waste my time."
[BUZZER – violates rules of engagement. TRY AGAIN]
Why? #3 redo

DANA: "I suppose they get something out of the complaining itself."
Why? #4

DANA: "Maybe it helps them reach a solution on their own."
Why? #5

DANA: "Probably because in the course of complaining, they end up talking through the details of the problem and laying out the various perspectives, and that helps them work it out."

Now we're getting somewhere. Instead of feeling frustrated that people are wasting her time, Dana has now deduced that people are simply trying to work out the problem on their own by talking it through with her. That actually sounds like a pretty good use of her time!

Once you get in the habit of asking "Why?" you probably won't need the formality of the Toddler Challenge. You'll have trained yourself to seek more insightful motives rather than jumping to conclusions.

Understanding where someone is coming from is the start of empathy. Next you need to *show* that person that you understand. You can begin by asking them questions: How did that work out? Were you worried? What were you hoping would happen? Then you can make statements that don't try to solve a problem but that simply demonstrate that you are listening and recognize the underlying feelings. Try sentences like: "It sounds like you were really frustrated," "That must have been really disconcerting", or "I imagine that felt great."

ALL ABOARD!?

Once a Driver gets focused on a goal they tend to move quickly toward it, putting all their energy into its pursuit. But as we mentioned earlier, one danger for a Driver is that they can end up driving a bus with no one on it. In other words, they might be barreling ahead in the pursuit of a goal without realizing that somewhere along the way they've lost some people. It's a good idea to check in with the team along the way, to make sure everyone else is still moving along as well. One idea is to schedule a regular check-in with the team. To make that meeting more palatable to you, have it be a quick stand-up meeting, or a focused scrum. Come prepared with some standard questions like, "Is the goal still clear?" "Have any new roadblocks popped up?" "Have any new concerns arisen?"

The disconnect can often come at the individual rather than team level though. As a Driver, you're probably likely to ask for what you need in order to get a job done, but not everyone is so direct. Take some time to ask what people need. A Guardian may need clear expectations. An Integrator may need context. A Pioneer may need some room for creativity. People won't necessarily tell you these things unless you ask directly, and since directness is a strong Driver trait, go ahead and ask!

GET A SIDEKICK

At the end of the day, you may not be able, or willing, to bend beyond a certain point. Luckily, you might not need to. Just look at the leadership ranks of many Fortune 500 companies to see examples of leaders of all types teaming with others who complement their skills. For Drivers this can be particularly powerful. Not only because they can rely on that individual to round out their edges and fill in their gaps, but also because that person is optimally placed to provide the second opinion we mentioned earlier.

Take the classic example of Sherlock Holmes and his sidekick Dr. Watson. Holmes has the ultimate Driver mind—analytical, unemotional, and rational. As Watson describes him, "He was, I take it, the most perfect reasoning and observing machine that the world has seen." Watson, on the other hand, while intelligent, was the humanizing balance to Holmes' aloofness. He served as the whetstone upon which Holmes sharpened his thinking. Watson is also the reason that Holmes was not just brilliant, but beloved. He gave voice to Holmes' genius, literally, and literarily, as his biographer. Without Watson, Holmes might have remained an unknown recluse shooting up and playing the violin in the shadows of his Baker Street apartment.

A distinction important to the success of this model is that a sidekick is *not* a lackey. Watson was not Holmes' servant; he was a partner in crime-solving. Drivers, in seeking a sidekick, you're not just looking for someone to do your bidding. You want someone who is, if not on equal standing hierarchically, at least someone for whom you feel a lot of respect. After all, you're looking for someone who rounds you out, a true better half, as perhaps non-Drivers might argue. Matching cape and tights optional.

RED FLAG: WHEN TITANS CLASH

We've highlighted how Drivers delight in debate, thrive on competition, and don't shy away from confrontation. All these traits can be productive, helping contribute to Drivers' hard-earned reputations for getting things done. But they can also be detrimental if two or more Drivers go head to head on a course of mutually assured destruction.

If you're a Driver in a Driver-heavy culture, or if your boss is a Driver (particularly the Commander variety), you might engage in a fair share of minor scuffles or outright skirmishes to determine who has the best or the biggest...well, anything really. These are matches designed first and foremost to establish superiority. If the fights are fair, that's probably not a big deal and might even be a lot of fun, but here are some things that should give you pause:

- Competitions escalate to the point where it becomes all about winning, regardless of the cost.

- You notice the system seems to be engineered to stack the odds against you Vegas-style; the house always wins.

- Your boss believes there should only be one top dog and likes to make examples of people who challenge his or her alpha position.

If you see these patterns emerging, we're not saying you should turn tail and head for the hills, but you should factor them into your calculus. After all, it could be possible to shift things to your advantage if you bide your time. History is rife with examples of leaders who have emerged after two powerful rivals went head to head and destroyed one another. But history is also full of examples of those who decided to go their own way and set a different path to success. Either way, as a Driver knows well, only to the victors go the spoils.

**Integrators in Hell:
How to Stop Killing
Their Potential**

15

An Integrator we know and love, Hans, once embarked on a career journey that seemed like it could be the trip of a lifetime, but turned out to be a bust. He joined up with a boss who, let's just say was not his ideal work companion. In fact, when things really started to heat up, Hans wished he'd never decided to work with him at all.

Things started out all right when Hans was hired. He was excited about the new opportunity he'd been offered to build out the company's sales network and the work seemed interesting and engaging. His boss was smart and successful and, as Hans developed his own skills and career, he thought his boss would be a great coach. But as the first days turned into weeks, Hans soon grew concerned.

His boss never said, "Good morning" or "How was your weekend?" He didn't ask Hans about his family or where he grew up or went to college. He didn't even ask about his goals and aspirations. He didn't ask much of anything at all.

That included not asking for Hans's thoughts, opinions, or input. His boss *told* him things, and when Hans asked questions, whether work-related or a little more personal, the look his boss gave him seemed to say, "Why do you need to know that?" Hans felt his boss wasn't interested in him as a person, or even as an employee, and he certainly didn't seem to value what Hans might have to offer in the way of ideas. In fact the boss seemed to go out of his way to interrupt or talk over Hans any time he tried to speak.

> ✳ HE FELT HIS BOSS WASN'T INTERESTED IN HIM AS A PERSON OR EVEN REALLY AS AN EMPLOYEE.

Since Hans was new to the job, he wasn't sure what the boundaries were for how he should spend his time, so he erred more toward checking in than not. He thought he was being responsible, but his boss just seemed annoyed and responded in a way that was brusque, or even rude if Hans was being honest. As one particular project was kicking off, Hans made a concerted effort to spend some time with key stakeholders, asking for their thoughts and input on how to proceed. Hans found it hugely valuable. Several people identified areas where the company had stumbled in the past, and one revealed a possible competitive threat that hadn't been on the radar. When Hans shared what he'd been doing, his boss told him in no uncertain terms that he considered such efforts a waste of their time. Getting the project done was the only priority; there was no reason to bring others along for the ride. When Hans tried to say that it was about more than just that, his boss didn't even let him finish the sentence. He just dismissed him and walked away.

Hans had accepted the job thinking he'd be working in a team environment with others in similar roles. He had expected they would collaborate and help each other out, learn from each other, and even become friends. He tried to pitch in and offer his assistance when he saw someone else was overwhelmed. He thought anything he could do to help the organization would be appreciated. But when his boss caught him doing so, Hans wasn't praised for his helpfulness; instead he was scolded. The boss made it hard for him to forge any relationships to speak of, and Hans started to feel very isolated. Things really got uncomfortable when his boss started to criticize how Hans was managing some vendor relationships. He said Hans was too friendly, that he needed to be more aloof so the vendor wouldn't try to take advantage of them.

Hans started to feel he couldn't do anything right and he began questioning his own judgment. He stopped trying to take any initiative, because it always seemed to get him into trouble. He no longer reached out to collaborate with others, and when someone asked for a little bit of help with something, he apologized but said he just didn't have time, which made him feel bad and not at all like the best version of himself.

This job just wasn't at all what Hans had been hoping it would be and he shared his disappointment far and wide with his large network of friends and family. When he received a survey from one of those "great workplace" lists he shared this story in full, even agreeing to talk to an interviewer about his experience. When the list and accompanying article eventually came out highlighting the best and worst workplaces, it prominently featured one of Hans's quotes about his organization: "While misery loves company, I wouldn't want anyone to suffer my fate, even if it would ease my own loneliness. On the journey that is your career, I strongly recommend you skip this stop."

Let's talk about it

As we begin our conversation, remember that Kim is a Pioneer-Driver (specifically a Scientist) and Suzanne is a Guardian-Integrator (specifically a Dreamer).

SUZANNE: Ouch. Poor Hans! This is not at all the kind of work environment that's going to support an Integrator, in particular, in doing their best work. Of all the types, Integrators most want to collaborate and help others. They even think of it as their *duty* to do so. And here Hans is learning that not only is his helping others not appreciated by his boss, but he's actually punished for it. That's going to totally go against the grain of who he is and how he wants to work.

KIM: The underlying challenge here is that some leaders dismiss many of the Integrator characteristics as just being nice. They are considered nice to have, but not essential. Being friendly, teaming with others, and building networks are extremely important in business, but they can be easy to dismiss because, by their very nature, they make things operate more smoothly. Hans's boss clearly doesn't see the value in what Hans is doing, whereas Hans feels he can't add value without doing those things.

SUZANNE: To really engage Integrators, a leader should look for ways to allow and encourage them to work closely with others and lend a hand where they're needed. We know it's important to Integrators that they can do work they enjoy with people they enjoy, and also that they know their work matters. Hans is experiencing none of these things.

KIM: Right, Integrators are nothing if not team players. More than any of the other types, Integrators like to work with others. And they are the most willing to put common goals above self-interest. To your point, leaders need to give them the opportunity to form a team. In Hans's case, his boss explicitly constructed barriers to teaming, but that's not the only reason Integrators could face a problem here. I worked with one Integrator whose company moved to a virtual team model. Instead of the traditional, hierarchical structure of cascading leaders and direct reports, this organization took more of a scrum approach, pulling people together for specific projects (often across different geographical locations), and then dispersing them again once the project was done. This Integrator was beside herself. She felt like she no longer had a "home base" of people she could count on, and who could count on her. The projects were so short that even though she had a team in name, they weren't together long enough to forge a deep connection. While she used to be able to see how her group fit within the broader organizational picture, this wasn't always the case with the individual projects she worked on. Sometimes she found it difficult to get a sense of the value of what she and her virtual team were doing.

Many companies are moving to more remote work and virtual teaming. For Integrators it's particularly important to help ensure that there's still a mechanism to build relationships in these constructs, and a way to nurture links back to the organization.

SUZANNE: This makes me think about some of the research suggesting that having a best friend at work is predictive of higher satisfaction, engagement, and performance, as well as a sense of being able to take on anything.[1] I'd venture to guess that this is even more true for Integrators than for other types, and that it's getting more difficult as teams become more temporary and more virtual.

Since these trends related to virtual teaming are not likely to be reversed, what can we do to help Integrators, and everyone else, continue to feel connected to others? Well for one thing we can elevate *connecting* as a crucial team goal, not just a nice to have. Some explicit effort put into getting to know each other, particularly at the start of a project, could go a long way toward building that connection. Ideally a new project would be kicked off in person—this is still often the quickest and best way to get to know people—but this isn't always possible. Another effective strategy can be video-conferencing, which has come a long way from the days when you needed high-tech equipment and dedicated rooms to use it. Now there are solutions you can use right on your laptop to give a meeting more of an in-person feel.

KIM: It's true that technology is increasingly providing options to simulate the feeling of in-person meetings. In our sessions with executives, we will occasionally have a person join us by robot for instance. The remote person can drive the robot around and see the room, and the people in it, through the robot's eyes. And everyone in the room can see and hear that individual in a live feed through the robot's display "head." I just wish they made them with arms that let you gesticulate as you speak! While robot representation certainly isn't a perfect replacement for actually being in the room, if physical attendance isn't an option, it's a great way for someone to feel included, and for others to feel like that person is a part of the group.

Some sort of visual engagement is also particularly important to Integrators, because they glean so much from non verbal communications. The way someone is sitting, where they are sitting, the expressions on people's faces, who's having sidebar conversations with whom, who's checking their phone surreptitiously—all of these things are gems of information for Integrators. And for the people physically in the room, having a visual reminder of the Integrator's presence increases the likelihood of that person's inclusion in the discussion, especially if that person is a Dreamer who might not be quick to speak up (and could be more easily "forgotten" on a conference call). Human-sized robots are still uncommon enough that they're hard to ignore.

SUZANNE: Another good strategy is to include a little bit of explicit *getting to know you* time in each meeting. One of our teammates, Selena, who is an Integrator, is particularly good at this. At some point during each of our team meetings she asks a question that helps us learn something more personal about each other. Recent questions she's asked include: "What's the origin of your name?" and "If you had the use of a private jet for one month where would you go?" While it's particularly important to Selena to feel connected with the rest of us, even the Drivers on our team seem to appreciate the quick moment we take to share something with each other beyond progress on our team goals.

KIM: It's interesting that you say that Drivers seem to appreciate it. Small talk tends to be one of the minor points of complaint that emerges about Integrators, and it's usually voiced by Drivers. Drivers tend to see this kind of chitchat as a waste of time, an unwanted attempt to get personal, or both. Whereas for Integrators a deeper feeling of connection is essential. It helps them better understand people's motivations, determine appropriate ways to collaborate, and, frankly, just feels better to them. In general I wouldn't expect this kind of thing to necessarily be welcome to Drivers. For your team, Suzanne, it probably isn't creating a problem (and perhaps is even appreciated), because the activity is timeboxed, with enough for the Integrators but not too much for the Drivers. Plus, all the team members are disciples of Business Chemistry, so they recognize and respect the Integrator's need for those sorts of conversations, even if it's not their own personal preference.

SUZANNE: Actually, I like to think that the reason everyone, even the Drivers, appreciate it is because our answers are so interesting and engaging! But yes, you're right, typically Drivers aren't so fond of this kind of thing.

KIM: Regardless of whether you truly enjoy these things or not, as a leader, it helps to make space for these kinds of interactions. Just approach it in a measured way to avoid alienating other types. I recently worked with a team who replaced a poorly attended monthly conference call with an interactive video call. In the new format, the meeting would be hosted by a different individual, who would determine a theme for the call that reflected a personal interest (e.g., travel, cuisine, etc.). In advance of the call, they would ask the group to share a photo related to the theme. Then the first five minutes of the call they would quickly cycle through the submissions and have people say a little bit about them. The rest of the 55 minutes were all business-agenda focused, though still on the theme of the month. Because it was a video link, you could see not only the photos but the people's faces reacting to them. Attendance dramatically increased after this new format was implemented (it's also easier to notice someone's absence when you're using video). Feedback was very positive; not only from the Integrators, but from all types.

■ **SUZANNE:** That sounds a lot more satisfying than many of the meetings I've sat through! And it brings up something else that's important to Integrators—context. Knowing a bit about a colleague's life outside the office, seeing photos, and being able to view body language are all ways Integrators get context about the people they're working with. And context is important to Integrators in other ways as well. Consider the Integrator whose organization moved to virtual project teams. You suggested that part of the reason she was struggling with it was because she couldn't always see how these projects fit in with the broader organizational picture. That's about context too.

Another example of the importance of context is how Integrators make decisions. In order to make a decision, an Integrator will want to understand how the past, present, and future relate. What relevant decisions were made in the past and why? What other decisions that need to be made might impact this one? What do various stakeholders think is the best course? What are the potential future implications of the various options? This is one of the reasons Integrators get accused of being indecisive. If something about the context changes, their decision is likely to change too. (Which can drive some of their other-type colleagues crazy!) Leaders should make sure there are ample opportunities to get this information.

■ **KIM:** One of the main sources of information for Integrators, not surprisingly perhaps, is other people. Integrators love talking to people and hearing their perspectives. As we've mentioned, relationships are important to them, but this outreach is also essential for them to get the lay of the land and have that context you're talking about. The thing is, to engage with all the critical stakeholders takes time, so if you spring a topic on an Integrator, don't expect them to immediately turn around with a decisive answer. (Unless it's something like, "You want to go out with the team later this week?" Which will likely yield an immediate and enthusiastic "Yes!") They will weave together their insights from a variety of conversations and sources in order to form their answer. Integrators also believe it's important to socialize ideas with others, so they will also want to reach out to ensure that everyone understands what's happening and is bought in. Integrators tend to get uncomfortable when there isn't a full consensus. The interesting thing is, that means they'll sometimes go along with an idea they themselves are not particularly fond of because the rest of the group is heading that way. They hate confrontation, so even if they were going to contradict the group, they probably wouldn't be overly direct but would wait and talk to people individually to try to make their point.

■ **SUZANNE:** As a secondary Integrator myself (and a born and bred Minnesotan who's spent the past 25 years on the east coast), I'd like to pick up on your point about hating confrontation and relate it back to the issue of "nice" that you raised earlier, Kim. I often think people are being less than nice and I really can't understand why it should be so difficult! I know I'm not the only one—it seems a lot of Integrators share this perspective. Whether or not others sometimes think they're *too* sensitive, the reality is that Integrators seem to be more affected than others by how a message is delivered; things like tone and word choice matter to them. So if you have any Integrators around, it might be helpful to pay particular attention to these things. For example, instead of saying "You did that wrong. You need to fix it," a leader could try something like "Thanks for doing that. We need a few tweaks to make it just right. Would you try it this way?" Same message, a few additional words, and a very different tone.

While a little bit more niceness will generally make the world a better place to be, that's not the only reason for digging deep here. If an Integrator (or anyone else) is busy processing the meaning of your brusque tone or protecting themselves from what may feel like an attack, you can bet their focus isn't on whatever message you're trying to deliver. Furthermore, it's hard to build trust with someone if they still feel bruised from their last interaction with you. You'll get a better response from an Integrator if you put some effort into considering both what you say and how you say it.

KIM: I agree that words matter, and not only for Integrators. We know that certain words appeal to, and are used by, each of the Business Chemistry types, and that if you use those words intentionally, you're more likely to connect.[2] But with Integrators it's not the words alone, it's the intent. I suspect Integrators sometimes react to bluntness because it indicates a singular focus on a particular objective as opposed to connecting, appreciating, or any of those more human-oriented things that Integrators feel are important. What Integrators might not understand is that other types don't necessarily find it *difficult* to be nice. As you suggest Suzanne, it really shouldn't be. But it does *take effort* to think through every word and how it might be interpreted in order to avoid potential hurt feelings. For leaders, I think the best guidance here is to follow social norms (say please and thank you, for instance), and be aware of how your message might be received, and how the context might change how it's received. For instance, an Integrator who has just been celebrated by her team might respond very differently to a correction or criticism than one that's been working extra nights and weekends without acknowledgment.

SUZANNE: Ain't that the truth. Speaking of working without acknowledgment, I'll add that often Integrators' contributions go unacknowledged, since the value they bring can sometimes be invisible or difficult to quantify. When a team's engagement and commitment are raised by an Integrator's team-building efforts, what's the value of that? When an Integrator notices a client's subtle hesitation, asks about it, and finds out they're worried about something and can now be reassured, how much is that worth? Often performance management systems and reward structures don't really capture this kind of subtle work, which can leave leaders underestimating the value of their Integrators, and leave Integrators feeling unappreciated.

KIM: I'm reminded of the rows and rows of greeting cards you see that say something like "I know I don't tell you often enough, but you're really great." Maybe we don't always tune into everything Integrators do for us, but perhaps leaders should consider, every once in a while, explicitly recognizing their contributions. Hmmm, "Integrators' Day" has something of a ring to it. So who's ready to celebrate?

That's a wrap

We just made a bunch of suggestions for how to create an environment where Integrators excel, and we thought a summary might be helpful. But while focusing on the needs of Integrators, you may be in danger of turning off the other types. You don't want that, so we've included some ideas for how to keep things palatable for Drivers, the Integrator's opposite.

To meet the needs of Integrators	To make it palatable for Drivers
Support Integrators in their desire to help others and reward them for doing so.	Even Drivers might occasionally benefit from an Integrator's help!
Provide opportunities to work in teams.	Don't make teamwork the only option in all cases.
Help Integrators see the meaning in their work.	Interpret meaning as contribution toward goals.
Spend time connecting.	Keep it short, state reasons for doing so.
Use technology to make virtual teams and meetings more personal.	Drivers like technology— no problem. Keep the personal stuff brief.
Enable them to socialize issues and gather info from stakeholders.	Provide a chance to socialize prior to meetings so it won't cause delays.
Be nice and say thank you.	Come on Drivers, you can do it.

ACCEPT TRADE-OFFS

Martin Luther King Jr. once said that "a genuine leader is not a searcher for consensus but a molder of consensus." If you're an Integrator, chances are you agree. Of all the types Integrators, both Teamers and Dreamers, are most likely to prioritize doing the work to get everyone on the same page. There are many benefits of doing so, including an increased level of commitment and engagement that can result when people feel their input has been sought out and listened to, or that care was taken to do things in a way that everyone can agree with.[3] But while it's great to have everyone on board with a project or decision, getting there is both time consuming and labor intensive, and it's not necessary in every case. So take some time to determine whether a particular project or decision requires everyone's buy-in, or whether speed is more important, because it's difficult to attain both. Ask yourself whether balancing everyone's input is likely to lead to a superior decision, or are there particular individuals who have unique expertise or perspectives that can really decide? When you're tempted to ask for broad input, consider why. Is this a situation where everyone will have an equal say? Will you really consider people's input in making the decision? Are you asking more to make people *feel* included? What are the trade-offs of doing so and are they worth it?

MAKE A DECISION ALREADY (AND STICK TO IT!)

Among the criticisms of Integrators is that they're indecisive. Indeed, Integrators are more likely than some of the other types to worry about whether the decisions they make are unpopular with others, and they're also more likely, especially Dreamers, to say that they change their minds frequently. This can be frustrating for others who want to make a decision and move forward. And here's the thing, by keeping things open and considering decisions to be changeable, not only might you be making others feel frustrated, but you may also be making yourself less happy. Research shows that second-guessing decisions—looking too hard for the very best option rather than a good-enough option—leads people to feel less committed to that decision and less satisfied with it.[4] So Integrators, go ahead and do what you do before making a decision (gather input, consider the people implications, and so on), but once you've made a decision, popular or not, try to stick with it.

ARTICULATE MEANING

Integrators are more likely than the other types to say that they thrive when they know their work matters. At the same time, they sometimes say that the value of their strengths goes unseen or unappreciated by their colleagues and leaders. We've seen that Integrators, more than other types aspire to be team players and mentors, and that they think it's more important to help others. Often it's Integrators who do the kind of invisible work that connects people and helps teams gel.

If you play some of these roles and suspect the value of that work is going unnoticed, it may help to take a little time to articulate how your work makes a difference. What is the impact of your work—for the team and for the organization as a whole? What are some specific examples that illustrate the value you bring? What would be the negative effect if you *didn't* do that work? Articulating the meaning of your work has several possible benefits. First, doing so is likely to make you feel more engaged and connected to the work you're doing, since it will help you clarify for yourself why it matters. It may even lower your stress levels, because focusing on the meaning of your work and how it helps others represents the type of mindset shift that has been shown to mitigate some of the negative effects of stress.[5] It may also help you at performance management time. Depending in part on *their* Business Chemistry type, your leader may not be particularly attuned to the ways in which you add value beyond your assigned responsibilities. Go ahead and tell them, now that you've clarified it for yourself.

While you're articulating why the work you do matters, make sure to do so in a way that relates specifically to the goals of your leaders, your organization, and your team. As an Integrator, you may have strong convictions about doing things—giving everyone an opportunity to have input, molding consensus—because you see them as the right thing to do for the people around you. Integrators are the type that feels the most responsibility to society, and they're the most likely to be focused on the people-related implications of decisions and actions. You may see building strong relationships as a worthy end goal in and of itself. But others won't always agree, or, their attention and focus may simply be elsewhere, based on what they're held accountable for. Think through your business case and follow the impact of those stronger relationships all the way through to how they can boost team performance, promote project success, facilitate organizational change, and positively affect the bottom line. *These* are likely the impacts that your leaders will care most about.

—————

TOUGHEN UP

Integrators are the most likely type to sense others emotions and to be concerned about how they make others' feel. And if you're an Integrator who's expending your energy worrying about these things, it may sometimes surprise you when others' don't seem to do the same. While it's not an unreasonable expectation that other types should also consider people's feelings, it's a reality that they're not always going to. And, pouring salt in the wound, they'll sometimes accuse an Integrator of being oversensitive!

If you're in this kind of situation, you can certainly try to explain to the culprit why you find their behavior off-putting or upsetting, or alternatively, you might focus on your own reaction. Remember that others aren't always as naturally attuned to people's feelings as you are. They may not even realize that they're rubbing you the wrong way, and may be acting more out of ignorance than disregard. If their own feelings are not particularly sensitive, they may not grasp how their behavior affects others. Try to put their behavior in context. Is it likely that they're purposely trying to offend you? Or is it more likely that their focus is simply elsewhere? If it helps, go to your empathy place—what must it be like for someone to go through life not even realizing that they're laying a trail of little (or big) offenses as they go? If it's less a matter of someone being offensive and more a matter of them seeming a bit standoffish, consider reaching out and taking the lead to get to know each other better. Sometimes others don't really know how or feel awkward doing so, but will welcome your efforts. Give it a try, but use that Integrator spider-sense to gauge their reaction and determine whether you're getting too close for comfort.

─────

BE. CLEAR.

Speaking of worrying about people's feelings—sometimes this can lead to one of the most common complaints about Integrators, which is that people don't know where they stand, because they're so busy being diplomatic rather than direct. But there are some very clear benefits of directness and sometimes even of conflict. For instance, directness is efficient. Speaking directly allows one to deliver a message quickly and helps ensure that the message is clear, which benefits both the speaker and the listener. You may avoid directness out of consideration for your listener's feelings, but a direct message can actually make things easier for the listener by removing the burden of having to interpret your message before processing it and responding. Moreover, directness can help teams avoid Groupthink, a phenomenon characterized by subpar decision-making that results from a desire to maintain harmony and avoid conflict. Since effective decision-making requires critical evaluation of various options or perspectives, team members must be free to state their opinions and to disagree with one another. In fact, research shows that cognitive or task-related conflict, that is conflict that's focused on the tasks of the group rather than its people, can actually make teams more creative and productive.[6] Keep thinking before you speak, but consider whether a bit more directness might not actually be a kindness.

RED FLAG: BENDING OVER BACKWARD

Wikipedia defines gymnastics as a sport involving the performance of exercises requiring balance, strength, flexibility, agility, endurance and control. Sounds to us a lot like being an Integrator! Often Integrators are practicing all these moves in response to and in the service of others. But make sure to take care of yourself as well. Being in an environment where people don't treat you the way you want to be treated is likely to be particularly hard on you. As the type that's most likely to prioritize working with people you enjoy, it may be worth determining whether the people around you are focused on meeting your needs while you're so busy trying to meet theirs. We can't always choose who we work with or for, but days can get pretty long for an Integrator working with people who aren't a good fit. And life is short. If you've tried the strategies we've offered and still don't feel good about the interactions you're having on a regular basis, it might be time to consider whether greener pastures await elsewhere.

REFERENCES

1. "The Impact of Excellent Employee Wellbeing." O.C. Tanner - Appreciate Great Work. 2016. http://www.octanner.com/landing/offers/the-impact-of-excellent-employee-well-being.html.

2. Goldberg, Lewis R. "From Ace to Zombie: Some Explorations in the Language of Personality." Lawrence Erlbaum Associates, 1982.

3. Gallup, Inc. "State of the American Workplace." Gallup.com. 2016. http://news.gallup.com/reports/178514/state-american-workplace.aspx.

4. Sparks, Erin, Joyce Ehrlinger, and Richard Eibach. "Failing to Commit: Maximizers Avoid Commitment in a Way that Contributes to Reduced Satisfaction." *Personality and Individual Differences* 52, no. 1. January 2012.

5. McGonigal, Kelly. *The Upside of Stress: Why Stress Is Good for You, and How to Get Good at It*. New York: Avery, 2015.

6. Nemeth, Charlan J., Bernard Personnaz, Marie Personnaz, and Jack A. Goncalo. "The Liberating Role of Conflict in Group Creativity: A Study in Two Countries." *European Journal of Social Psychology* 34, no. 4 (July 2, 2004): 365-74. doi:10.1002/ejsp.210.

16

Creating Powerful Relationships with Colleagues, Customers, and Everyone Else

By now it's no doubt clear to you that each type can contribute significant value—as a partner, within a team, and
to an organization—and that the needs of each differ, often
dramatically. We've shared lots of details about each type's
nightmare work scenarios, how these situations can negatively affect their performance, and what can help make
things better for them (and for you). Now we're going to
tackle this issue from a slightly different angle. In this chapter
we'll specifically address how your type impacts the ways in
which you should flex to best work with others.

Flex is a funny word, because it can mean seemingly con-
tradictory things—to bend and stretch, but also to tighten
and contract. We like that apparent incongruity because
the concept here is that sometimes you need to tweak your
style to adjust to other people's needs, while also being
true to yourself. There's an inherent and healthy tension
in that. You shouldn't become a different person and act
completely out of character, but you should make an effort
to accommodate others' preferences and needs. That's
how you exercise that gem-grade empathy mentioned in
Chapter 1, and how you ultimately create powerful relationships. And hopefully the other person is flexing too
so you can meet in the middle, like the rubber bands Kim
talked about in chapter 14. When it comes to one-on-one
relationships, how you go about flexing, and how challenging it's likely to be, depends on your type and that
of the other person.

___

When opposites
don't attract

We'll start with flexing to your opposite type, because it's
often the most difficult for people, particularly if one or
both of you are on the more extreme end for your type.
Flexing to your opposite usually requires conscious focus
and lots of practice. It's worth it because the strengths of
your opposite type are often in the areas where you have
weaknesses, so working together can be really powerful.

Just like a certain pair of twins from another planet—remember that cartoon? "Wonder Twin powers activate!" When the twins were out of each other's reach they couldn't activate their shape-shifting powers. It was only together that they were super heroes. But you don't need to be a shape-shifter to flex to your opposite type. We've already given you lots of clues for how to do it. Remember?

Let us remind you, just in case. We suspect as you read the previous four chapters you may have paid particular attention to the chapter about your own type, sort of like when you look through your old high school yearbooks. *That's me! There I am again!* But may we gently suggest you tear yourself away from your own image and do a thorough read-through of the chapter about your opposite type. There, you'll find lots of ideas about what your opposite type wants and needs, and how you might contribute to making conditions right for them to perform at their best. After all, isn't that what you want from all of your colleagues, team members, and stakeholders?

We know that more information is sometimes better—especially when doing something that may be unfamiliar—so the next four pages offer more specific hints for how to go about flexing to your opposite type.

Engaging a Pioneer if you're a Guardian

As a Guardian you may not realize that imposing too much structure or specifying too many details about a project can box a Pioneer in and leave them without the space they want to get creative. Backing off and providing more high-level guidance instead of detailed instructions might be the key.

TRY TO...

- **Keep things moving.** Quicken the pace of pretty much everything. Pioneers can be fast talkers and thinkers, and they can be prone to boredom. Build variety into meetings and projects to keep them engaged.

- **Whiteboard it.** Since ideation is in their blood, let them explore big ideas in a visual way. Think brainstorm.

- **Don't push details.** Keep things high level and expansive so that Pioneers don't tune out. Too many details or rules make them feel constrained.

- **Silence your skeptic.** To avoid shutting a Pioneer down, temporarily suspend your disbelief or doubts and just go with it. If you have concerns share them later, rather than sooner.

- **Deliver an experience.** Change things up. Present a new idea to Pioneers by allowing them to experience it—play a song, let them experience something via touch, hold a meeting outside of the office. Seriously.

- **Tolerate the chaos.** Pioneers have their own processes for creation and they may seem to go all over the place. Build time into the agenda for them to do so and wait a while before trying to bring them back to earth.

- **Bring passion!** Show the excitement in your idea by bringing conviction and interest. Sell it!

Our overall recommendation for engaging a Pioneer is *go big, buckle up, and enjoy the ride!*

Engaging a Guardian if you're a Pioneer

If you're an anything-goes Pioneer, you might be challenged to provide an environment where a more practical Guardian will thrive. You may want to give more consideration to the structure they crave and the time and information they need to make a decision.

TRY TO...

- **Give them time to process.** Guardians don't appreciate being put on the spot. Provide materials or expectations in advance so they can make careful considerations and come to a discussion prepared.

- **Provide data.** Point them in the right direction to find the details they need, and anticipate that they're going to ask additional questions.

- **Cite your sources.** Rather than making sweeping generalities, be precise and cite evidence for how you reached your conclusion.

- **Make it linear and concrete.** Rather than speaking at a theoretical level, make your idea practical. Follow a logical and linear, step-by-step approach to help Guardians understand what's been done and how you got to where you did.

- **Respect the agenda.** Be punctual, stay on task, and run your meeting using a clear structure.

- **Honor precedent.** Guardians may be more comfortable with what is tried and true. Relate your idea to something familiar or that's worked in the past.

- **Keep emotions in check.** Be calm and thoughtful in your approach.

Our overall recommendation for engaging a Guardian is *be prepared.*

Engaging a Driver if you're an Integrator

DRIVER

INTEGRATOR

As an Integrator, you may be so diplomatic and dead-set on providing lots of context that a Driver loses patience or is left not understanding what your stance on an issue actually is. You may need to work toward being more direct and concise so they know where you stand and you don't lose their attention before they get there.

TRY TO...

- **Get your facts straight.** Make sure you know what you're talking about, and then don't be afraid to strut your stuff a little bit.

- **Assert your point of view.** Bring a recommendation and stand by it. Drivers expect you to have a point of view, and you may lose their respect if you don't have one.

- **Lead with the punchline.** Structure a discussion backwards; start with your main point and then provide facts to support your message.

- **Build a logical argument.** Concisely take them through your thought process and bring the evidence.

- **Anticipate pushback and preempt objections.** Drivers will challenge your stance as they think it through and they will poke holes in their attempts to validate it. Be ready to back it up. Drivers appreciate critical thinking, so talk through obvious counterarguments to your proposal or idea.

- **Keep it tight.** Avoid excessive small talk, prolonged scene-setting, or too much pomp and circumstance. Don't carry on too long—Drivers appreciate you getting to the point, and doing so quickly and directly.

- **Propose an experiment.** Appeal to both their scientific side and desire to move fast; prototype an idea sooner rather than later.

Our overall recommendation for engaging a Driver is to *be smart, be quick, be gone.*

Engaging an Integrator if you're a Driver

As a Driver you may mistakenly try to push an Integrator in a particular direction with a black-and-white, logical argument, since that tends to work best for your own Driver-nature. Instead, slow down and focus in on the person in front of you to bring them along more gradually.

TRY TO...

- **Ask questions and listen.** If an Integrator expresses discomfort or displays resistance, ask for clarification. Listen to their response and reflect it back to check your understanding of their true issue.

- **Share context.** Integrators have the greatest need for the big picture. Help them see how things fit together so they understand the purpose of a project or task.

- **Co-create.** Work together to build on an idea or plan in a collaborative format.

- **Don't rush.** Create room for them to synthesize separate data points and socialize ideas and opinions before coming to a conclusion.

- **Be open to alternatives.** Integrators prefer an iterative and collaborative process, and they're prone to changing their minds; anticipate an alternative solution or compromise.

- **Get personal.** Humanize the proposal or idea you're putting forward, pointing out the impacts on actual people. Involve the heart and head. Don't just ask Integrators what they think about a matter, ask them how they feel about it. One way to captivate an Integrator and give them context is to tell a compelling story, making a concept real and relatable rather than theoretical.

- **Don't be a jerk.** Integrators like to play nice; if you're overly aggressive, rude, or abrasive, they will shut down. Be aware that the Integrator thinks you're acting like a jerk much sooner than you do.

Our overall recommendation for engaging an Integrator is to *practice a bit of give and take.*

When you've got
too much in common

You may think that when you're working with someone who's the same type as you, you're on easy street. But like-type pairs can quickly find themselves in trouble. Two Drivers might end up in a power struggle, while a pair of Integrators may get stuck in an endless loop of considering and reconsidering every option in light of all the input they've gathered. A couple of Guardians together may analyze a problem to death and never make a decision, while a Pioneer duo might make very little progress on some really great ideas because they come up with even more great ideas before they can implement the first ones.

If you find yourself in a situation with someone of your same type, your goal is still to flex, but not to get closer to the other person's style. Instead, you want to get a little bit further away. You might do this by digging deeper and channeling your secondary type, like we talked about in Chapter 7. For example, if you're an Integrator working with another Integrator, lean into your Pioneer or Guardian traits to bring a different perspective into the mix. The great thing is, if you and your colleague are both in the Business Chemistry boat you can acknowledge what you're trying to do. You might say something like, "Since we're both Integrators I'm afraid we're going to have a hard time landing on a final answer, so I'm going to channel my secondary Pioneer to help get us there." Your fellow seadog will know just what you mean.

The next page offers some quick tips for each of the types to help prevent your greatest strengths from becoming your greatest weaknesses.

If you're a Pioneer working with another Pioneer

Try to bring things back down to earth. After you've enjoyed some time brainstorming cool ideas, focus on developing actionable next steps so the path forward becomes clear.

If you're a Driver working with another Driver

While debating an issue, avoid tunnel vision by bringing up context or the human implications to get a broader view. Otherwise you may end up driving a bus together with no one else on board.

If you're an Integrator working with another Integrator

Temper your shared desire to explore all alternatives and settle on a direction. If there's an elephant in the room address it, even if it's uncomfortable.

If you're a Guardian working with another Guardian

Challenge yourself to ask whether the current way of doing things is really the best way to reach your goal. Avoid fixating on unknowns and instead focus on what is necessary to move ahead.

When you need to flex just a little

So we've covered how you might need to flex to your opposite type and flex away from your own type. But what about the other types—those with whom you share some traits despite your differences? We'd like to invite you to sit on the floor for a moment. Come on, give it a try... chances are you've been sitting in that chair too long anyway. Now, put your feet straight out in front of you and reach for your toes (without bending your knees!). Is it challenging? Probably. (If not, then we'd like to know your stretching regimen so we can adopt it.) Now reach for your shins; it should be easier. Flexing to your adjacent type is more like reaching for your shins than your toes. You might feel the pull a little, but likely not too much. Here are some tips.

If you're a PIONEER working with a DRIVER...

Your naturally bold and quick thinking is likely to engage a Driver. Go ahead and bring your out-of-the-box ideas; Drivers like to explore too. And feel free to spar a little, you're both likely to thrive on it. But don't lose sight of logic or practicality. Pie-in-the-sky isn't going to work here and ill-considered risks will likely not be embraced.

If you're a PIONEER working with a INTEGRATOR...

You're likely to have a lot in common with an Integrator, including a tendency toward big-picture thinking, an appreciation for context, and an expressive, collaborative style. Your storytelling skills will be an asset, and if you can make your stories about people, even better. The Integrator is likely to move a bit more slowly than you and to spend more energy on gauging the opinions of other people, so hold your horses and indulge their desire to bring others along for the ride.

If you're a GUARDIAN working with a DRIVER...

Start with the punchline. Drivers appreciate logic, data, and analysis just like you do, but you'll lose a Driver's attention if you try to take them through your full thought process. Come prepared with the facts, but once they've gotten the point, stop talking.

If you're a GUARDIAN working with a INTEGRATOR...

The Integrator shares your distaste for confrontation, so make sure any issues that need to be discussed are surfaced and not ignored. Be patient with discussions that may seem tangential, an Integrator's way of thinking through an issue may be more roundabout than yours. Start with some personal connections before launching into planning, and then provide the facts and structure that an Integrator may not naturally seek, as well as the context they need.

If you're a DRIVER working with a PIONEER...

You and a Pioneer may find a groove by exploring new approaches and experimenting together. You can help bolster the ideas you co-create by providing the facts to support them, but be careful not to go too deep into logic; Pioneers are more interested in possibility. You may also need to be cautious about being overly direct or trying to run the show. Pioneers are very collaborative but they also like to be in charge and bristle against feeling controlled.

If you're a DRIVER working with a GUARDIAN...

You may need to access your reserve tank of patience. Like you, Guardians thrive on facts and data, but they're likely to need more of both than you are, and they'll probably take longer in considering them. Be prepared to continue reviewing the details even if you've already reached a conclusion yourself, and don't attempt to take shortcuts.

If you're an INTEGRATOR working with a PIONEER...

You and a Pioneer could be great collaborators, as you both value working closely with others. You may also enjoy thinking big together, but don't forget to address critical details, something neither of you is likely to do naturally. You might need to pick up the pace, as Pioneers like to move quickly and they may feel impatient with your tendency to consider things more thoroughly.

If you're an INTEGRATOR working with a GUARDIAN...

A Guardian will likely appreciate your tendency to be introspective and considered; it's something you have in common. Your nonconfrontational style can also be an asset, because a Guardian is likely to be as con-flict-avoidant as you are. Just make sure that important issues get addressed when needed, even if they're difficult to broach. You may need to adjust your level of structure and focus a bit to fit with a Guardian. Your non linear thinking style can feel scattered to them and your big-picture focus won't give them the specifics they're likely to need.

Flexing with strangers

One final note about flexing. So far we've focused primar-ily on how to flex in one-on-one relationships. In the next chapter we'll address how to make Business Chemistry work on your teams, those you interact with on a somewhat regular basis. In both cases you're likely able to observe people over time to develop a hunch about their type, and you probably have the opportunity and incentive to adapt your style, and/or the broader environment, to be more effective together. But what about situations where you're interacting with a group of people that you don't know, or that you've met only once?

Take for instance, a sales presentation. You enter a bland conference room, and around the table eyeballs stare back at you. You might know the names of a few people in attendance, but others you've never met before. How do you use Business Chemistry in a context like that?

Well, to start, it helps to have a sense of the power dynamics. Who is the decision maker in the room? Who is the influencer? Try to do some homework in advance to get a sense of their Business Chemistry; the Internet is your friend in times like this. If you can develop a hunch based on what you find, great (look back at our tips in Chapter 7). You want to tailor your style to those people if you can. If you don't know who has the power, watch the others in the room. Who are they deferring to? Who do they look at most frequently? These are small clues that can give you a sense of the dynamics you're dealing with.

If you really don't have much to go on or aren't confident in your hunch, it's best to assume you'll have all types in the room. Here are some things to consider doing when going in blind:

- Drivers and Pioneers often tune out quickly if you don't capture their interest right away. Consider opening with a quick stat or short engaging story that clearly sets up the point of your discussion.

- Integrators and Guardians appreciate context. If you didn't cover it in your opening, consider briefly setting the scene with how what you're talking about fits in the broader picture.

- Guardians and Drivers may ask detailed questions, particularly if you've been keeping things high level, so bring an appendix of detailed information that you can reference if needed.

- Pioneers and Integrators will likely be more engaged by things that are visually stimulating. Consider including videos, prototypes, or evocative photos to pique their interest.

Ultimately, our recommendation is to prepare like a boy or girl scout would. Make sure you have something for each of the types, try some of the tips we've proposed, and then watch the room. See how people respond and then go from there. We've given you lots of suggestions for how to relate to each type already, but here's one last cheat sheet.

- **SENSING GUARDIAN** – double down on the data and follow a linear path.

- **SENSING DRIVER** – get to the point and make sure you can defend it.

- **SENSING INTEGRATOR** – use positive body language and share options and implications.

- **SENSING PIONEER** – make it fun, paint the art of the possible, and get them contributing their own ideas.

Sure, you can't please everyone all the time, but that doesn't mean you shouldn't try.

17

Putting Business Chemistry to Work On Your Teams

If you've made it this far we like to think you've learned a thing or two and now have a variety of options for flexing to individuals of different types. That will take you a long way, but what if you're dealing with multiple people at the same time? How do you go from focusing on the needs of one to addressing the needs of two, three, or maybe even four types at once? How can you practice diplomacy with the Integrators without sacrificing the directness the Drivers prefer? How can you provide the structure the Guardians want without making the Pioneers feel penned in? Maybe you're wondering: Would it be better to stick with one or two types on a team so you can more easily create an environment that will meet everyone's needs? Is it really better to have lots of diversity? What's the best composition for an effective team anyway?

Good. Questions.

We're asked similar questions all the time, and the answers, of course, depend on a number of things. When we're asked about how to make a team effective, our response usually involves asking a series of questions in return to help leaders take a step back and consider the issue in a different way.

Before we pose our questions, we'll mention that others have also attempted to tackle the issue of team composition and effectiveness. Perhaps most significantly of late, Google's People Analytics team has explored it, and in the end, with all the data, computing power, and analytical chops they have available to them (and they have a lot), they didn't arrive at an ideal team composition. Instead they concluded that a team's norms and ways of working matter most.[1] We'll share a bit more about these ideas as we go along, but we offer that context now as a bit of foreshadowing. We really don't think there is one ideal team composition. We *do* think it's important to consider your team's composition in the context of the team's current environment and ways of working, as well as your team's goal, and the preferred working style of your most important stakeholders. Once you have a better sense of how all that fits together, you can make adjustments so that all types on your team can thrive. By the end of this chapter we hope you'll have a good sense of how to do that. Now on to our questions for you.

1. What kind of environment do you have today?

Every team has certain ways of working, from how often they meet to the way they communicate to what they value. Chances are, your team's current practices are creating an environment that's meeting the needs of some types better than others. Ask yourself, does our team's culture or way of working enable all types to thrive? This is important because, you can add all the diversity you want to a team, but if it's set up to work in a way that's more accommodating to some types than others, you're likely to get inconsistent performance. For example, a team that relies heavily on a consensus-based approach to decision-making may be so frustrating for a Driver—who is uber focused on moving things forward—that he or she checks out entirely. Likewise, a team with a very fluid process that changes direction frequently may make it tough for a Guardian to fully contribute.

* YOUR CURRENT TEAM ENVIRONMENT IS YOUR STARTING POINT.

In our experience, the way a team ends up operating is often more organic than intentional. Sometimes it follows the leader's preferences, or the dominant types on the team. Other times it is influenced by organizational culture. Whatever the source, your current team environment is your starting point, so it helps to give it a good hard look to know what, if anything, you might need to adjust.

When it comes to assessing the ways your team works, here are some questions you and your team members might ask yourselves:

■ Do you typically dictate all aspects of a project? Or do you define what needs to happen and then set team members free to determine how they accomplish it? Pioneers, in particular, crave more freedom and autonomy, and your approach here is likely to impact them most.

- Are roles and expectations crystal clear? Does everyone know what a raging success or dismal failure would look like? Or are things left open to interpretation? These answers may be particularly relevant for Guardians, who perform best when they have clarity.

- Are those expectations also set high? Do you push your team to excel and then hold people accountable? These practices may be most critical for Drivers, who sometimes feel held back by what they see as the subpar performance of others.

- Is your door open? *Really* open? Is it clear to your team that it's okay for them to check in, ask questions, get your input, or even engage in a conversation that's a bit more personal? Knowing this is the case might be particularly important for Integrators, who thrive when they can forge real connections with people.

While those questions can give you a great start, there are many others you might pose to better understand whether your team's ways of working are more suitable for some types than others. Here are a few:

- Does your team rigidly stay the course or constantly change direction, go back on decisions, or chase the next big idea?

- Is it all teamwork all the time or are people working away in lonely solitude?

- Is making a mistake no problem on your team or is it grounds for banishment, punishment, or at least a good scolding?

- Is there a bias toward acting first and thinking later or toward looking before leaping?

- Do you check in with people to make sure things are A-okay, or leave them to their own devices?

- Are people recognized for contributions big and small, or are only heroic efforts worthy of acknowledgment?

- What does your team respect and reward? Individual or team success? Results or effort? IQ or EQ? Agility or expertise? Quiet competence or bravado? Putting out fires or preventing them?

We bet by now you get the picture. If you've realized your current team environment is more suited to some types than others, you have some work to do in order to get the most out of all types on your team. Don't be lulled into thinking you're sitting pretty as long as you're meeting the needs of *most* of your team members. As we'll soon discuss, meeting the needs of those in the minority may be even more critical to your team's success. We'll get to what to do about all of that soon, but first, now that you're more aware of your current environment, you can move onto the next question.

---

2. What's your team's goal?

Each type has preferred ways of working and particular kinds of tasks that are likely to be more natural for them. Depending on what a team is trying to accomplish, certain types might add extra value. Need meticulous, high-quality work? A few extra Guardians might be a good idea. Looking for lots of big ideas? More Pioneers might be important. Need to navigate some tricky political waters? Maybe an Integrator-heavy team is what you'll want. Have a big goal to reach in a very tight time frame? You might benefit from including more Drivers.

So maybe it's just that simple? Who you want on a team just depends on what you're trying to do? Well, not really.

＊

IT WOULD RARELY BE IDEAL TO HAVE A TEAM HEAVILY DOMINATED BY JUST ONE TYPE.

For one thing, it's important to recognize the complexity involved in reaching most any goal, which means it would rarely be ideal to have a team heavily dominated by just one type. As an example, we often associate Pioneers with innovation, but innovation involves multiple phases. Some phases require an expansive orientation where imagination and blue-sky thinking are really beneficial (that's where a Pioneering perspective is key). But other phases require an orientation toward narrowing down or prioritizing. In fact, in his book *Originals*, Adam Grant suggests that the biggest barrier to originality is not idea generation, but selection.[2] In these phases a more Guardian-like perspective, emphasizing practicality or thinking through implications in a detailed way, can really help.

Further, beware, our stereotypes about the value each type brings or doesn't bring to a team may prevent us from recognizing that people can flex as the situation calls for. Remember we cautioned you about this in Chapter 8? We shouldn't assume, for example, that an Integrator can't rise to the occasion of driving toward a big goal within a tight time frame, or that a Pioneer can't think through the detailed implications of a decision. Of course they can; it just might require them to put in a little extra effort.

So, if your team has goals related to innovation, transformation, collaboration, strategic re-engineering, sound decision-making, high productivity, or implementation of a complex plan—and what team doesn't—what you'll probably want is a good diversity of perspectives.

Now onto another question.

─────

3. Who are your primary stakeholders and what's their perspective?

Most teams have a number of different stakeholders, from internal and external clients, to leaders within the team's overall organization, to the broader community. And just as your team is made up of individuals who have particular perspectives, stakeholders have perspectives too. Trying to get a sense of what they are can provide useful information for determining how your team can be most effective.

As we've discussed, sometimes it's easiest to work with those who are just like you. In those cases you *get* each other and things feel good because they go smoothly. For this reason a *like-type* team or individual may be effective when working with an important stakeholder. With those of the same type, your stakeholder is likely to feel at ease and to enjoy this working relationship.

Other times what stakeholders most need is a perspective that's different from their own. Your team's client might be a big-picture thinker, who needs help sorting through the details of an implementation plan. Or they might prefer to avoid conflict and want some support in making the right decision even when it's unpopular with others. In these cases, a *different-type* team or individual may bring more value, but only if you can offer a different perspective in a way that's palatable to the stakeholder. For example, this might mean providing a Pioneer, who prefers a big-picture perspective, with a summary that allows them to be confident you have all the details covered, but doesn't actually force them to get into the weeds with you. For help with getting the tone just right, a team with a stakeholder of a different type might seek out a friendly colleague who shares the stakeholder's working style to help prepare for that interaction. For example, if the stakeholder is a Guardian, check in with a Guardian colleague to determine whether a proposal includes the right level of detail.

Regardless of who the stakeholder is, understanding their perspective is an important first step. Then your team can attempt to work and communicate in the style of the stakeholder, but push their limits or offer a different take where needed (e.g, encouraging some risk-taking for a stakeholder who seems risk-averse to a fault). It may seem obvious that a diverse team could deliver the best of both worlds, but it's not always as simple as it seems. To get the most value from diversity, it needs to be actively managed. We'll talk a bit more about that soon. But first, onto our final question.

4. What's the current composition of your team?

While people often ask us about the best Business Chemistry composition for a team, we also hear that creating a team with a particular composition is more of a pipe dream than a real option for most leaders. Often you're stuck with the team you've got. Sometimes you might be able to change things up a bit, but there are many factors to simultaneously consider when choosing team members—like their knowledge, skills, and experience; who's available when; what the budget is; the balance of gender and other types of diversity; and a multitude of other complicating factors. So even if you *wanted* to select your team based on their Business Chemistry types, in most cases it would be a real challenge to do so. Instead, we usually recommend carefully assessing your team's composition in the context of the issues we just explored, and then actively managing it by making adjustments to *how* your team works. This fits in with Google's findings that what matters is not so much the specific combination of people on a team, but how everyone works together.

When it comes to team composition there are a range of possibilities, but they can mostly be broken down into two broad categories. Either your team will be relatively well-balanced across the various types, or it won't. If it's not balanced, that usually means it's primarily dominated by one or two of the types and lighter on the remaining types, or maybe even missing those types entirely. And there are potential benefits and challenges associated with any of these combinations. Let's start with the dominant scenario.

NOT BALANCED: EFFECTS OF A DOMINANT TYPE

One potential benefit of a team that has many people with the same type is that, because of their similarity, working together likely feels pretty good—at least for those in the majority. Similarity between people can contribute to group cohesiveness and more satisfied team members.[3][4] When people on a team share a particular perspective, work is likely to go smoothly. People will tend to agree on what to do and how to do it and the team will feel connected. For example, a team dominated by Drivers will likely embrace a fast pace and revel in a feeling of accomplishment as they push hard to meet goals and deadlines. A team with Integrators in the majority will relish high levels of collaboration as they all focus together on connecting.

✱ MINORITY TEAM MEMBERS AND TEAM EFFECTIVENESS MAY BOTH SUFFER ON AN UNBALANCED TEAM.

It sounds pretty good, right? Unless of course you're in the minority. Then you might feel a bit left out in the cold. We'll discuss that further in a moment, but it's not just the minority team members who are likely to suffer on an unbalanced team—the team's effectiveness may as well. Research suggests that while decisions made in a homogeneous team feel good, they're often inferior to those made in more diverse teams.[5]

Why? Well... picture a waterfall. And now picture trying to change the direction in which the water flows. Without a feat of engineering, it would be practically impossible to do so. This is how a *cascade* works on a team. Once ideas, discussion, or decision-making start moving in a particular direction, momentum often keeps them moving in that direction, regardless of whether it's the *best* direction.[6] Even if some diverse views exist on the team, they're unlikely to divert the team's direction once it's been set, in part because people hesitate to voice disagreement with an idea that gets early visible support. While this isn't a great thing, it doesn't necessarily feel bad in the moment. In fact, it can feel pretty good when everyone is going with the flow.

These kinds of cascades can happen on a team for two primary reasons. *Reputational* cascades occur when people fear that voicing disagreement or a different perspective will make them look bad or even lead them to be punished in some way. Remember our discussion of psychological safety in Chapter 10? A lack of psychological safety could lead to a reputational cascade. *Informational* cascades, by contrast, occur when people assume early speakers who are in agreement with one another must know something they don't.

In other words, people don't offer their differing opinion because they suddenly suspect they might actually be wrong. After all, their colleagues who spoke early and so confidently are smart people, right?

Either way, cascades lead those with differing opinions to self-censor, which means the team can't benefit from their diverse perspectives because they remain undercover. As a result, decisions made by the team end up looking more unanimous than they actually are. While those unanimous-seeming decisions feel pretty good, they're often not the best decisions. This phenomenon is commonly known as groupthink.

You might imagine it happening like this: A team of high-energy, outspoken Pioneers starts talking excitedly about a new direction for a project. They whiteboard frantically and speak in rapid-fire fashion, bouncing ideas off one another and possibly bouncing around the room. The sole Guardian in the group feels a niggling sense that the idea can't work, but it's hard for her to piece together exactly why when there are so many people talking at once. By the time she pinpoints the major flaw that she's been circling around, the Pioneers are well down the path with their idea. And they're so damn excited! So does the Guardian speak up and burst their bubble? Or might she first pause (she's a Guardian after all) to consider the potential personal benefits and costs of doing so, before deciding to stay silent?

The majority type often determines the form that groupthink will take, so understanding what perspective a team is likely to have can be as simple as identifying which type is most strongly represented.

While most of us find it easiest to work with those who share our type, when it comes to teams, it's far from a fool-proof recipe for success. It's important to note that an overwhelmingly dominant type isn't required for these things to happen. Sometimes a smaller concentration of members with extreme types can have a similar effect. Or even just a single person, for instance...a leader.

**Potential blindspots and likely outcomes
of teams dominated by each type**

Potential Blindspot	Likely Outcome
A Pioneer-heavy team may get a little too outlandish with their ideas and fail to consider whether there's any realistic way to actually implement them.	Potentially a big waste of time and money.
A group of Guardians can get into trouble by falling into a state of analysis paralysis and erring toward keeping things the way they are rather than experimenting with something new.	May be left in the dust by their competition.
Together, a bunch of competitive Drivers may lock themselves into the fierce pursuit of a goal on a strict timeline.	Possibly fail to consider new information that suggests a change of direction would lead to greater success.
A team dominated by conflict-avoidant Integrators may adopt a subpar idea because no one wanted to criticize it.	May work harmoniously toward the wrong goal.

What people say about leaders of each type

STRENGTH "I enjoy working with Pioneers because they bring energy to the room and they're unbounded in their thinking, which pushes me to be more innovative."

WEAKNESS "The Pioneers I've worked with are quite unrealistic and often very manic, jumping from idea to idea without pause."

STRENGTH "They keep the team grounded and make sure ideas are feasible."

WEAKNESS "I love big ideas and creativity, which can be stunted by the practical thinker in the room."

STRENGTH "Drivers can take ideas from concept to action and keep the team on track."

WEAKNESS "I feel bulldozed by Drivers."

STRENGTH "They listen generously and bring people together."

WEAKNESS "They're too concerned about what other people think and can't make a move without consensus."

NOT BALANCED: EFFECTS OF A DOMINANT LEADER

A leader's type can have as strong an impact on a team's perspective as having a majority type—especially a leader who states their opinion early or often.

For example, as leaders, Pioneers' imagination and focus on possibilities can inspire creativity in others, but at times they move so quickly that important details and processes are overlooked by the whole team. Guardian leaders can provide a stable foundation that mitigates risk and makes people feel secure, but their teams may end up being more cautious and inflexible than is ideal. Drivers in leadership roles often push their teams to excel and rise to a challenge, but they might also prioritize results over people with detrimental effects on the way team members relate to one another. And Integrators as leaders frequently build trust by prioritizing people and collaborative cultures, but they might also over-emphasize getting everyone to agree, which can discourage differing opinions.

NOT BALANCED: EFFECTS OF MISSING A TYPE

* MISSING PERSPECTIVES CAN HAVE A MAJOR IMPACT ON HOW A TEAM FUNCTIONS.

If your team has a dominant type or two then the other types will be more lightly represented or even missing entirely. And those missing perspectives can also have a major impact on the team's decisions and the way the team functions. For example, a team with no Guardians could be overexposed to risk without the more cautious perspective that Guardians are likely to bring. A team with no Integrators may have a tough time working through a difficult interpersonal challenge without the relationship focus that Integrators are likely to emphasize. A team with no Pioneers might miss opportunities because they aren't stretching their thinking enough. And a team with no Drivers might miss key deadlines without that Driver-like discipline.

Even if the team has a token individual or a small group of a particular type, it may not be enough to actually represent that perspective, especially if those people are not particularly outspoken. This is because of the cascading effect we discussed earlier. And even if these tokens *are* willing to state a differing opinion in the midst of a cascade, there's another effect that tends to make their bravery futile, a phenomenon known as *hidden profiles*.[7] When working in groups we tend to focus on information that is shared by many and dismiss information that is held by a few, even if that exclusive information is the key to the kingdom. That means the minority perspective becomes virtually invisible (i.e., their differing *profiles* are *hidden*). As a result, we often benefit little from unique perspectives that could improve our decision-making.

It might look like this: Let's say a team of Guardians, who tend to stick with what's tried and true, intentionally seeks out the perspective of a Pioneer to help them expand their horizons. The Pioneer shares their thoughts and describes a vision of a bright new future. The Guardians smile and nod thoughtfully. But then Guardian A points out a potential risk of going in the direction the Pioneer suggests. And Guardian B piles on with another potential risk, followed by Guardian C. Then the Guardians look at each other and revert back to their prior, shared perspective (which now overwhelms the new, different perspective) and conclude that the Pioneer's idea is *too risky*.

Add to all of this that the types in the minority might be trying to succeed in an environment that feels like a poor fit, or even downright hostile to them—like the stories we shared in Chapters 12-15. If you answered the questions we asked about your team environment you might have identified some practices that are less ideal for some types than others. Together this all means that if you're not paying very close attention to the minority types on your team you're likely not benefitting from their diverse perspectives as much as you could.

A BALANCED TEAM

After all that discussion about minorities and majorities, it seems like a diverse and balanced team would be the holy grail of team composition. Indeed, among the most powerful benefits of a balanced team is the potential to mitigate risks associated with cognitive biases like groupthink, leading to better decision making and problem solving. But while diversity enhances creativity and encourages people to search for novel information and different perspectives, it can also bring challenges like greater conflict, difficulties with communication, and lower levels of trust and cohesion.[8][9][10] It can also be difficult for leaders and team members to navigate the many preferences of people on a very diverse team. The work environment that most suits a Guardian, for example (highly structured, detail-focused, solitary work), is the opposite of the one that most suits a Pioneer. As a leader, how can you provide them both with the environment that best enables them to succeed? How do you meet the needs of one type without turning the others off?

*
HOW DO YOU MEET THE NEEDS OF ONE TYPE WITHOUT TURNING THE OTHERS OFF?

Working with what you've got

Before we discuss what to do about all of this, we'd like to note that the value of the strategies we're about to suggest may be most obvious in a diverse team that's balanced across types. But they can be equally beneficial, and perhaps even more critical, on an unbalanced team, because to have any real hope of benefitting from the perspectives of your minority types, you need to create an environment that suits them. And yet, you obviously don't want to turn off the majority of your team.

To illustrate how you might work toward creating a team environment where all types excel, we'll focus on meetings, because let's face it, most of us spend more time than we'd like in meetings. Endless. Meetings. There are many aspects of what makes a meeting successful or not (and in fact we spend a lot of time studying that in the Deloitte Greenhouse). Here, we'll offer just a few practical perspectives that have particular relevance to Business Chemistry. We hope these examples, paired with the questions you previously answered about your current team environment, will set you on a path to exploring many different aspects of how your team works now and might work differently in the future. First, some level-setting.

We all know what a meeting is, right? You gather in a conference room with a group of colleagues. If you're lucky there are some windows, but you're not always lucky. You sit in chairs around a table that has some less-than-fresh bagels plopped in the middle of it. You don't want to eat those stale baked goods but you do anyway—because they're right there in front of you and you're possibly a bit bored. People may or may not have their laptops open, depending on the culture of the team, and some people may be half asleep due to the bagels (or are they surreptitiously looking at their phones? It's hard to tell). You talk to each other around the table, or maybe watch and listen to someone presenting a PowerPoint deck. (Or you don't, because you're too busy with your phone. Or the bagels.) Maybe someone takes notes. Maybe there are handouts. Or, maybe it's a conference call and absolutely everyone is multitasking whenever they're not actually talking. We've all been there and that's just how meetings are, right? We'd suggest, no.

Meetings don't have to look like that, and if your meetings do, then you're probably not meeting the needs of *any* of the types on your team! We won't go through all the ways you can engage different types in meetings, but we will make some suggestions that can set you on the right path. Who knows? Maybe you'll even manage to make meetings enjoyable, or at least more effective.

NAIL THE ESSENTIALS

Everybody has preferences for the way they like things to be, but each Business Chemistry type has specific things that are *essential* for them to be able to contribute to their fullest potential. Your meeting structure and approach should address as many of these "bare minimums" as feasible to engage all the types.

* **ADDRESS "BARE MINIMUMS" TO ENGAGE ALL TYPES.**

For Guardians, what's essential is having a clear agenda with specific expectations sent out *in advance*. This helps them plan ahead, from what they'll bring to how they'll contribute. If you have pre-work or materials they can review, even better. Guardians, in particular, process things more deliberately than other types and are more reserved about sharing their thoughts. Making sure they have a chance to do some of this processing in advance is a gift to them more than a burden. Finally, start and end on time!

For Pioneers, what's essential is having visuals that bring the content to life. This will hold their attention and spark their imagination more than text or number heavy presentations. As much as possible build some flexibility into your agenda to allow for a tangent or two—Pioneers tend to shut down when they feel too boxed in. While few people love boring conference rooms, Pioneers in particular will appreciate a less confining setting with natural light.

For Integrators, what's essential is having time for interpersonal connection and sharing of ideas. Make sure that you make room for a bit of small talk or connecting in smaller groupings (like pairing up for some discussions versus only plenary settings). If you want a decision made, you'll not only need to make time in your agenda to accommodate people's input, but you should also factor in time for Integrators to get input from others, either teeing the topic up prior to the meeting or building in time after the meeting so the Integrators have an opportunity to make their rounds.

For Drivers, what's essential is having clear objectives, and achieving them. Articulate how the various pieces of the agenda are contributing to meeting those goals and push for some level of closure before moving on to the next topic. Include data to back up any key points, and provide opportunities for productive debate. Bonus points if you can conclude the meeting early.

PROVIDE OPTIONS AND CREATE HYBRID APPROACHES

Once you address the essentials for each of the types, you'll then want to make sure that meeting the needs of one doesn't come at the expense of another. You can do so by making various aspects of your meetings optional, and by creating hybrid approaches that are designed to meet the needs of several types at once.

Make pre-work optional

Pre-work, one of our Guardian essentials should be optional to review. You don't want the success of your meeting to depend on people doing pre-work, because certain types aren't likely to do it, and asking them to may tint the whole event the color of drudgery. Guardians will likely welcome the opportunity to prepare in advance, and alone, so that they're more able to fully participate when with the group. Integrators, too, might appreciate the chance to consider issues in advance and maybe even discuss them with others before they're asked to comment in a meeting or to make a decision. Providing these opportunities will benefit the whole team by getting more concerns out in the open early, speeding up decision making, and reducing the likelihood of revisiting decisions since they've been thoroughly considered in advance by those who prefer to do things that way. All of these benefits are likely to be appreciated by Drivers, and by Pioneers too. Offering the option of prework without forcing the issue is likely to mean everyone gets what they need and everyone wins.

✳

WHEN EVERYONE GETS WHAT THEY NEED, EVERYONE WINS.

Make brainstorming smarter

Some people love a good brainstorming session, where energy is high, the pace is brisk, and ideas bounce around, collide, and shoot for the moon. But others, not so much. With their more reserved natures, introverted types sometimes find it challenging to contribute in this kind of setting, either because they can't get a word in edgewise with all those Extroverts talking, or because they don't feel safe sharing their ideas (as we discussed in Chapter 10). And it turns out that on-the-spot group brainstorming is actually not the most effective way to get the highest-quality ideas, (or the largest number of ideas, for that matter); individual brainstorming is.[11]

That doesn't mean your team should never engage in those kinds of brainstorming sessions, especially if some members of your team find it valuable. Instead of throwing the baby out with the bathwater, meet the needs of more of your team members by adding some additional bells and whistles to the way you brainstorm. One idea is to let people know in advance what you want to brainstorm about in an upcoming meeting. Like offering the option of pre-work, giving people a heads-up as to a brainstorming topic will allow those who have a hard time being creative in the middle of a hurricane to get a head start. That will likely increase the chances of getting some of their ideas into the mix before a cascade takes hold of the discussion. And it can have an added benefit—research has shown that people tend to be more accepting of creative ideas if they've first tried to get creative themselves.[12] So give those more practical types—Guardians and Drivers—the chance to do so and some of the more innovative ideas proposed by others might go down a little easier!

But if the more introverted types feel less safe offering their ideas, they might not share even if you make space for them to do so. To address this challenge, consider making the initial stage of brainstorming confidential, so those who feel less safe sharing won't hide their light completely under a bushel. There are many digital tools, for instance, that allow people to provide input anonymously. Once some of these techniques have been implemented to help surface the ideas of those who're more hesitant to fight for the floor, you can go ahead and hold a free-for-all brainstorming discussion as your Extroverts might prefer.

Make detailed tasks visual and interactive

Sometimes there are tasks that simply need to be accomplished—like creating complex work plans or Gantt charts—whether or not someone on the team thinks it's boring. And you can't always relegate these tasks to your Guardians or Drivers alone. But instead of everyone sitting around together squinting at tiny fonts in tiny boxes, could you accomplish these kinds of tasks in a way that gets the job done but also integrates elements of movement, visuals, or interactivity? Imagine creating your work plan on a huge wall chart where various pieces can be added, removed, or relocated during the discussion. Your Guardians will get the focused attention to details that they need and the Drivers will clearly see how the goals are going to be accomplished. This would also be an easy way for people to see individual points within the broader context, something important to Integrators. Even your Pioneers might be able to stay on task while working through details in more interactive and engaging ways. And all without straining anyone's eyes.

Make stage crew an acceptable choice

When working through a really tricky problem, there are lots of ways to approach it. You could have a long discussion, bring various experts in to share their perspectives, or review a few reports and position papers. Or, you could ask your team to try out techniques such as role plays, skits, improv, or other versions of play, which can increase cognitive fitness and enhance creative problem solving.[13] If you're a Guardian, those last activities may strike fear into your heart (they do for Suzanne and she'll do just about anything to stay off the stage). If you're a Driver maybe they feel a bit frivolous. But Pioneers and Integrators, in particular, often love the opportunity to actively engage with an idea or challenge by getting up and acting it out. For many of these folks, the chance to use their creativity and acting chops keeps them interested.

The key when asking a group to try some of these less traditional activities is to offer multiple ways to participate. Don't force a more introverted person onto the stage or in front of a video camera—instead of a healthy stretch this may be too far for comfort. And if someone's totally preoccupied by performance anxiety, they're probably not focused on learning. While some people can't wait to get into the spotlight (ahem, Pioneers), others are more comfortable participating offstage, developing a script, suggesting an improv scenario, creating a prop, recording a video, cheering their colleagues on, or summarizing learning in a wrap-up conversation. Offer these as ways to be part of the action.

Make your meetings work for humans

From our work in the Deloitte Greenhouse, we've discovered that there are lots of other ways to make meetings better by focusing in on some of the basic things that can enhance the human experience regardless of Business Chemistry type (but in ways that traditional meetings don't always address). Consider things like movement and comfortable seating options; humor and use of metaphor; lighting, music, even scent. And one last tip for your meetings: While we agree people need sustenance, if you want your team energized rather than in a carb coma, you might want to rethink those bagels.

SPECIAL CONSIDERATIONS FOR
AN UNBALANCED COMPOSITION

While the ideas we've just offered are relevant for any team composition, when your team is dominated by one or two types and light on others, there are some special considerations that can further help to avoid those groupthink-style cascades we told you about.

Switch up the order

One idea is to encourage minority types to speak first. Doing so will give them some chance of influencing the direction of the conversation before a cascade takes hold. Psychologist Solomon Asch's classic experiments on conformity demonstrated that even one person going against the majority can greatly increase the likelihood that others will offer divergent perspectives.[14] Take advantage of this phenomenon to help promote healthy dissent on your team, and make it easier for your minority types to go against the tide by encouraging them to do so before the direction is obvious.

Wear different hats

You might also ask others to "think like" the missing type. Do this early in the conversation, too, before the majority viewpoint takes hold. You know how you'll sometimes hear someone say, "Just playing devil's advocate"? In this case one might say, "Just playing Driver here…" or "If we had an Integrator on this team I think they would likely say…" Once your team is well versed in Business Chemistry it's usually not too difficult for them put themselves in the shoes of others when asked to do so.

Look inside

You could also suggest that people lean into their secondary types. Remember our exploration of primary-secondary type combinations in Chapter 7? It's rare that a team is missing a perspective altogether, even if you're missing a primary type. Since we're all a mix of the four types, and most people have a relatively strong secondary type, someone with the secondary you're missing might be especially good at doing what we've suggested above.

Lead together

What if you're the leader of the team? First, you should acknowledge that you have a type, just like your team members, superiors, and stakeholders do, and understand that your type is likely impacting how you view the world, how you prefer to work, and how you lead. It may also be influencing how you relate to others, which types thrive under your leadership, and who you see as most effective or most challenging to work with.

In addition to the suggestions we have for flexing to other types in general, as a leader, you might consider taking on a leadership partner, or co-lead, with a different type. If a co-lead of equal rank isn't the right solution for you, a second-in-command of a different type can also be a good balance. If you're an Integrator who gets bogged down in considering too many perspectives, a Driver or Pioneer may help you decide when to cut off discussion and make a decision. If you're a Driver who tends to push your team too hard or fast, a Guardian or Integrator might be able to help you see when it's important to take a breather.

Once you start looking for it, you'll likely start seeing examples of these power pairings in successful companies across industries, maybe even within your own company, leaders who work together like peanut butter and jelly. After all, as the saying goes, two heads are often better than one. But beware: Leaders of two different types can also cause confusion if the team experiences their differences as they would a two-headed monster—while they're trying to anticipate what one head is going to do, the other is suddenly moving forward with jaws open. When co-leading with a different type, make sure you put a bit of extra effort into communication with one another and with your team.

Creating a whole that's more (not less) than the sum of its parts

To bring to life how you can get the most out of a diverse group in real life (#BizChemIRL), let's look at an example of two companies going through a merger, we'll call them Piotech and Newco. Piotech was a large software company with a reputation for being bold and innovative. They were acquiring a start-up, Newco, known for its commitment to quality, deep relationships with customers, and industry-leading brand loyalty. The integration team was made up of people from each organization, with joint leads representing each company.

Claire (an Integrator-Pioneer) was the lead for Piotech. She was outgoing and enthusiastic, constantly rushing from one commitment to the next, leaving a trail of Post-Its and pens behind her as she went. Her Newco counterpart for the integration was John (a Guardian-Driver), a strong silent type who always carried around his own coffee mug stamped with one word: Java. Overall the working team had a relatively good balance of types, which sounds like a positive thing, but it didn't seem to be working in their favor if you take one of their first meetings as the case in point.

As the two leads tried to establish priorities and expectations it was almost as if they were speaking different languages, which of course, if you think of working style as a language of sorts, they were! John was quiet, almost withdrawn, except when he spoke up to aggressively critique a point. Claire was speaking even more rapidly than her usual rabbit pace and seemed flustered as she kept bouncing between topics.

While the leaders were caught in an unproductive back and forth, the team wasn't faring much better. The Pioneers were shooting off ideas for how things could proceed without waiting for input from anyone else. The Drivers were having a side debate about one particular aspect of the deal. The Integrators kept tentatively suggesting things that everyone ignored. And the Guardians just kept to themselves. One of the team members told us after the meeting that it was like trying to learn calculus during lunch in a high-school cafeteria. None of it was working.

After learning a bit about Business Chemistry, this team committed to trying out some new techniques. Claire made an effort to put in more structure, clarify responsibilities, and define desired outcomes more explicitly. John began trying to spend more time with the members of the integration team and other employees, gathering and incorporating feedback. He also tried to be more open to adjusting priorities based on emerging needs.

Together, Claire and John began experimenting in team meetings with dividing up responsibilities and playing distinct roles that reflected their complementary styles. Claire would open the meetings with a quick, usually funny, story about the team's progress to date. Then John would lay out the agenda for the meeting, which they had shared with the group in advance (to give the Guardians in particular time to prepare). He then would start with a brief summary of key stats relative to objectives (designed to satisfy the Drivers in particular). After that summary, they wouldn't necessarily follow the agenda sequentially. Instead, Claire would call on people in a random sequence to mix things up (keeping things a bit more interesting for the Pioneers). And they always had a "wild card" portion of the agenda, which provided open time to talk about whatever was on the group's mind (which the Integrators in particular loved, but everyone appreciated).

As these process changes started to become their new way of doing things, they also asked people to take on specific lenses as they worked through the integration, lenses that were essential to the team's success and which also suited their individual strengths. One of the Integrators was asked to be the "Voice of Employees," a Driver was asked to be the "Voice of Competitors," a Pioneer was asked to be the "Voice of Customers," and a Guardian was asked to be the "Voice of the Market." This construct provided them with a platform not only to contribute valuable insights from their assigned "voices", but also to ensure that their own voices would be heard as well.

Fast forward several weeks, and Claire and John had turned a corner in their relationship. Beyond just acknowledging that they came from different perspectives (which in and of itself helped a lot), they both were flexing toward the other. Claire learned to view John's directness as a sign of his dedication to the project, versus a criticism of her. John in turn made an effort to connect with Claire more often, not just when he needed something from her.

As you can imagine, all of this contributed to the success of the integration, but the feedback from the team also indicated that it was one of the more productive and enjoyable projects they'd ever been part of. Win–win!

Don't try this on your own

Whatever your team's composition, you don't have to do any of this alone—and you really shouldn't! Bring others into the effort by letting them know what you're trying to do. Learn together about the Business Chemistry types, adopt a common language for talking about working styles, and get a sense of each other's styles and those of your most important stakeholders. Where are the similarities and differences? Where are the points of complementarity and conflict?

There are several reasons for making this effort an ongoing team project or way of being. First, there's no reason for you to carry the burden all by yourself when you can share the load with others. Really, sharing is not just for Integrators. Carrying heavy stuff can be exhausting! And you need your energy to do lots of other things.

Second, chances of making a meaningful difference in the strength of your working relationships and the effectiveness of your team are much higher when you're all working from a common point of reference. Say you have an Integrator team member experiencing challenges with a particular colleague. If you point out that it seems a like a classic Integrator-Driver conflict that they could address by flexing a little bit in the Driver's direction, it's going to be a lot more helpful if they already understand what an Integrator is, what a Driver is, and how their preferences differ.

Third, people are likely to have a lot more patience with team practices and ways of working that go against their natural preferences when they understand that you (and everyone else on the team) are trying to accommodate diverse needs so that everyone can succeed together. Kim mentioned in Chapter 13 that she finds it challenging to organize herself in advance of a meeting so her Guardian colleagues can get what they need, but she makes the effort because she understands that it matters. With such a shared goal, most people are more willing to go along with things, if not always good-naturedly, then with fewer complaints.

Ultimately, an effective team leader can learn a lot from a great choir conductor. Give the group shared sheet music with multiple parts. Celebrate different ranges and contributions of members. And let them discover the power of the resulting harmony as they start weaving their diverse voices together.

REFERENCES

1. Duhigg, Charles. "Group Study." *The New York Times Magazine*, February 28, 2016.

2. Grant, Adam M. *Originals: How Non-Conformists Move the World*. New York: Viking, 2016.

3. Hackman, J.Richard. "Group Influences on Individuals in Organizations." In *Handbook of Industrial and Organizational Psychology* edited by M. D. Dunnette & L. M. Hough. Vol. 3 (2nd ed.) Palo Alto: Consulting Psychologists Press, 1992.

4. Hogg, Michael A. "Group Cohesiveness: A Critical Review and Some New Directions." *European Review of Social Psychology* 4 (1) (1993): 85–111. doi:10.1080/14792779343000031.

5. Rock, David, Heidi Grant, and Jacqui Grey. "Diverse Teams Feel Less Comfortable — and That's Why They Perform Better." *Harvard Business Review*. September 22, 2016.

6. Sunstein, Cass R. and Reid Hastie. "Making Dumb Groups Smarter." *Harvard Business Review*. December 2014.

7. Ibid.

8. Page, Scott E. *The Difference: How the Power of Diversity Creates Better Groups, Firms, Schools, and Societies*. Princeton, NJ: Princeton University Press, 2007.

9. Phillips, Katherine W. "How Diversity Makes Us Smarter." *Scientific American*. October 2014.

10. See Note 5.

11. Chamorro-Premuzic, Tomas. "Why Group Brainstorming Is a Waste of Time." *Harvard Business Review*. March 2015.

12. See Note 2.

13. Gilkey, Roderick and Clint Kilts. "Cognitive Fitness." *Harvard Business Review*. November 2007.

14. Asch, Solomon. "Studies of Independence and Submission to Group Pressure: I. A Minority of One Against a Unanimous Majority." *Psychological Monograph* 70. 9 (1956): No. 16.

e.g. Seminal Research [handwritten annotation]

18

Got Chemistry?

We're pretty sure that at some point in your life, you've been asked a version of the following question:

If you were stranded on a desert island (with plenty of food and water), what *or* who *would you most want with you?*

As Business Chemistry practitioners, we suspect that your answer to *what* you would like to have says a lot about your individual style and preferences. For now, though, let's save that particular exploration for a future team-building event. Instead, let's focus on the question of *who*. And let's assume that you're limited to a handful of people.

Setting aside the consideration of whether or not it's cruel to subject anyone else to your island fate, most people would probably answer with some combination of family and friends. Or perhaps you would choose a collection of intriguing, famous personalities (after all, this *IS* a hypothetical, so why not hang out with A-list movie stars and gurus?). Or maybe you'd opt for people with relevant skills, like a survivalist, an engineer, or a doctor, for instance. Maybe if you're lucky, your individual social sphere captures the Venn overlap of each of these categories. Most of the time, though, you'll likely have to make trade-offs between categories in selecting your fellow castaways.

Of course this is a contrived scenario, but in a work context we'd argue this question is not so hypothetical. We don't want to be overdramatic and suggest that business efforts are the equivalent of being stranded on a deserted island (at least not typically), however in many work environments the expectation is that groups of people who do not know one another well, if at all, will come together to use whatever limited resources are available to achieve specific goals. With plenty of sharks in the water around them if they go astray.

So now let's revisit the original question again, with the island setup as a metaphor for a work effort, and the *who* pertaining to your potential team. What do the trade-offs look like now? Do you choose the people you know really well and are comfortable with—the friends and family equivalent? Do you choose people who have a history of success in their respective domains—the business-version of movie stars and gurus? Do you choose people who have essential skills and expertise—the survivalists and doctors? How will you make your decision? And how will you get the most out of your choice once you do?

Since this is the concluding chapter of a book entitled *Business Chemistry*, it should be obvious that at least *one* of the factors we think you should consider is the individuals' working styles. Whether you're launching a raft to reach civilization or launching a new product to increase market penetration, your success can hinge on having diverse perspectives available and on crafting the kind of powerful working relationships that make those differences a boon rather than a bust.

Hopefully, by this point in the book, you've also gathered that there isn't a single *right* answer for how to use Business Chemistry to compose a team and foster relationships that work. There's an element of art as well as science to this. Consider that:

1) Every type brings unique strengths (and unique limitations). While it might be easier to work with similar types, there are clear advantages to diversity if you're willing to make the effort to tap into it.

2) Where and how you use Business Chemistry depends on your objectives. You might take a very different approach, and tap into a different mix of Business Chemistry perspectives, if your goal were to establish a sustainable settlement on that deserted island, for instance, than if your goal were to escape it.

3) People's types are relative and represent preferences *in general* in a work environment, and might vary depending on the context or with the passage of time. Types are the launch point for understanding others, not the last word on who they are, or what they can or cannot do.

Throughout this book we've offered a number of ways for you to think about, and address, these considerations. As you start to look at the world through a Business Chemistry lens, we suspect you'll begin to expand that list. We also hope that you'll start to consider the relevance of Business Chemistry, not only for the workplace of today, but for the workplace of the future.

So for instance, when you read an article about rapid innovations in bioengineering, you might quickly think about how Drivers might advance the technology, or how Pioneers might embrace such dynamic change, but also how Guardians could create guidance around ethical concerns, or how Integrators could help people understand the potential societal impact and consider options to mitigate negative outcomes.

Or when you think about how to build artificial intelligence into your operations, you might think about what it will be like to have robots interacting with people. Will they be programmed to be perfectly rational, Spock-like beings (extreme Driver-Scientist types)? Or more diplomatic and cautious C3PO-like creations (Integrator-Guardian types)? Or should their working styles be dynamic, adjusting to flex to the person, and the situation, they're interfacing with?

Can you guess which option we're rooting for?

The thing is, unless robots do one day become our overlords, humans will remain a key factor in the emerging business landscape. Indeed, we could, and do, argue that the more digital, virtual, and tumultuous the world becomes, the more humans become *the* differentiating factor—in the business world and beyond. Algorithms and data are incredible raw ingredients, but their business value depends in large part on people's ability to transform them into something valuable. To create alignment around where and how to use them. To inspire adoption and change. To build powerful relationships that can unleash the potential of both technology and people.

This is the kind of transformation we hope you'll seek after reading this book, whether you're looking to change the world or just your next meeting. Whether your goal is to turn difficult relationships around, to manage your boss or your reports more effectively, to influence and connect with clients, customers, and stakeholders, or to tap into the unique strengths of different people, Business Chemistry can get you there. The suggestions we've provided throughout this book may be nuanced, but they're also practical, based on years of research and real-world application. This is something you can start doing today, whether you simply start using Business Chemistry as a common language to talk about different preferences, or whether you re-architect your team to engage all the types.

Regardless of how you adopt Business Chemistry, we believe that from now on you will look at the world around you a little differently. Like a hidden pattern revealed, once you've become aware of Business Chemistry, you'll see it everywhere. And therein lies the magic.

About the Authors (or When a Pioneer and a Guardian Work Together)

We considered writing a typical "about the authors" section, but then we thought maybe you've heard quite enough about us already. On the other hand, maybe you're wondering what our qualifications are for writing this book. So in case you're asking, "Who the heck are these people?" we'll share just a little more about our professional and personal selves here. We also thought it might be fun to tell you a bit about our working relationship generally and in writing this book together. After all, we're opposite Business Chemistry types, and as you've probably learned through your own experiences, that's not always a picnic! But it seems to us like working through a few differences has paid off.

Who are we?

After almost pursuing a career in medicine, Kim shifted gears to explore the business world, first in a PR/marketing agency and then joining Deloitte as a systems analyst. After getting her MBA from the Stanford Graduate School of Business, Kim returned to Deloitte. She spent the next 18+ years in a variety of roles, from delivering strategy projects to leading merger and acquisition engagements to defining new customer-engagement models. She now heads the Deloitte Greenhouse team in the United States, a group that delivers interactive experiences expressly designed to shift thinking, activate teams, and accelerate breakthroughs.

Suzanne started out her career focused on health psychology research and program evaluation in various organizations including Sloan-Kettering Cancer Center, Mount Sinai School of Medicine, and Planned Parenthood Federation of America. She then shifted her focus to organizational culture and employee engagement, moving on to the Great Place to Work Institute and finally Deloitte. Along the way she has earned a PhD in social-personality psychology from the Graduate School and University Center at CUNY (so she's a psychologist, but more of a researcher than a clinician), and then an MBA from the Stern School of Business at NYU. Now she quite happily lives, eats, and breathes Business Chemistry.

Just in case you thought it's all work all the time for us, we've got lives outside of work too! Kim lives in California and Suzanne in New Jersey (but with strong Minnesota roots). We've each got a couple of kids and some hobbies as well— painting, architecture, and hiking for Kim, and reading, gardening, and walking for Suzanne.

In the beginning

Now on to our work together. As a reminder, when it comes to Business Chemistry, Kim is not only a Pioneer, but she's also a secondary Driver, and specifically a Scientist. Suzanne is a Guardian and an Integrator, specifically a Dreamer. When Kim originally began architecting Business Chemistry, her team was composed mostly of Pioneers like her. They had all sorts of ideas about what they could do with the emerging system, but they didn't necessarily wake up in the morning eagerly anticipating cross-referencing the various pieces of research or sifting through the data sets. They knew *someone* needed to be doing those things, so they thought it could be a good move to bring in a researcher. Along came Suzanne, a social-personality psychologist with a love for research and data-sifting. And from the word *go*, she was definitely a bird of a different feather, especially when compared to Kim.

Since there were many areas of the Deloitte Greenhouse where Suzanne's background and skills were relevant, Kim and team got her involved in lots of projects right away. It should have been good for them and good for her, right? But it wasn't good for her, so in the end it wasn't good for anyone. Being deployed against multiple workstreams necessitated constant topic- and task-switching, which made it hard for her to get traction on any one thing. As a result, Suzanne's frustration levels were rising, as were Kim's.

Then we had our *eureka* moment. In theory we were trying to take advantage of Suzanne's strengths by putting her on multiple projects that needed her expertise. But by spreading her across so many activities and not providing her opportunities to really dig in, she wasn't set up for success, because that's not how she performs at her best. So we decided to take our own advice and change the model in a way that would better suit her Business Chemistry. Suzanne would stop being a Jill-of-all-trades and would become a master of one. She would work only on Business Chemistry, balancing out the original Pioneer-heavy team with a totally different skillset. The result? Suzanne was happier and more productive, and so was everyone else. Leaning into complementary workstyles meant everyone could contribute to the best of their abilities. Suzanne still won't join Kim in karaoke and sometimes she sequesters herself in a corner during loud social events (where Kim can often be clearly heard, even over many other voices), but there's a lot more great work getting done, as we hope this book will attest.

───────

We should write a book together. Wouldn't that be fun?

Perhaps the first clue to what it's like working on a giant project across this particular opposite-type partnership is that Suzanne has kept an ongoing file of conversations and telling moments that have occurred along the way, in preparation for writing this section at the end. Meanwhile, Kim has no such file. Perhaps because she knew Suzanne had one?

Suzanne's file tells us that one key point of divergence happened early on, when we were thinking about the timeline for the book. Neither of us had written a book before, so in the beginning we were feeling around in the dark a bit. Suzanne built a timeline by imagining every possible step she thought might be required, outlining them in a sequence that seemed to make sense, and including a complicated back and forth process of drafting, reviewing, and revising multiple chapters, in different stages, all at once. As she figured it, the book would take a year and a half to write.

Kim took a quick look at Suzanne's timeline and said "That seems overly complicated. Why don't you draft half the chapters and I'll draft half, and then we'll switch." She then suggested we could write the book in, oh…let's say…six months. "After all," she said, "we know what we want to say!"

Suzanne is a big enough person to admit that, OK the original timeline *was* overly complicated and we *did* write the book in six months or so, but she spent the entire time just barely containing her anxiety about getting it done.

Here's a typical, illustrative email exchange about our timeline:

_____

■ **SUZANNE:** "I know it's a lot (I'm trying to keep my own panic at bay) but if we can dig in now to stay on track we can keep things from spiraling out of control. I've attached the most current version of the book plan/timeline."

_____

▪ **KIM:** "Thanks for keeping us organized but I think we're making great progress and am not concerned."

And that's pretty much how it went throughout the writing process. Suzanne was the taskmaster and queen of details. She sent Kim hundreds of very long, elaborate emails about timelines and deadlines, research findings and analyses, permissions and citations, drafts and edits. (Sorry Kim!) Suzanne shared lots of feedback and usually thought a chapter could benefit from just *one more revision*.

Kim's deep and varied experiences with executives on the ground balanced Suzanne's more research-focused perspective. And she was the enthusiastic navigator with her eye always on the horizon: Where are we trying to go, and is this winding path really the best way to get there? What are we trying to say, and is it really necessary to use quite so many words to say it? She also sent a number of "sorry this is late but something came up!" emails. (Sorry Suzanne!)

You'll get the picture pretty quickly through the following quotes from emails we exchanged while drafting chapters and reviewing each other's work:

■ **SUZANNE:** "We've got two weeks until risk review. We need to complete the following, listed here in order of priority. I'm sending this now in case you can complete any of them before tomorrow, and also making sure you have most updated versions all in one place in case you want to print anything for our meeting…"

"We need to think about a few (more) things related to the book. Key questions follow. We can discuss on a call, but initial answers now would help with planning. I've attached the most recent book plan and timeline (Gray text means these things have been accomplished. Bright yellow highlighting means currently in process. Light yellow highlighting means we're revising)…"

"I think we will want to work on this chapter a bit more to perfect it. It's the key to everything and I'm not quite satisfied yet."

■ **KIM:** "Ok, I think I may have completed everything on this list apart from what the visual TOC might look like—is that true?? SO EXCITING!"

"Phew. That was the most work I've ever done for 6 pages of output. I explored a number of different directions for this but felt that this was the most non-typical business book direction while still hopefully being compelling for a businessperson to read."

"Eureka! Well, maybe not QUITE that exciting, but I did start exploring a different approach for the intro…"

"Just an update so you don't worry—I am working on this!!"

As we went along and produced some solid drafts of the chapters, we asked for feedback from colleagues of all Business Chemistry types. That was telling as well. We heard that our writing styles are quite different. In a nutshell, we were told that Kim's writing is more direct and declarative, while

Suzanne's is a bit softer, with more qualifications, questions, and citations. Occasionally we heard that a section was too heavy or too long. Some of them maybe still are, but Suzanne drafted those and she simply couldn't imagine robbing you, our readers, of all that important and interesting information! And it's not just Suzanne; some of our reviewers, depending on their own type, indicated that the level of detail or the presence of supporting research was appropriate and helpful, and lent credibility to our work. Others suggested shortening the text. (Kim promises she did not put them up to it.) Still others, we suspect, politely skimmed over the denser parts. And our goal, of course, was to meet the needs of those who like the details without losing the attention of those who prefer things short and sweet.

And did you know, readers, that when you write a book, you need to market it? You probably did know that, and we knew it too on some level, but once it started ramping up we had very different responses to some of the events that put us out there in different ways (webcasts, podcasts, speaking engagements, etc.). Here are our respective responses to a suggestion from our marketing lead that we do a live-feed event:

■ **SUZANNE:** "I'll ponder it even though it makes my blood pressure rise. I'll look at the one you shared as an example so I can see what it's like..."

■ **KIM:** "I'd love to do this."

We hope our example has demonstrated that making the effort to work with your opposite type can be effective, but can also be fun, if you keep a sense of humor about it. Perhaps one final quote from each of us, recorded along the way, will give you just a little more insight into our partnership.

■ **SUZANNE:** "I'm already upset about the imperfections of the book we haven't written yet."

■ **KIM:** "Suzanne, you need to write down some of your own quotes."

Appendix

Details of the Business Chemistry System

Hello to our detail-oriented and technical friends! To everyone else, we're a little surprised to see you here, and frankly quite flattered that you made it to this page, so welcome! Here's where we put information about the development of the Business Chemistry assessment and system, the specifics about our research samples and methodologies, and the properties of Business Chemistry. All of that is important to document and consider when interpreting our findings and using Business Chemistry, but it's maybe less than fascinating to read about (depending on your type). Still, we'll do our best to keep you awake and if we can't end with a bang, hopefully at least it's not a whimper.

About the assessment

When we first decided that a working style assessment might help our people strengthen their working relationships, we started by reviewing the existing fields of related research and the currently available assessment tools. And let us tell you, there is tons of research and there are plenty of tools, so that took quite a while.

We also consulted with biological anthropologist Helen Fisher, of Rutgers University. Her research on brain chemistry in romantic relationships sheds light on how people's temperaments can impact their interactions. We even tried out a version of Dr. Fisher's assessment with a large group of Deloitte leaders to see how the idea of understanding different styles in order to strengthen relationships would resonate with them. It definitely did.

We didn't find a tool that quite met all our needs through this process of review, consultation, and piloting, but from it we were able to identify a set of behaviors, preferences, and traits that seemed to have the most potential to affect working relationships. So we decided to create our own tool, working with a survey development company to craft original assessment items designed to measure these key behaviors, preferences, and traits, and homing in on those that could either be observed directly, or inferred from people's behavior at work. Remember, our goal was to develop a tool that people could use to understand their own working style and, but even more importantly, the styles of others.

As an example, the item "I focus on the big picture and leave the details to others" is something that can be observed directly. Do you do this? Does your client or colleague do this? Whereas the item "It's important to take time to help others" is a belief that you can reasonably infer from someone's behavior. Do you actually take time to help others on a regular basis? Does your client or colleague do so? If so, it's likely that you do (or your client or colleague does) see it as important.

We tested these initial items with a sample of 1,000 individuals and then refined them before retesting them with a second sample of 1,000 individuals. Once we were confident we had a solid set of assessment items, 68 in all, we used the data from this second sample to conduct an Eigen analysis. If you don't know what Eigen analysis is, no need to worry, we needed a little help with it too so we collaborated with molecular biologist Lee Silver, of Princeton University, on this step. Dr. Silver adapted the statistical models he uses for genetic population analysis to look for patterns in our data about people's working styles. Specifically, the analysis Dr. Silver conducted allowed us to mathematically derive the Business Chemistry types by determining the associations among all of our items, and identifying how the items cluster together in multidimensional space. If you're not sure what that means don't panic, there's an example coming.

For example (told you), the analysis indicated that our items measuring empathy, relationship orientation, and respect for traditions clustered together on one dimension. This means if you're empathic, you're also likely to place a high value on close relationships and to think it's important to respect traditions (as you've already learned, these traits are representative of the Integrator type). The analysis also told us that our items measuring directness, competitiveness, and logical thinking clustered together at the other end of the same dimension (these traits are representative of the Driver type, the Integrator's opposite). This means if you're very direct you're also likely to be competitive and to approach things in a logical manner, but also that you're *not* likely to be particularly empathic, relationship oriented, or traditional.

And this is one of the key properties of Business Chemistry. It takes into account both what you're attracted to (which items you think describe you and your preferences), as well as what you're repelled by (which items you think really don't describe you and your preferences). Because the thing is, we're defined both by what we are and what we're not.

So through our analysis we were able to identify these clusters of items that formed the basis of the Business Chemistry types, but remember when we mentioned multidimensional space? We really meant it. Eigen analysis identifies clusters in as many different dimensions as there are items, which in our case is 68. Since that is far, far too many dimensions for our human minds to comprehend, we focused in on just a few dimensions that showed the most robust clusters (and explained the most variance, for you more quantitatively oriented types). In doing so we identified one dimension with traits clustering at opposite ends characterizing the Pioneer and Guardian types, and another dimension with traits clustering at opposite ends characterizing the Driver and Integrator types. But we also identified two other dimensions with identifiable clusters that added some important nuance to the Driver and Integrator types—those ultimately become the Commander and Scientist subtypes of Driver and the Teamer and Dreamer subtypes of Integrator.

We've found that the main four types work great for day-to-day business uses—four types are easy for people to learn, remember, and use, and our goal in developing Business Chemistry was to create something both memorable and actionable. But we've discovered that for our research on specific topics like stress or leadership, we gain additional insight by breaking the types down further to include that additional layer of subtypes.

Our next step was to confirm that the types were reliable—that they weren't some fluke or trick of the data. So we verified the structure of the system by repeating the Eigen analysis with a third sample of 1,000 individuals. We found that the same items clustered together along the same dimensions, replicating 96% of the Eigen values.

Here might be a good place to pause and address the issue of how our types compare to the types identified by the other personality and working style systems out there. The short story is they're sometimes quite similar! We think this is pretty interesting, given that various systems have used different methods for arriving at their types. In the case of Business Chemistry the types are mathematically derived through the analysis we just told you about; we developed items measuring things we thought were important and then used Eigen analysis to determine how they clustered together. Then we looked at the clusters and named the types appropriately. Some other systems are theoretically derived; they started out with certain categories or types they wanted to identify and then created items designed to characterize them. While at first it seems a bit unexpected that these different methods would produce similar types, in a way it's not so surprising because the systems are trying to get at the same underlying thing—human behavior.

In brief, far from seeing it as a short coming, we see the overlap with other systems as a good sign because it suggests that we're getting to something that's real. Remember, we weren't seeking points for originality for Business Chemistry, but rather for utility.

We'll now get on with sharing more details about how we compute Business Chemistry scores, but there's one more thing we want to share first. While we think Business Chemistry is pretty awesome, as practitioners of it we're more than aware that people have different preferences. If you have a different assessment or system that you like to use, that's fine—whatever floats your boat! Regardless of what specific tool you prefer, if your goal is to work better with others, there's plenty in this book that could be of use to you. With a few tweaks, much of what we'll say could fit with your favorite system. Business Chemistry is about inclusivity after all, and all are welcome here.

IDENTIFYING BUSINESS CHEMISTRY TYPES

There are two main ways to identify a person's Business Chemistry type—the low-tech way, which you can apply right now after reading this book, (or even glancing through it), and the high-tech way, which we use in our research studies and client engagements. We'll explain both here, starting with the low tech.

If you've read all the chapters of this book, you've learned everything you need to know about the Business Chemistry types and how to recognize them. At this point we bet you have your own type identified and those of the people around you. If for some reason you're reading this appendix first, just take a close look at the summary descriptions of the types in Chapter 1, or at the figure located directly after Chapter 6, and pretty quickly you'll likely know your own type and that of others. If you haven't already, you could also read Chapter 7, where we describe the process for developing a hunch, which can be applied to identifying your own type or someone else's. Speaking of developing a hunch about someone else's type, we've also created an online tool designed to help you do that. The tool guides you through 20 questions that narrow down someone's likely type.

While most of you will identify your type through the low-tech method, since our research is based on data collected with the high-tech method we want to provide you with some of the details about that here. Essentially, people use our online Business Chemistry tool to respond to each of the 68 assessment items by using a slider to indicate how accurately the item does or does not describe them. And then a bunch of math happens and they get a report telling them their type.

What kind of math you ask? (If you're reading this appendix you're likely one of the types that would ask that question.) We're happy to oblige; two main calculations happen.

First we normalize a person's ratings of each item to account for individual response biases. We do this because when taking a survey some people tend to respond to everything in a very extreme way while others tend to be a bit more moderate across the board. There's nothing wrong with that, but what we're trying to get at is how a person responds differently to one item versus another (not whether or not they respond in an extreme way to everything). Basically, we adjust a person's scores in a way that accounts for this (we use their average and standard deviation across all the items to do so, if you really must know).

Once that's done we go back to those Eigen values we told you about a few pages ago and use them to transform a person's normalized scores for each item into raw scores for each dimension. Those raw scores tell us whether a person is closer to the Pioneer or Guardian end of one dimension and whether they're closer to the Driver or Integrator end of the other. Now we're getting somewhere.

Finally we compare a person's raw dimension scores to our baseline sample to determine in which percentile they fall for each of the types. You can read more about the composition of our baseline sample below, but basically it's a sample of about 1,500 men and 1,500 women of varying organizational levels who work in the United States in one of more than 700 different companies representing a variety of industries.

Why do we do this? As we discussed in Chapter 7, Business Chemistry is relative. That is, there's no such thing as a Pioneer (or any of the other types) in a vacuum. A person is a Pioneer in relation to how Pioneer-like those around them are. The same goes for the other types. That means someone may be a Pioneer in comparison to the typical professional, but an Integrator compared to the typical leader. In a similar way, they may be considered tall in a room full of kindergarteners but short in a room full of basketball players, even though their height hasn't changed.

A person who completes the Business Chemistry assessment receives a percentile score for each of the four types in relation to this baseline, with the highest percentile representing their primary type, and the second highest their secondary type. They also receive percentile scores in relation to the Dreamer, Teamer, Commander, and Scientist subtypes.

Samples and methodologies

Most of the samples for our research studies come to us in similar ways—they're made up of professionals who work for organizations that are clients of Deloitte or that have other types of relationships with us. They typically complete our online assessment in preparation for participating in an interactive Business Chemistry session. There are just two exceptions here: 1) Our stress study, highlighted in Chapter 10, includes Deloitte professionals as well as those from outside organizations; and 2) many of the quotes and the perspectives about how people view the various types come from our large group of certified Business Chemistry facilitators within Deloitte.

Once someone logs on to take the Business Chemistry assessment, we offer them the opportunity to participate in our research by answering a few additional questions about topics like psychological safety or career aspirations. So if you're one of those people—thank you for your help!

We also give people the option of answering a few questions about demographics like their gender or generation. Many people answer these and some don't, so for our analyses that consider these variables, samples are sometimes a bit smaller. As you're about to see, we're generally working with quite sizeable samples. Just know that when we report representation of demographics among our samples we're calculating percentages considering only those for which we have the information.

In addition to basic information about how many respondents make up each sample and what we know about them, we'll provide you with details about margins of error so you can get a sense of the statistical significance of any differences. But generally speaking we only highlight in the chapters differences that are significant. Now on to the details.

BASELINE SAMPLES (featured in Chapters 9 & 11)

Our Business (U.S.) Baseline sample is used in two primary ways. First, we use it as the comparison sample representing the *typical professional* when we calculate respondents' Business Chemistry scores and identify their types—the process we just described in the previous section. Second, we use this sample to explore introversion/extroversion (described in Chapter 9) and Business Chemistry differences by gender, generation, and organizational level (all described in Chapter 11).

The reason for using this sample for these analyses rather than some of our larger samples is that this one was specifically selected and stratified with particular attention paid to how variables may overlap. For example, we made sure that there were roughly equal numbers of men and women at all organizational levels so we didn't end up with a confounding effect of higher levels being male dominated. Our other samples aren't selected, rather we include everyone who responded to our questions. We often repeat demographic analyses with our larger samples to confirm the patterns we identify with this baseline sample, but we report results from this sample because it's cleaner.

Our Business (U.S.) Baseline is comprised of 2,958 U.S.-based professionals, 50% male and 50% female. We included professionals from a representative mix of 714 companies across industries, ensuring that no particular company made up more than 5% of the sample.

The margin of error for this sample is less than +/−2 percentage points at a 95% confidence level. In other words, we can be very confident (95% confident!) that were we to assess Business Chemistry across a large swath of the U.S. professional population, the proportions of the Business Chemistry types would be within a couple of percentage points of what we're seeing in this sample (which is a relatively even distribution across types).

One caveat here is since our sample was deliberately selected rather than chosen randomly, we might expect patterns to differ a bit more depending on the overall demographic make-up of the large swath we assessed. For example, while Millennials are now the largest generation in the U.S. workforce,[1] our Business (U.S.) Baseline sample includes fewer millennials because we intentionally selected for more professionals at the manager and leader levels. Our other samples all include higher proportions of Millennials.

Margins of error for men and women in this sample are +/– 3, and for organizational level and generation as follows:

Business (U.S.) Baseline Sample Demographics

Category	% of Sample	MOE (+/–)
Staff	11%	5
Manager	45%	3
Leader	34%	3
Academic, legal, medical, entrepreneur	10%	6

Category	% of Sample	MOE (+/–)
Millennial (born 1981-1997)	18%	4
Gen X (born 1965-1980)	54%	2
Baby Boomer (born 1946-1964)	28%	3

In addition to the Business (U.S.) Baseline, which is our default baseline and offers respondents the chance to understand their Business Chemistry type relative to the *typical professional*, we have a second, optional baseline. Our Leadership (U.S.) Baseline allows respondents to compare themselves to the *typical leader*. Because remember, as we discussed in Chapter 7, Business Chemistry is relative.

Our Leadership (U.S.) Baseline is comprised of 1,000 U.S.-based leaders, 52% male and 48% female, serving at the director level and above. We selected leaders from a representative mix of 453 companies across industries, ensuring that no particular company made up more than 5% of the sample.

Leadership (U.S.) Sample Demographics

Category	% of Sample	Category	% of Sample
SVP/EVP	12%	Millennial	6%
Director	50%	Gen X	55%
C-suite role	28%	Baby Boomer	39%

The margin of error for this sample is less than +/−4 percentage points at a 95% confidence level. We have not reported margins of error for the demographic categories because we do not use this sample for demographic comparisons, but only for calculating Business Chemistry scores in relation to the *typical leader*.

STRESS STUDY SAMPLES (featured in Chapter 10)

Our stress study includes two samples of professionals working at varying organizational levels in the United States and elsewhere. Participants represent more than 1,300 organizations across various industries, including Deloitte, and 120 countries overall.

Stress Sample 1 is comprised of 23,597 professionals who, during the period of November 2014 to June 2015, completed the Business Chemistry assessment online and also answered questions about their current and general stress levels, and about how stressful they find 15 workplace events and situations to be.

Stress Study Sample 1 Demographics

Category	% of Sample
U.S.	46%
Outside U.S.	54%

Category	% of Sample
Student/Intern	3%
Staff	51%
Manager	34%
Leader	12%

Stress Sample 2 is comprised of 17,008 professionals who, during the period of June 2015 to October 2015, completed the Business Chemistry assessment online and also answered questions about how effective they are under stress and how often they use 12 different coping strategies.

Stress Study Sample 2 Demographics

Category	% of Sample
U.S.	50%
Outside U.S.	50%

Category	% of Sample
Student/Intern	13%
Staff	57%
Manager	22%
Leader	9%

The margin of error for both samples is less than +/−2 percentage points at a 95% confidence level, for all Business Chemistry types, including subtypes.

We do not have sufficient information to report gender, generation, or organizational level in these samples because we did not gather this data at the time these studies were conducted.

PSYCHOLOGICAL SAFETY AND LOCUS OF CONTROL STUDY SAMPLE (featured in Chapter 10)

This study includes 11,294 professionals working at varying organizational levels, in the United States and elsewhere. Participants represent more than 2,000 organizations across various industries, and 88 countries overall. No one organization represents more than 5% of the sample.

Psychological Safety and Locus of Control Sample Demographics

Category	% of Sample	Category	% of Sample
U.S.	64%	Female	53%
Outside U.S.	36%	Male	47%

Category	% of Sample	Category	% of Sample
Student/Intern	13%	Millennial	40%
Staff	16%	Gen X	44%
Manager	41%	Baby Boomer	16%
Leader	30%		

During the period of November 2016 to July 2017, participants completed the Business Chemistry assessment online and also answered questions about how often various statements about psychological safety were true for them.

The margin error for this sample is less than +/−3 percentage points at a 95% confidence level, for all Business Chemistry types, including subtypes.

The sample for the locus of control analysis was a subset of 9,336 of these respondents.

CAREER ASPIRATIONS, CAREER PRIORITIES, AND THRIVING CONDITIONS STUDY SAMPLE
(featured in Chapter 10)

This study includes 13,885 professionals working at varying organizational levels, in the United States and elsewhere. Participants represent more than 1,200 organizations across various industries, and 115 countries overall. No one organization represents more than 5% of the sample.

Sample Demographics

Category	% of Sample	Category	% of Sample
U.S.	66%	Female	51%
Outside U.S.	34%	Male	49%
Student/Intern	19%	Millennial	43%
Staff	19%	Gen X	39%
Manager	34%	Baby Boomer	18%
Leader	27%		

During the period of February 2016 to November 2016, participants completed the Business Chemistry assessment online and also answered questions about their career aspirations, career priorities, and the working conditions under which they thrive. For each topic, respondents were asked to select their top 3 options out of a list of 10.

The margin error for this sample is less than +/−2 percentage points at a 95% confidence level, for all Business Chemistry types, including subtypes.

C-SUITE STUDY SAMPLE (featured in Chapter 11)

Our sample of CxOs is made up of 853 U.S.-based executives who have self-identified as holding a C-suite role in an organization of more than 100 employees. Most of them serve moderate to large organizations. More than 500 organizations are represented overall, with a relatively even distribution across industries.

Each participant took the Business Chemistry assessment online between the periods of October 2012, and July 2017. Participants and their roles were validated using external information sources such as LinkedIn and organization websites.

The margin of error for the full sample of 853 CxOs is +/−4 percentage points at a 95% confidence level. In other words, while 36% of the CxOs in our sample were identified as Pioneers, a four-point margin of error means we can be reasonably confident that, were we able to assess a large swath of C-suite leaders in the United States, the percentage of Pioneers would be somewhere between 32% and 40%. Likewise, the range for the percentage of Drivers would be 25% to 33%, for Guardians would be 14% to 22%, and for Integrators would be 13% to 21%.

Margins of error are higher for the various sub-samples of CxOs categorized by function, organization size, and gender.

C-suite Study Sample Demographics

Category	% of Sample	MOE (+/−)
Function		
CIO	33%	6
CFO	18%	8
CEO	14%	9
CHRO	8%	12
CMO	5%	16
Other C-suite role	22%	7
Gender		
Male	69%	4
Female	31%	6
Organization Size (Employees)		
<3,000	29%	6
3,001 – 10,000	18%	8
10,001 – 100,000	34%	6
> 100,000	19%	8
Organization Size (Revenue)		
<$1B	30%	6
$1B-$5B	16%	8
$5.1B-$10B	7%	12
>$10B	28%	6
N.A. (Govt.)	19%	8

Because the sample included a disproportionate number of men compared to women, and of CIOs compared to other C-suite roles, we explored how the representation of the Business Chemistry types in the C-suite might be impacted by a more equal distribution between women and men and across CxO roles. Weighting scores to reflect such distributions resulted in slight changes in the proportions of Business Chemistry types, but the overall representation was similar, with Pioneers being most common, followed by Drivers.

**Adjusted for Overrepresentation
of Position and/or Gender**

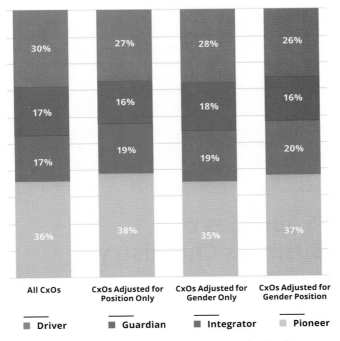

	All CxOs	CxOs Adjusted for Position Only	CxOs Adjusted for Gender Only	CxOs Adjusted for Gender Position
Driver	30%	27%	28%	26%
Guardian	17%	16%	18%	16%
Integrator	17%	19%	19%	20%
Pioneer	36%	38%	35%	37%

Percent of Group Represented by Each Business Chemistry Type

QUOTES

More than 900 Deloitte professionals are trained and certified to deliver Business Chemistry sessions within Deloitte or with our clients. Officially known as our *certified network*, they are more like Business Chemistry black belts, having earned their stripes with plenty of real session facilitation. Many of the quotes we offer in this book are drawn from a study we conducted with 140 certified facilitators who completed the Business Chemistry assessment online and, in September of 2015, answered a series of open-ended questions about perceptions of the Business Chemistry types. Other quotes come from interviews we've conducted and conversations we've had with executives as described below.

FACILITATED INTERACTIONS

As part of our broader Deloitte Greenhouse activities, our team works with thousands of executives each year in thoughtfully crafted immersive experiences we call Labs. These Labs cover a range of topics geared to address our clients' toughest challenges; one component of which is often the dynamic between individuals, within a team, or with broader stakeholder groups. These Labs give us the opportunity to apply, refine, and extend our core research studies both through observation and through direct interviews and feedback. In addition, many of our clients have themselves adopted Business Chemistry for use across their organizations, and work with us to continue to gather insights.

Properties of Business Chemistry

We get all kinds of questions about the properties of the Business Chemistry system, so we'll address some of the most common here.

DIMENSION CORRELATIONS

Let's start with the question of correlations between dimensions because this one is particularly easy. Eigen analysis produces orthogonal dimensions, which means dimensions that are not correlated with one another. In other words, while having a high Pioneer score means, by default, that your Guardian score will be low (because they're opposite ends of one dimension) your Pioneer score won't affect your Driver or Integrator scores since the two dimensions are independent. So you might have a high Pioneer score along with a high Driver score and a low Integrator score. Or you might have a high Pioneer score along with a low Driver score and a high Integrator score. Or you might have a high Pioneer score along with modest Driver and Integrator scores. Or, of course, you might not have a high Pioneer score at all.

However, things look a bit different when we consider the Integrator and Driver subtypes, because, after all, a subtype is generally related to the type it's a "sub" of. Overall Integrator scores are correlated with both Dreamer and Teamer scores, and overall Driver scores are correlated with both Scientist and Commander scores, all at approximately the same level: Pearson's $r=.70$. Correlations run from 0 to 1, so this is generally considered to be a relatively strong correlation.

─────

INTERNAL CONSISTENCY

People also sometimes ask about the correlations among individual items on the Business Chemistry assessment, a form of reliability known as internal consistency. Are all the items doing a comparable job of measuring the underlying construct they're designed to measure (in this case working style)? Are they all pulling their weight equally? We use the split-half method of measuring internal consistency, which compares scores on one half the items to scores on the other half. The Spearman-Brown coefficient is an indicator of this type of reliability, and for the Business Chemistry assessment it's .83, which is generally considered to signify a relatively high level of internal consistency.

─────

TEST-RETEST RELIABILITY

Another question we get in regard to the Business Chemistry assessment is about its overall stability, another type of reliability. In other words, if you take the Business Chemistry assessment twice, will you get the same scores and be identified as the same primary type both times?

We tested this with a sample of 1,420 individuals who completed the assessment twice, a year apart. We decided on this intervening time period because we wanted it to be short enough that people wouldn't reasonably be expected to have significantly changed their working style preferences, behaviors, and traits. We also wanted it to be long enough that people wouldn't have a clear memory of the assessment items or how they had responded to them previously. Since Business Chemistry is a self-report assessment, the reliability of scores depends in part on whether people are answering the questions honestly and through a similar lens each time. For example, if the first time you complete the assessment you're being very honest about how you think, feel, and behave, but the second time your answers are a bit more, shall we say *aspirational*, you may end up with different scores or be identified as a different type the second time around. While we'd like to assume everyone responds to the assessment with complete honesty, we wanted to reduce the chances that anyone might attempt to "game the system" to end up with a different result. We thought a year in between assessments was sufficient for doing so.

We used two methods for determining test-retest reliability. The first was comparing dimension percentiles on the first and second assessments using a simple correlation. Pearson's *r* for the two primary dimensions was .71 for the Pioneer-Guardian dimension and .72 for the Driver-Integrator dimension. In other words, people's results didn't come out exactly the same both times, but they were similar.

Then we took a look at how often respondents were identified as the same primary type when they took the assessment a second time. The answer to that was *it depends*. What *it depends on* (apart from honest responses) is how extreme a person's scores were on the first assessment. Let's unpack that a bit with an example.

Two people might have the following scores on their first assessment:

	Person A	Person B
Guardian Percentile	85th	56th
Pioneer Percentile	15th	44th
Driver Percentile	45th	51st
Integrator Percentile	55th	49th

In both cases the Guardian percentile is the highest of the percentiles, so the person is identified as a Guardian. But person A, at the 85th percentile, is a more extreme Guardian than person B, at the 56th percentile. Now you might imagine that when a person responds to the assessment a second time a year later, even if they answer honestly both times, their scores still might change a little bit (we're not robots after all). On the one hand, if person A's scores change a little, they might end up in the 80th or even 75th percentile for Guardian (and maybe their other scores will change at similar levels), but they're still going to be identified as a Guardian, because it will still be their highest score. On the other hand, if person B's scores change a little they might end up in the 51st or even 46th percentile for Guardian. And if their other scores change at similar levels, this person may now be identified as another primary type.

In fact this example is a good illustration of what we actually find. (Imagine that!) The more extreme someone's scores are on the first assessment, the more likely they are to be identified as the same primary type the second time they take the assessment. This is just what we'd expect.

Putting some real numbers to this, overall 63% of people in our study were identified as the same primary type the second time they took the assessment a year later, but among those with stronger scores on their primary type (above the 80th percentile) that number was 72%. For those with even more extreme scores (above the 90th percentile), 79% were identified as the same primary type on the second assessment.

So what about the others? If they weren't identified as the same type, what type were they likely to be identified as on the second assessment? Usually, they wind up being the type that was their secondary type the first time they took the assessment; this was true in 24% of the cases overall. In our example above, if person B was identified as a different primary type the second time they took the assessment, chances are they'd be identified as a Driver (which was their secondary the first time).

Overall, in 87% of the cases, people were identified as their initial primary or secondary type the second time they took the assessment. That number rises along with more extreme scores, with 93% of those above the 90th percentile being identified as their initial primary or secondary type when they took the assessment again.

OTHER SIGNS OF INTEGRITY

At this point we'll loop back to highlight two points we made earlier that speak to the integrity of the Business Chemistry system. First, the fact that we replicated 96% of the item coefficients when we repeated the Eigen analysis with a second sample is a strong sign that the types themselves are stable. Second, the overlap with the types identified by other systems, based on different assessment items and derived in different ways, is a good sign of the same thing.

As we shared in Chapter 10, our research consistently reveals statistically significant differences between the types in most every area we explore, from experiences of stress and feelings of psychological safety to career aspirations and the conditions under which people thrive. Finding significant differences between the types in all of these areas suggests that the types themselves are meaningful categories.

Finally, we've seen that Business Chemistry has what's called face validity, which basically means that it seems to measure what it's designed to. We know this because time and again when we work with teams who have completed the assessment, we hear people say how well the system has managed to boil down to its essence who they are (at least at work). We can also see the light dawning as people find out the types of their colleagues, which often gives them a clue as to why it's easy for them to work with some while they experience conflict with others.

REFERENCES

1. Fry, Richard. "Millennials Surpass Gen Xers as the Largest Generation in U.S. Labor Force." Pew Research Center. May 11, 2015.

Acknowledgments

As with any book, there are many people we're grateful to for contributing to this project in so many different ways. We'll start with our Deloitte colleagues, present and past.

For transforming a spark of an idea into a reality, creating Business Chemistry from the ground up, thanks to Brian Fugere, Jennifer Juneau, Naomi Bagdonas, and Neda Shemluck. And for being part of the evolving team that has shepherded Business Chemistry through its early years and made it what it is today, thanks to Grace Lee, Danielle Fowle, Kristin Pech, Rebecca Adams Zuteck, Devon O'Malley, Jake Lewitz, Cree Scott, Leigh Otey, Sarah Snow, and Swati Kundu.

For helping get the story of Business Chemistry out of our heads and onto paper/screen by reading chapters, making suggestions, checking our work, and generally keeping us out of trouble, thanks to Sean Kelly, Stephanie Quarls, Nick Murphy, Katie Baird, Jim Guszcza, Kimmerly Cordes, Kristi Loughran, Tony Scoles, and Debbra Stolarik. Thanks in particular to Selena Rezvani, who played an especially central role in the development of this book as resident thought-partner and hand-holder, and to Joanne Ruelos Diaz, who helped wrangle the many minute details that brought it over the finish line. For getting the word out about Business Chemistry and this book, thanks to Shelley McNeill, Grace Pai Leonard, Michelle DeZabala, and John Connors. For making our work look beautiful, thanks to Patricia Mozetic and Randy Yoshio Okamura. Thanks to Punit Renjen for helping to make Business Chemistry a global phenomenon and for writing the foreword. For their constant support and guidance, and championing of Business Chemistry, special thanks to Diana O'Brien and Ken Clinchy.

There are far too many other people at Deloitte (thousands) to thank for bringing Business Chemistry to our colleagues and clients over the years, but we especially want to recognize our global network of certified Business Chemistry facilitators and the entire Deloitte Greenhouse team for sharing the Business Chemistry love far and wide, and bringing back experiences that have enriched our own understanding of working styles and relationships.

Finally, thanks to the team at Wiley, especially Richard Narramore, Danielle Serpica, Vicki Adang, Peter Knox, Christina Verigan, Jocelyn Kwiatkowski, and Pete Gaughan.

FROM SUZANNE: Thanks August and Sinikka for keeping me laughing and allowing me the time to get this book written, even when you would rather have had my attention! At least now you have something to point to when someone asks, "What does your mom do?" For the rest of my family, thanks for your ongoing love and support: Nancy and Mike (that's Mom and Dad), Michelle and Jemma, Shannon, Jim and Toivo, Phon, Sambok, Matthew, Catherine, Michael and Edward, Tim and Ana (whom I particularly appreciate as my work-from-home partner and frequent sounding board). To my many amazing friends who have listened to me talk about this work (and everything else) over so many cups of coffee and glasses of wine—you all know who you are—what would I do without you? And to MJ, thanks for being there to listen, talk, and offer suggestions. (You are a patient and brave man. ☺) Finally, to Kim, I'm grateful for the space you've given me to focus on what I love to do, and for all you've taught me about how to make my work interesting and compelling (rather than just thorough and accurate).

FROM KIM: Thanks to Suzanne for being a fantastic co-author and for helping make this book-writing project both productive and enjoyable. Thanks to my mom and dad (John and Gale) for enthusiastically reading everything I've ever written, and providing input and encouragement. Thanks to Oliver and Alex, my amazing sons, who delight me every day and who have been so understanding when I need to work. (*They also are a hit at dinner parties, guessing the guests' Business Chemistry types.*) And finally thanks to my husband, Jacob, for everything, including being my test *Driver* helping inspire and improve my work.